BEN JONSON

BEN JONSON

His craft and art

Rosalind Miles

Barnes & Noble Books

Savage, Maryland

First published in the United States of America 1990 by
BARNES & NOBLE BOOKS
8705 Bollman Place
Savage, Maryland 20763

Library of Congress Cataloging-in-Publication Data
Miles, Rosalind.
Ben Jonson, his craft and art/Rosalind Miles.
p.   cm.
Includes bibliographical references.
ISBN 0-389-20944-9
1. Jonson, Ben, 1573?–1637—Criticism and interpretation.
I. Title.
PR2638.M55   1990
822'.3—dc20   90-8311 CIP

Printed in Great Britain

FOR
LORNA FLINT
IN GRATITUDE AND AFFECTION

MY PRAISE IS PLAIN, AND WHERESOE'ER PROFESSED
BECOMES NONE MORE THAN YOU, WHO NEED IT LEAST

A poem, as I have told you, is the work of the poet, the end and fruit of his labour and study. Poesy is his skill, or craft of making.

Ben Jonson, *Discoveries*

CONTENTS

PREFACE

Despite his undisputed status as one of the giants of English literature, Jonson is known to most people only as the author of three or
four plays. When *Ben Jonson: His Life and Work*, the companion
volume to this book, appeared in 1986, it was kindly greeted as an
important step forward in increasing the general awareness of an
unjustly neglected great man. The present study attempts to take the
process a stage further, by offering the first completely comprehensive
critical account of Jonson's creative career, taking account of every
piece he wrote from his angry literary apprenticeship to what Jonson
himself called 'the close or shutting up of his circle'.

This story has long deserved to be better known. During a working
life of more than forty years, over twice as long as Shakespeare's,
Jonson produced or was connected with upwards of thirty plays, the
same number of masques, a dozen royal entertainments and several
collections of poetry – plus works of translation, criticism, philology
and philosophical reflection. Perhaps understandably in view of this
massive and varied output, previous critical studies of Jonson have
been either thematic or selective, concentrating on one phase of his
career or on the highest achievement of his mature art. The result
has been to perpetuate the common misconception of Jonson as a
dramatist pure and simple.

But Jonson's relation to that role was, like Oscar Wilde's truth,
rarely pure and never simple. For his chosen role was always that of
'the Poet', a far higher calling than that of 'Playwright', in his own
contemptuous coinage. Poetry was the supreme, indeed to Jonson the
only true art. Equally, however, the height of art was only to be
attained through conscious and unremitting *craft*. For the perfection
of a poet, he wrote in *Discoveries*, 'we require exercise of those parts,
and frequent'. No man can think to 'leap forth suddenly a poet'; he

must 'bring all to the forge and file again, turn it anew'. Only 'labour' will ensure that works 'will last their age'; and 'in the making of our maker, it is only Art can lead him to perfection'.

A full survey of Jonson's output, then, will reveal him as a relentless and self-conscious craftsman, who gave his life to the work demanded by his art. Nor is this any diminution of his achievement. It reveals his unswerving dedication both to self-improvement and to the improvement of the forms in which he was working; it provides a detailed portrait of the growth and development of a creative artist unique in its own time and rare in any other; and it enhances our respect for his dogged professionalism and devotion to the service of his capricious and often unrewarding muse. The more we know, the more there is in Jonson to admire. For one wedded to 'the Ancients' he was refreshingly avant-garde, and as his chosen motto *Tanquam explorator* indicates, he remained to the end eclectic and experimental, willing to try new forms and themes in the restless search for the perfection and high status that he craved.

The long-term perspective also renders us a much more truthful and vital figure than the Jonson of literary and critical tradition. As a writer Jonson was undoubtedly committed to the Chaucerian formula of the making of poetry, 'the lyf so short, the craft so long to lerne'. But in his impatience to attain the finished role Jonson did not scruple to rewrite his own creative history, suppressing *The Case Is Altered* and countless other plays (he told Drummond in 1619 that 'the half of his comedies were not in print'), and reworking *Every Man in his Humour* to create a grand sweep of 'his studies in that kind'. One result of all this strenuous self-modification and self-promotion has been to produce the rather cold and repellent notion of Jonson as an intellectual giant and consummate artist; and this in turn has ensured that for all too many, his work is as coldly known, or rather *known of* from afar, and never taken to the heart. A far more attractive picture emerges when we see Jonson at work, share his struggles with form and content, with reader and audience, and experience with him the erratic pattern of his failure and success.

This book brings to a close over fifteen years' biographical and critical study of Jonson, during which I have incurred innumerable debts of gratitude to friends throughout the academic world, and the libraries that minister to us – my heartfelt thanks to all. Another immeasurable debt is to the work of other Jonsonians, and especially his editors ancient and modern: above all the eleven-volume edition of his works by C. H. Herford and Percy and Evelyn Simpson (Oxford,

1925–52), cited here under the abbreviation HS throughout. For ease of reading I have normalized in all quotations contemporary forms like the long s, the i/j and u/v, and have also modified punctuation where necessary to simplify the often over-elaborate contemporary conventions, some of which have in themselves provided obstacles to the better appreciation of Jonson and helped to thwart his own professed desire 'to make readers understanders'. If this book can make any contribution to that most Jonsonian of aims, my work will be well rewarded.

Rosalind Miles,
Corley Hall,
Corley

LIST OF DATES

xiii

1

A MERE EMPIRIC

Great Lord of Arts, and Father of the Age!

So begins one of the numerous tributes to Jonson written after his death. That event set in motion the combination of strenuous eulogy and misdirected hagiography that still conspires to make Jonson the greatest English writer almost never read. 'Alas that bard, that glorious bard is dead!' lamented his admirers. Reverently they crept about the feet of this colossus, the 'King of English poetry', invoking the magnitude of his achievement in terms of uncritical adulation. 'Great Jonson' appeared at last in the roles he had so persistently sought, those of consummate artist, towering classicist and custodian of the sacred flame, the poet-didact who had 'taught the ruder age / To speak by grammar, and reformed the stage':

> So great his art, that much which he did write
> Gave the wise wonder, and the crowd delight.[1]

So great was Jonson's art, his elegists urged, that he was for his own and later ages a source and oracle, 'to whose most rich and fruitful head we owe / The purest streams of language which can flow'.

It is salutary to recall, however, that this posthumous picture of Jonson as a great artist would have been greeted with derision and disbelief by many of his colleagues and contemporaries. To the author of *The Return from Parnassus* he was '*a mere empiric*, one that gets what he hath by observation'. To others he was a shameless plagiary, especially from the classics; Marston accused him of 'filching by translation'. Dekker too derided Jonson's working methods, attacking him in *Satiromastix* (1601) as 'a mere translator' who laboriously patched up his own work out of bits of others' efforts, a costive compositor and no true creator. Nor was this view of Jonson simply the product of the vicious infighting of the Stage Quarrel, the so-called 'War of the Theatres' at the outset of Jonson's dramatic career. At the very end of his life Thomas May, who had had nothing but kindness at Jonson's hands, flouted him as 'that plunderer, Ben', while even loyal friends complimented Jonson on his 'laboured works' and assured him that time would devour 'the abortive offspring of [his] hasty hours'.[2]

These attacks are more remarkable for their spite than accuracy, but their malice is illuminating; they point towards an important truth. For Jonson was never gifted as a writer with the spontaneous upsurge of a ready poetic inspiration. Apart from the countless taunts of slowness in all the satires made on him, Jonson himself acknowledged his want of Dekker's 'overflowing rank wit', or Shakespeare's legendary flow. His compositions, as he confessed in the *Apologetical Dialogue*, were

> Things that were born when nought but the still night
> And his dumb candle saw his pinching throes.

The vivid image here of the monkish scholar struggling alone in his cell contains a literal reality. Jonson was always a student of life, even when most vigorously a participant. He used his varied experience of the human comedy to back up the truths he had gained from his reading, rather than the other way round. Although always enriched with topical or local detail, almost every one of Jonson's plots, characters and themes can be traced back to types and motifs popular in the literature he had studied, whether classical or contemporary.

For Jonson was a self-declared 'empiric', a patient, laborious, substantially self-taught *craftsman*, whose lifelong struggle 'to come forth worth the ivy, or the bays', is entirely obliterated under the monolithic designation of 'great artist'. Even in his highest comic moments, his method remained one of patchwork assembly or collage, here shown to its best advantage in Wasp's splendidly surreal description of the interior of the brain of his bird-witted pupil, Cokes, in *Bartholomew Fair*:

> He that had the means to travel your head now, should meet finer sights than any that are i' the Fair, and make a finer voyage on't, to see it all hung with cockleshells, pebbles, fine wheatstraws, and here and there a chicken's feather and a cobweb.
>
> (I.v.87–92)

Art such as this both demands and betrays a craft of a highly conscious order, self-conscious even; and Jonson's writing does not always escape the charge of being cold, mechanical, betraying the effort that has gone into it through its pervasive sense of strain. In Jonson, creative production was always at the mercy of the current intellectual credo; as a result his raw materials can seem imperfectly assimilated, their constituent elements not emotionally converted into a harmonious whole. Episodes of attitudinizing rhetoric such as this all too irresistibly evoke Yeats's indictment of 'the will performing the work of the imagination':

> To you that are by excellence a Queen!
>   The top of beauty! but, of such an air
> As, only by the mind's eye, may be seen
>   Your interwoven lines of good and fair,
> Vouchsafe to grace Love's triumph here tonight!
>   (*Love's Triumph through Callipolis*, lines 66–70)

Jonson's effects only succeed in full when each of their parts has been turned and turned again until it dovetails smoothly into the original design, when each word has been weighed, selected and fitted into place. Then and only then comes the triumph of the perfectly crafted piece, one that carries the grave poise and authority of achieved art, like the justly famed epitaph 'On My First Son':

> Farewell, thou child of my right hand, and joy,
> My sin was too much hope of thee, loved boy . . .
>   (Epigram 45)

This 'truth to nature', however much he valued and cultivated it, did not come easily to Jonson. He would have been suspicious if it had; for, as his advice to a young poet shows, he saw the 'labour' as inherent in the craft: '[therefore] let him not fall out with it, quarrel, or be over-hastily angry . . . but come to it again upon better cogitation; try another time, with labour. If then it succeed not, cast not away the quills yet, beat not the poor desk, but bring all to the forge and file again, turn it anew. . . . If it come in a year or two, it is well.' Jonson here sums up not merely his own poetic method of painstaking selection and revision, but beyond that his unflinching acceptance of the Chaucerian formulation of the destiny of the poet: 'the lyf so short, the craft so long to lerne, / Th'assay so hard'. How did Jonson approach the desired but daunting 'profession of poesy'? What were the raw materials from which he worked, and how far did his

3

training and intellectual background help or hinder him in the long hard 'assay'? Only by assessing the making of the craftsman can we understand the growth and progress of Jonson's art.

In a very real sense, and unlike the majority of his contemporary writers, Jonson consciously trained to be a poet. His education at Westminster School concentrated very heavily on 'exercises of style', the formal orientation only reinforced by a constant stress on grammar, syntax and the parts of speech. All these were practised daily in spoken and written assignments, in speech-making, in debate, in composition, in translation, in rote repetition and copying out. Jonson's own view of the value of these exercises may be gauged from the fact that he not only continued them into his adult life, but insisted that they were essential to the making of a poet:

> before we handle the kinds of poems, with their special differences, or make court to the art itself as a mistress, I would lead you to the knowledge of our Poet by a perfect information, what he is, or should be by nature, by exercise, by imitation, by study; and so bring him down through the disciplines of grammar, logic, rhetoric and the ethics.
>
> (*Discoveries*, HS VIII, 636)

Almost any Renaissance writer or thinker would have paid lip-service to these precepts. Where Jonson differed was in the steadfast consistency with which he absorbed them and applied them to all his work. In addition Jonson also received at Westminster a formal training in versification and the techniques of poetry-making that remained his constant literary practice for the rest of his life: as an old man of 45 he told Drummond of Hawthornden that he still 'wrote all his [verses] first in prose, for so his master Camden had learned him' (HS I, 143). Subsequent commentators have seen in this habit the source of Jonson's tendency to lapse from his 'high style' into the prosaic and pedestrian. But Jonson saw no shame in having been taught how to parse a poetic conceit; especially when his teacher, Camden, was one of Europe's most respected scholars.

Camden also taught Jonson to see the craft of words as a serious study, demanding whole-hearted, lifelong commitment. Throughout his life Jonson despised would-be writers, the dilettantes or 'smatterers, that are busy in the skirts and outsides of learning, and have scarce anything of solid literature to commend them' (HS VIII, 570). Serious lessons, though, could also be taught in light-hearted ways. Another vital element of Jonson's early intellectual and creative training was his exposure to drama. All Elizabethan schools made use of acting and play-reading as educational tools, to develop confidence, clear speech and good carriage in their boy pupils. Westminster School built upon this convention to achieve a unique distinction. From the age of 7, then, Jonson was exposed to at least three plays a year, two in English and one in Latin, by both classical and contemporary dramatists. His own dramatic characters and structures, from his first stage success *Every Man in his Humour* (1598) to the end of his career, consistently betray the workings of an imagination fed on the plays of native dramatists like Nicholas Udall, author of *Ralph Roister Doister* (*c.*1553) and above all on Plautus, Terence, and other great classics, his abiding love.

Jonson's classicism has always bulked large in any consideration of his work, not least because he himself always vigorously promoted his own claim to fame in this regard. In reality, the boy Jonson had no more than the grammar-school grounding conventional at this period; Westminster introduced him to Terence, Plautus, Sallust, Cicero and Ovid in a variety of forms ranging from plays, through letters and speeches, to history and poetry. In addition, the boys were diverted by less exacting works like *Aesop's Fables*. Although short and easy to read, these had the dual merit of instilling the terse and epigrammatic use of Latin, as well as a moral lesson.

This raw material certainly stocked the shelves of Jonson's mind for his maturity. Where he differed from his contemporaries was in his view of classical studies as an ongoing process of self-reflection, so that even after he left school he clung to his 'wonted studies'. Throughout the academic wilderness of enforced bricklaying and the conflict-ridden occupation of public 'playwright', Jonson continued his search through the classics for the writers who could supply him with the idea, the image, the form, the phrase even, that he needed. Most of these sources of new creative materials he found by himself; of the writers he praised to Drummond (Pliny, Quintilian, Horace, Tacitus, Juvenal, Martial and Hippocrates) only Martial and Horace had been on the syllabus of Westminster School.

There were then limits to Jonson's mastery of the ancient greats, limits which clearly highlight the nimble 'empiric' rather than the august classicist of his preferred pose. As a self-taught amateur his range was inevitably restricted in comparison with academic classicists, the products of 'the schools'. Further, he was always primarily a Latinist rather than a classicist in the full sense of the term. Westminster boys were unusual in that they were introduced to the study of

Greek, at a time when many Tudor grammar schools confined their pupils exclusively to Latin. But the young Westminsters did not attempt any Greek until the fourth form, by which point Jonson may very well have left, since he was not staying on into the upper forms in order to proceed from school to university. The study of Greek always remained subordinate to Latin, and, had Jonson remained at Westminster to enjoy the full course of study up to the sixth form – even with his known ability and dedication to his 'studies' – it is doubtful if the brightest linguist could pick up enough Greek in three years to enable the language to be read or written with any great range or confidence.[3]

In common with most Renaissance intellectuals then, Jonson's access to the Greek writers was via the many freely available Latin translations, and Latin texts were his much-valued key not only to the wisdom of the ancient world, but also to any hopes of making a creative mark in his own. On the primary level he relied solidly on them for subject-matter. From the earliest plays he drew on Plautus for plots, Terence for comic technique. In the satires, the on-stage persona may be Horace, but the off-stage presence is unmistakably Juvenal.[4] The character of Asper in *Every Man out of his Humour* expresses Juvenal's satiric pose, echoes Juvenal's reasons for writing satire, and Juvenal's feelings of contempt for his own age. Jonson's anti-feminism is imported lock, stock and barrel from Juvenal's sixth satire into this play, and the chorus, Macilente, quotes Juvenal at length. The later 'comical satire' *Poetaster* invokes both the spirit and presence of the calmer, more urbane satire of Horace, in addition to the mellifluous love-notes of Ovid, but an authentic Juvenalian snarl frequently cracks open the façade of amused tolerance:

> Mischief and torment! O my soul and heart
> How are you cramped with anguish! Death itself
> Brings not the like convulsions. O this day,
> That ever I should view thy tedious face . . .
>
> (III.ii.22–5)

On the former level then, Jonson's classical reading supplied him with ideas and structure, characters, situations, theme and tone. Of equal importance to the development of his craft was the inherent emphasis on self-reflection that constantly directed Jonson to examine and perfect his own working methods and artistic life. Hellenistic and Latin poetry from its dawn into consciousness was always intensely self-conscious, given to reflecting upon itself, its authors, its aims and

6

its accomplishments. The great Horace himself had perfected the use of poetry to this end; he in his turn was relying upon an even older model, that of a Roman poet so ancient that nothing but his name has withstood the tooth of time:

> There are many men in the world, and just as many varieties of taste and ambition. My own personal pleasure is to string words together in verse, as Lucilius, a better man than you or I, did before me. It was his way to tell all his secrets to his poems, which he regarded as his trusty and faithful friends. Whether things went well or ill for him, he always flew to his own lines for sympathy. Thus it comes about that the whole life of the old bard is there set down for all the world to look at as in a picture.[5]

In modelling himself upon these words of his 'great master' Horace, Jonson was embracing the opportunity of using his poetry as a vehicle for exploring himself and his preoccupations, both artistic and emotional; for exercising his craft, in short.

One final contribution of the classics to the formation of the young craftsman-poet deserves to be considered. In the widest terms, Jonson's classical studies established for the duration of his working life his artistic standards and horizons. From 'the ancient great' he derived his working concept of 'decorum', the excellence proper to the thing chosen. Jonson was always conscious, in both his dramatic and non-dramatic writing, of the occasion and function of his compositions. Yet each piece, no matter how carefully tied in to the moment of its creation, was still expected to have relevance to the wider world of the spirit. It had to establish standards, and to nurture and reward the desire to live up to them. It had to serve the only true purpose of art, that of giving plausible and pleasing expression to that controlled statement of the normative that we still term 'classical'. Even in the heat of his most ill-tempered and ill-judged disputes, Jonson never lost faith in the cool restraint of these aims and ideals.

To Jonson, the classics were pre-eminent; but they were not all-in-all. The traditional over-emphasis on Jonson's classical inheritance obscures both his native independence of thought and the success of his eclecticism. His reliance on these texts was never servile. He never advocated, for instance, a return to pure sources, and was happy to reach the ancients through the medium of Renaissance criticism; Scaliger crops up in *Every Man out of his Humour* (III.iv.14–18), as does the hand of Minturno, from whose *De Poeta* he took his idea of comedy.[6] Hence Jonson's employment of his classical raw materials was never as uncritical as is often assumed. On the contrary, to Jonson it was one of the marks of the 'true poet' to be able to return any borrowings from original sources with the interest of some addition, variation, or improvement all his own:

> I know nothing can conduce more to letters than to examine the writings of the Ancients, and not to rest in their sole authority or to take all upon trust from them . . . for to all the observations of the Ancients, we have our own experience: which if we will use and apply, we have better means to pronounce. It is true they opened the gates, and made the way that went before us; but as guides, not commanders.
>
> <div align="right">(<i>Discoveries</i>, HS VIII, lines 129–39)</div>

In the Induction to *Every Man out of his Humour*, Jonson argued that since the comedy writers of the ancients altered the form of comedy to suit their needs, there is no logical reason why English writers of the modern age should not do the same:

> I see not then but that we should enjoy the same licence or free power to illustrate or heighten our invention as they did; and not be tied to those strict and regular forms which the niceness of a few . . . would thrust upon us.
>
> (lines 266–70)

Nor need the search for the appropriate techniques by which to 'illustrate or heighten invention' be restricted to the great texts of the past. Faithful to one of the Latin tags he carefully preserved and analysed in *Discoveries*, 'nulla ars simul et inventa est, et absoluta' (no art is perfect the day it is born), Jonson seized upon and consumed any and every definition of 'regular form' as an aid to formulating his own definition. As tradition has consistently overstressed the importance of the classics in Jonson's thought, so it has tended to underestimate the key part played in the evolution of the apprentice poet by the native influence. Though travelling much in the literature of another time, Jonson was keenly aware of the current manifestations in his own; and he encountered them in the same spirit of wide eclecticism in which he had been trained.

In the formation of Jonson's emerging attitude to literature, and to his own place within it, one event was of profound significance, the publication in 1595 of Sidney's *Apology for Poetry*. Sidney's discussion of the essential nature of poetry, analysed according to classical notions of the art of imitation, echoed Jonson's chief preoccupations and facilitated their full articulation. This effort to classify the different types of poetry, to rebut the attacks made upon it by writers following in the footsteps of Plato, made him the mouthpiece of all Jonson wished to hear. Others beside Sidney were beginning to think along the same lines, and Jonson canvassed many opinions for what he needed; he read Puttenham, for example, carefully annotating a copy of his *Art of English Poesy* in the first edition of 1589. But it was in Sidney's systematic examination of the state of English poetry, the first ever to be undertaken, that Jonson encountered the literary work of his own country, from Chaucer to the present day, assessed and described as if it were important in itself, as important as the great classical literature of the past. The English language, too, was dignified not only by Sidney's adoption of it as the medium for the discussion, when scholarly or critical works had in the past always been in Latin, but also by Sidney's special consideration of the nature of English in relation to the demands of prosody.

Jonson's plundering of Sidney's thought, even of his words and phrases, is everywhere apparent in his work. The prologue to the revised version of the first of his plays he chose to preserve, *Every Man in his Humour*, has been called 'a positive collage of Sidneyisms', and at points within the drama Jonson simply paraphrases extracts from the book, especially when Sidney is expressing his vivid disgust with the non-naturalistic conventions of the contemporary drama:

> To make a child, now swaddled, to proceed
> Man, and then shoot up, in one beard and weed
> Past three score years: or with three rusty swords,
> And help of some few foot-and-half-foot words
> Fight over York and Lancaster's long jars . . .
>
> (Prologue, lines 7–11)

From this standpoint, Jonson enthusiastically borrowed Sidney's critical precepts, and applied them to his own ends. Sidney argued, for instance, that the ideal comedy should be didactic, an 'imitation of the common errors of our life'. These should be represented 'in the most ridiculous and scornful sort that may be; so as it is impossible that any one beholder can be content to be such a one'. In this sentence Sidney neatly encapsulates both Jonson's aim and his method in the later comical satires.

In essence, Sidney sought to insist on the high dignity of poetry both as a form and an occupation. To achieve this level, he believed, classical standards should be applied to all work in the vernacular.

Jonson pounced on this prescription and from the outset guided his course by its lights. From Sidney's stress upon the teaching function and high potential of poetry, Jonson derived authority to support both his own emerging concept of the messianic role of the poet and the treatment of the drama as poetry. Sidney's views, critical standards and ideals were imprinted upon Jonson and remained with him all his life; they passed through him like wine through water and altered the colour of his mind.

Sidney's critical precepts carried all the more weight with Jonson because he was no mere theorist but a poet himself. Jonson knew and admired Sidney's verses, despite the fact that he was not fond of the sonnet form in which Sidney excelled. Another poet of the time who caught Jonson's attention was Edmund Spenser (?1552–99), the first half of whose mighty *Faerie Queene* had appeared in 1589, the second in 1596. Jonson only genuinely admired epic poetry in Greek and Latin, and later told Drummond that 'Spenser's stanzas pleased him not, nor his matter' (HS I, 32). He disliked obscurity on the grounds that 'things farfet[ched] hinder to be understood'. Jonson was not alone in his doubts; he claimed that he had been obliged to explain Spenser's clouded allegories to Sir Walter Raleigh. But even in the difficult Spenser, Jonson found grist to his mill. Remarkably, he delighted in Spenser's early unabashed pastoral, *The Shepherd's Calendar* (1579), committing much of it to his phenomenal memory (he noted in *Discoveries* that he could 'repeat whole books', and every word of his own poetry that he had ever written). He particularly liked to recall an extract from Spenser's October eclogue in praise of wine, as an aid to poetic inspiration:

> O if my temples were distained with wine,
> And girt in garlands of wild ivy twine,
> How I could rear the Muse on stately stage . . .

Jonson later possessed a 1617 edition of Spenser's complete works, which he read and annotated very thoroughly, notwithstanding his reservations.

Yet the reference here to 'the Muse' on her 'stately stage' is a tell-tale indication of Jonson's perennial efforts to elevate his own much less dignified reality. At the same time as he was tasting the never less than elegant Sidney and Spenser, he was also gorging himself on the coarser fare of the younger writer, Thomas Nashe (1567–?1601). What were the qualities of Nashe's writing and thought that attracted Jonson? At first sight, there was little in common between them. Although only six years older than Jonson, Nashe seemed to belong to an earlier generation artistically. His main form was the prose pamphlet, and although he wrote one play, he was never a playwright. His medium, his element even, was the racy prose epistle, another fundamental difference between the slow, self-conscious stylist Jonson, and the headlong Nashe, who boasted that he could write as fast as his hand could trot. Finally, Jonson's aspirations to a classical restraint and tempered judgement would seem to have held little kin with the vivid vulgarity and flippant disrespect of Nashe, who 'flourished in all impudency'.

Nevertheless there was much that Jonson admired in and learned from Nashe's work. Nashe filled his fictional worlds with people, strikingly creating the 'crowded stage' that Jonson always favoured. Nashe's landscape was stuffed with characters covering the entire social range from courtier to carman. At times he startlingly anticipated what critics have seen as the uniquely Jonsonian world of discharged captains and draggle-tailed whores, of taverns and dicing-houses. Nashe's characters also express many of the attitudes that later emerge as peculiarly Jonsonian; the compelling need for money in a money world, for instance, coupled with a rampant contempt for those who deal in it, and sometimes simply for those who have it.

Stylistically, too, Jonson discovered an affinity with Nashe. Nashe was a master of the art of invective and denigration, perennially capable of fresh and unexpected grossness, and also of deploying the excremental in a creative comic mode – 'thou dunghill of obscurity' is one of his milder insults. Nor did he shrink from exploiting the comic potential of the gruesome or deformed, and his aggressive character-ization was rooted in a surreal intensification of observed actuality:

> At length, as Fortune served, I lighted upon an old straddling usurer, clad in a damask cassock edged with fox fur, a pair of trunk slops . . . and a short threadbare gown upon his back faced with moth-eaten budge. Upon his head he wore a filthy coarse biggin and next it a garnish of nightcaps . . . a fat chuff it was, I remember, with a grey beard cut short to the stumps as though it were grimed, and a huge worm-eaten nose, like a cluster of grapes hanging downwards. [7]

Nashe's chief gift to Jonson, however, was his sweeping satiric perspective. Nashe displayed a fearless and ferocious contempt for the multitude; it was his belief that 'the Vicar of St Fool's' would never want for occupation. Even more ridiculous, however, were those who

11

puffed themselves up above the common herd; Nashe viewed all pretension with derision, but especially the posturing of those in authority, and his self-important blunderers find their lineal descendants in Jonsonian characters like Justice Overdo in *Bartholomew Fair*, for instance. And like all satirists, Nashe found a sitting target in the female of the species; his parade of anti-feminism in the *Anatomy of Absurdity* (1588) provided Jonson with chapter and verse for his own attacks on the foulness of women, a key theme throughout his work. Equally, neither man could work up much genuine enthusiasm for the modest maids and mannerly matrons whom they formally commended.

Jonson's scorn was so peculiarly his own that it cannot be suggested that he copied it from any other writer. But in Nashe he found a fellow-spirit and an emotional source. The combination of the premier satirist of one generation with the emerging satirist of the next, formed a potent conjunction of talents, and the result was predictably explosive. Under circumstances now lost, Jonson took up an abandoned satire of Nashe's, and finished it for performance by the Earl of Pembroke's Men. This play, *The Isle of Dogs*, staged just before 28 July 1597, all but terminated Jonson's dramatic career before it had begun. For the play apparently attacked under thin disguise some person in high authority, and the queen's Privy Council, reacting with unprecedented anger and speed, ordered the arrest and imprisonment of all those associated with the play, and the suppression of all copies of it.

For over two months, while Jonson lay imprisoned in the Marshalsea, his interrogation entrusted to Elizabeth's notorious master-torturer Topcliffe, it looked as if he would pay dearly for his admiration and imitation of Nashe. But even an experience of this grim nature could not turn Jonson's feet from their chosen course. He was now determined to direct his poetic craft into the wider world of the theatre. He would not be a journeyman hack, turning out fodder for the groundlings, a 'playwright', in his own dismissive coinage. He would draw on his classical foundation for drama, satire and poetry and, working in the modern medium of the vernacular, would create a new higher form of 'comical satire', or dramatic poem. Given contemporary attitudes to play-making, Jonson could have been under no illusion that his dramatic productions for the public stage would be received as 'art'. Nor could they supply him with the artistic status that his nature craved. On the contrary, Jonson clearly recognized from the start that if he wanted to elevate that art of the drama

12

and dignify his own contribution to it, then he could do so only by the most strenuous efforts of his craft.

His first preoccupation then had to be with the nature of the drama that he had inherited. Indeed, it is hardly an exaggeration to say that Jonson embarked on his career as a dramatist in protest against the dramatic practices of his age. Pioneers like Marlowe had succeeded in regenerating the English drama, liberating it from its limited vision, crude didacticism and wooden techniques of characterization and construction. Old motifs had been not so much discarded as recycled, with the result that Senecan declamation jostled with broad farce, and romantic improbabilities took place between passages of sharp wit and wordplay. Elizabethan audiences, fed on ghosts, gods and golden lads and girls, clamoured for more of this multi-coloured action which other dramatists, even if they openly deplored popular taste, usually ended by giving them.

Alone among his contemporaries, Jonson was determined not to accommodate himself to what he regarded as the degraded taste of the multitude, nor to allow popular demand to enforce a split between his theory and his practice. As early as *The Case Is Altered* (1597–8) he refused to concede any authority to the opinion of the audience: 'A man shall have such a confused mixture of judgement, poured out in the throng here, as ridiculous as laughter itself' (II.vii.42–4). Similarly the prologue to *Every Man in his Humour* shows Jonson's contempt, learned from Sidney, for the stage effects of his theatre: the use of fireworks, rolling a ball to imitate thunder, and lowering actors and props on stage by a windlass located in the hut above – all these offended him. And *Every Man in his Humour* could only get under way after Asper had harangued the spectators about the good behaviour required of 'attentive auditors'; the opposite being stigmatized as *'more infectious than the pestilence'*.

Jonson used his battery of critical and literary gleanings to devise a variety of strategies to combat these drawbacks, and to shape up the raw material as he found it to something nearer to his own standards. He rejected the contemporary conventions that the dramatist should provide entertainment on all intellectual levels, offering like a shopkeeper something for everyone from illiterati to scholars, from prentices to lords. He dismissed crowd-catching comic devices like burlesque and the tomfoolery of farce, in favour of a solid base of stimulating subject-matter designed to provoke thought rather than thoughtless mirth. This proceeded from the distinction Jonson made between the ribaldry provoked by clowns and the 'high strain of laughter' in which follies were corrected. He never spoke of the former except with disdain, and in *Discoveries* quoted Aristotle that 'the moving of laughter is a fault in comedy', as trawling for 'the people's delight'.

But most consistently Jonson worked from the outset to re-create the status of the dramatist. His decision to raise the play-maker to the level of the poet rather than that of lowly mountebank with which it had previously been associated, firmly focused and eventually polarized the struggle between artist and craftsman. *Every Man in his Humour* staked the first claim by exalting poetry within the play itself, and also identified and expressed the same tension within the maker of the 'poem'. From this redoubt Jonson insisted on the total exclusion from the consecrated practice of all foolish and ignorant pretenders. These are at least handled with some affection in *Every Man in his Humour*, through the foolish Matheo's satisfaction with his 'rascally' mass-produced verses. Later, however, as Jonson's sense of his own mission deepened, he came more and more to feel that the profession of poetry was rightly entrusted only to 'the choice and master spirits of the age'; and he bitterly resented having to share with poetasters and balladeers the sacred name of 'poet'.

Attacks on false poets therefore became more intense in Jonson's 'comical satires', their prevalence stigmatized as irrefutable evidence of the corruption of contemporary values:

> O how I hate the monstrousness of time,
> Where every servile imitating spirit
> Plagued with an itching leprosy of wit
> In a mere halting fury, strives to fling
> His ulcerous body in the Thespian spring,
> And straight leaps forth a poet!
> (*Every Man out of his Humour*,
> Induction, lines 66–71)

This analysis, pursued through *Cynthia's Revels* (II.i.48 ff, and II.iv.15–18), reached its climax in *Poetaster*, where Jonson develops another technique to assert the high status of poetry and to clinch his rejection of inferior pretenders. This was the deliberate, self-conscious and essentially undramatic inclusion of Virgil and Horace as personae in the drama. These two establish the true standard by their own undying example. For only a 'wholesome diet' of real poetry can cure a poetaster, as Virgil claims at great length (V.iii.531–65). Through Horace in particular Jonson strove to demonstrate, indeed incarnate, authentic poetic genius in the teeth of base imitation, pretension and detraction.

As part of his professional obligation as a genuine craftsman, the 'true poet' of Jonson's definition has to discriminate on behalf of his audience, between drama good and bad. Jonson consistently attacked the old forms of popular comedy, as 'fustian protestations' and 'grey-headed ceremonies'. He was aware that his public had other tastes, making Mitis deal with the objection that *Every Man out of his Humour* is a failure because it does not deal with 'a duke in love with a countess, and that countess in love with the duke's son', with 'some such cross-wooing and a clown to their serving-man' (III.vi.196–9). But he was not to be deterred by the expectation of public disapproval from attacking the old forms either directly or by the use of parody – for example, of 'King Darius' doleful strain' in *Poetaster* (III.iv). He also pokes fun at the melodramatic ghosts who straggle through revenge plays shrieking '*Vindicta!*' (III.iv.230–5).

As this indicates, the play particularly singled out for disapproval on these grounds was *The Spanish Tragedy*. Jonson was deeply versed in this piece, both as an actor and as a writer. He had played the lead role, Hieronimo, at the start of his career in the theatre, and even after the stir he made with his 'comical satires', was still enough of a 'dresser of plays about town', as he scornfully categorized Dekker in *Poetaster*, to be hired by Henslowe to bring the old favourite up to date by writing new additions for it. Jonson's use of this much-loved play in his own work is entirely by way of ridicule. In I.iv of *Every Man in his Humour* he makes sport of Hieronimo's famous lament, 'O eyes, no eyes, but fountains fraught with tears', while in *Cynthia's Revels* he makes an old-fashioned theatregoer swear that *The Spanish Tragedy* is the best play in Europe. Several examples of Kyd's characteristic rhetoric are mocked in *Poetaster*, and Jonson's distaste for the play long survived his satirical springtime as a dramatist; the same jibes recur in *The Alchemist* and *Bartholomew Fair* very much later.

Paradoxically Jonson insisted that the poet's obligation to reject the old and to develop the new should derive from much older forms still, those of the classical writers. Only by adopting the ancient forms, like *vetus comedia* (see *Every Man out of his Humour*, Induction, lines 230–41 for Jonson's extended discussion of this), and by adhering to classical standards of execution, could the poet accurately reflect and comment upon the contemporary scene. Classical concepts like decorum and 'truth to life' should establish the level at which the investigation must take place; classical forms like satire would supply the subject-matter and framework. Classical writings afforded too the precedent of a significant philosophical and intellectual body of material wrought into an artistic whole. This must compose a harmonious unity – Jonson constantly stressed the subordination of detail to the overall concept – and consequently his plays became through-composed to a degree unique among the dramatists of his time.

Yet Jonson's critical theory could not always dictate successful literary practice, and in this early phase of eager eclecticism the result was often experimental, uneven and confused. In the course of trying to learn both how to make plays, and how to make those plays 'true poems', while wrestling simultaneously with currents of contemporary thought and the need to impose his own stamp upon his work and the world at large, Jonson came to identify certain radical difficulties both in his own approach and in the theatre of his time. In his assessment, everything finally came back to the question of the audience.

For side by side with Jonson's frequently expressed contempt for contemporary audiences was the conviction that they both could and must be improved. He used Mitis and Cordatus as an 'audience within the play' in *Every Man out of his Humour* to provide a living example of how the good audience should conduct itself. It is easy to see with hindsight that Jonson's vision of converting the average Elizabethan playgoer into the ideal interlocutor for an earnest and over-intellectualizing young playwright was doomed to failure. In addition, by insisting on himself as poet, and his play as poetry, Jonson was attempting to construct the recipient of his work as a *reader* rather than a spectator. Jonson was in fact determined to remodel theatre audiences into an entirely new role, and one that flew in the face of its own nature, being essentially undramatic.

Jonson's inability to realize the ideal audience was then implicit in the very terms that he himself established for the creation of it. The response he sought, of understanding, study and judicious consideration, was inescapably that of private study and response, not the public reaction of the theatre. From the outset Jonson was using the drama to pursue an essentially non-dramatic quest, even insisting, in the Prologue to *Poetaster*, for instance, that spectators at a play should disregard what they *see* and learn only from what they *hear*, like children in school. As a result he came more than once in his career as a playwright to a dramatic dead end, and found that he could go no further, at that time, with play-writing. In the course of his on-off love affair with the drama, Jonson was to find it necessary to withdraw into the less contentious worlds of pure poetry or masque-making, in order to clarify and consolidate his views, techniques and creative self-esteem.

Yet whatever he did, Jonson remained 'empiric' still. One key attitude hardened in him from his earliest days, and was summed up in the phrase he subsequently adopted as his personal motto: *Tanquam explorator*, 'Always an explorer'. Through his writing Jonson was always learning and pushing onwards, on a continual voyage of discovery. Judicious as ever in the analysis and justification of his methods, Jonson left a perfect description of his own eclecticism:

> For a man to write well, there are required three necessaries. To read the best authors, observe the best speakers: and much exercise of his own style . . . he must first think and excogitate his matter; then choose his words and examine the weight of either . . . and to do this with diligence, and often. No matter how slow the style be at first, so it be laboured and accurate; seek the best, and be not glad of the forward conceits or first words that offer themselves to us, but judge of what we invent, and order what we approve . . . the safest is to return to our own judgement, and handle over again those things. . . . So did the best writers in the beginning; they imposed upon themselves care and industry. . . . [But] as it is fit for grown and able writers to stand of themselves, to trust and endeavour by their own faculties, so it is fit for the beginner and learner to study others, and the best . . . rules are ever of less force and value than experiments.
>
> (*Discoveries*, HS VIII, 615, lines 1697–1758)

In these sober lines lies the secret of Jonson's creative growth, the story of his development from 'prentice wordsmith' to the 'Great Lord of Arts'. Craft into art; even as a young 'beginner or learner', Jonson accepted this distinction and the discipline it imposed. And from the very beginning it dictated his every step in the long, slow progress to the coveted status of 'poet'.

2

BEGINNING HIS STUDIES
IN THIS KIND

Jonson's literary apprenticeship has to be assessed with care. *The Isle of Dogs* was so firmly suppressed after its staging in July 1597 that only its title and the whiff of brimstone surrounding its reputation now survive. Jonson's earliest dramas, which included collaboration with others of Henslowe's team of hacks, were allowed to perish. One such was *Hot Anger Soon Cold*, a comedy written with Henry Chettle and Henry Porter in the first half of 1598. There were many more; Jonson told Drummond in 1619 that 'the half of his comedies were not in print' (HS I, 143). All we have now to judge of Jonson's work as a 'beginner or learner' are the pieces that he deemed worthy of the judgement of posterity, and so rescued from the jaws of time. This loss of so much of Jonson's prentice or hack work from the years before 1600 means that all observations on his early development have to be made with some reservation. But the evidence is not entirely wanting. *The Case Is Altered* is the first play of Jonson's to survive in almost its original form, having undergone a small change not long after writing; and it has much to tell us about this phase of Jonson's creative career.[1]

Most immediately interesting are the abundant signs of Jonson's immature stagecraft. To the young man who was at this time earnestly pursuing his 'wonted studies' in the classics, the idea of combining two plots from separate plays of Plautus must have seemed an excellent way of ensuring a double ration of dramatic intrigue and humour. The complex design so produced would also have held for a devoted classicist like Jonson the further merit of emulating the more sophisticated structuring of the other great Roman comedy writer, Terence. In practice, however, the joining of the story of the father who has lost his son with that of the miser who has lost his gold, does not result in a balanced whole. It is never clear to the audience of *The Case Is Altered* where the play's true centre of interest lies.

Additionally the young Jonson felt strongly that a romantic comedy must contain plenty of romance. Accordingly he maximized the love interest of the miser's story, Plautus' *Aulularia*, and inserted love themes of his own into *The Captives*, where Plautus has none. The effect of this is to bring about an absurd multiplication of incident as no fewer than five characters are in love with the principal heroine Rachel, and all have to have their chance to pay their addresses to her in the course of the play.

The combination of two plots in the hands of a prentice dramatist also results in some obvious structural difficulties. Jonson is clearly unsure where the climax of the action should be. Is it the unmasking of the miser's deceptions, or the restoration to Count Ferneze of his lost son? Neither of these alternatives allows for the resolution of the love business; this is in fact handled so perfunctorily in a twenty-line burst at the very end of the play that one of the secondary heroines is left dangling and unpartnered, while her sister is bestowed in marriage upon a man with whom Jonson has been unable to contrive for her one single word of prior conversation.

Nor is Jonson at this stage sure of where the internal climaxes of the action should occur. What are obviously intended to be high spots come over rather as examples of defective plotting. The long-lost son, Camillo, makes his entrance into the action only in Act IV; structurally just too late for a major character. Equally, when the Count Ferneze joins the list of Rachel's admirers, a potentially dramatic revelation is experienced as an awkward wrench of the plot to no particular purpose. The play's final scene aspires to be one of revelation, restoration and reconciliation, a type of which the climax of *The Winter's Tale* must stand as the supreme example. But it is simply fudged. The dramatic opportunities afforded by the plot are missed through tentative and inexpert handling; the reunion between father and son, for instance, is expressed in the hollow rhetoric of contemporary convention, after which Jonson reverts immediately to comic business:

COUNT: O happy revelation! O blest hour!
   O my Camillo!
PHOENIXELLA: O strange my brother!
FRANCISCO: Maximilian!

Behold how the abundance of his joy
Drowns him in tears of gladness.
COUNT: O my boy!
(V.xii.49–52)

The structuring of his drama overall is clearly Jonson's major problem. A survey of the play's opening scenes demonstrates his inability to construct forward-moving dramatic action which proceeds by its own momentum through its own internal dynamic, drawing in characters, or moving beyond them, in a natural and convincing way. When *The Case Is Altered* opens, Jonson's one character on stage is immediately joined by another, and a duologue ensues. As that character leaves the stage, another is brought on, and another duologue takes place. This 'on-off' shuttle movement of characters speaking exclusively in duologue is repeated throughout the first six scenes of the play. *The Case Is Altered* consequently gets off to an inconsequential and unconvincing start.

The limitations of Jonson's dramatic techniques are further revealed as the play progresses. He is genuinely at ease only with the straightforward and undemanding forms of soliloquy or duologue; when more than two people are assembled on stage, some of them fall unaccountably silent for long tracts of time, unless their contribution is required by the plot. Particular victims of Jonson's lack of assurance with groups are the female characters; because they are reactive rather than active characters, in the way of the contemporary convention to which Shakespeare is an ever-impressive exception, they are too often brought on and given virtually nothing to say or do. The predominant consideration of the young Jonson is to find the means throughout to advance his full and rather unwieldy plot, and characters not directly implicated in this tend to disappear from their creator's view.

Other problems of characters crop up, too. The introduction and establishing of characters, together with the dramatization of such exposition as is necessary for the play to proceed, constitute, even for experienced dramatists, a notorious dramatic pitfall which the inexperienced Jonson does not quite escape. In a clear foreshadowing of his later development he is at his best with the comic characters, so that the 'witty cobbler' Juniper succeeded in impressing himself on Nashe's memory, but the young heroes Paulo, Angelo, Camillo and Chamont are interchangeably noble and remarkably colourless. The initial choice of the romantic plot, with its lost children and mistaken identities, further imposed on Jonson the necessity of motivating some highly unconvincing characters and actions, like the betrayal of the hero by his best friend, and the hero's subsequent one-line forgiveness of this grave offence (compare Shakespeare's equally problematic handling of the same device in the last scene of *The Two Gentlemen of Verona*). It is, in one sense, no reflection on Jonson's mature stage craft that he does not at this point achieve these moments successfully; many of his contemporaries experienced the same difficulty. Jonson himself later came to feel that romantic comedy was inherently implausible and ridiculous.

A final uncertainty of handling appears in the fluctuation within *The Case Is Altered* between poetry and prose. Jonson moves from one to another without any obvious *dramatic* purpose. Clearly the count should speak in verse as he expresses the deep grief still alive after many years for the loss of his son. It is not quite so clear why the miser Jaques should introduce himself in a long and laboured verse soliloquy when he is handled throughout as a low and contemptible comic character; still less why the two sisters should converse, *tête-à-tête*, in stilted verse. The use of prose, except when spoken by the play's genuinely comic characters Juniper and Onion, is too often experienced as a descent, especially when the character is a high-ranking lord and, as such, socially the most elevated personage in the play.

To pick up the play's weaknesses, however, should not lead us to ignore its strengths. It is fascinating to observe how it improves as it proceeds; Jonson writes himself into it, learning and practising his dramatic skills within the course of the play. Juniper and Onion, for instance, are not particularly funny, either individually or together, in the opening scenes. But towards the end Jonson finds the way to create authentic comic interaction for them, increasing their comedy value enormously. Jonson's plot management in general becomes more confident and adroit as he goes along. While he never quite rises above the tendency to tell his story in little scenes, the action develops a much greater rhythmic flow when Jonson gets his teeth into his combination plot.

In character terms, too, Jonson's comparative failure with young and noble characters is compensated for by his evident gift with cranky old men. Both Count Ferneze and Jaques the miser are strongly characterized and deployed with confidence. The count's first appearance is heralded with some skilful anticipatory characterization – 'You know my father's wayward, and his humour / Must not receive a check.' But this passionate irritability is convincingly balanced against an equally passionate attachment to his two sons. The miser

Jaques, portrayed as half-cracked when the play opens, is convincingly but not painfully edged towards full-blown madness, as Jonson
gives him some marvellously demented utterances to express his
obsessional love of money-making and of each individual coin he
handles:

> O in what golden circle have I danced . . .
> Here blessed ghosts do walk, this is the court
> And glorious palace where the Gold of gold
> Shines like the sun, of glorious majesty.
> O my fair-feathered, my red-breasted birds
> Come fly with me, I'll bring you to a choir.
>
> (V.iv.1–8)

As an ex-actor himself, Jonson provided in these two parts absolute
plums for the performer. Inevitably this cannot hold true across the
range of all the characters, and the women's roles in particular contain
such pronounced areas of deadness that they would be little more than
a chore to act. Nevertheless Jonson the dramatist can be seen to be
bearing the interests of his actors in mind, and writing good parts for
them. In particular, Jonson was clearly able, from this early stage, to
write good comedy material. He did not rely upon the clowns to
create the play's humour through their own professional skills; he
wrote their comic lines down to the last 'Hey, catso!' and 'No sir, why
so sir?' Through Juniper and Onion, then, Jonson explored a wide
range of verbal humour; these two characters have a magpie curiosity
about new words and phrases, together with an ignorant inability to
grasp their meanings or to discriminate between them. Juniper's
crude attempts to ingratiate himself with the heroine Rachel under
the tutelage of Onion display Jonson's happy command of this type of
foolery:

JUNIPER: D'you hear? sweet soul, sweet Radamant, sweet
   Machavell? One word, sweet Melpomine, are you at leisure?
RACHEL: At leisure? What to do?
JUNIPER: To do what, to do nothing, but to be liable to the
   ecstasy of true love's exigent, or so; you smell my meaning?
ONION: Smell? Filthy, fellow Juniper, filthy! Smell? O most
   odious!
JUNIPER: How, filthy?
ONION: Filthy, by this finger! Smell? Smell a rat, smell a
   pudding! Away, these tricks are for trulls, a plain wench loves

plain dealing. I'll upon her myself. Smell to a march-pane,
wench?

JUNIPER: With all my heart. I'll be legitimate, and silent as an
apple-squire, I'll see nothing, and say nothing . . . and bag
pudding, ha ha ha.

(IV.vii.28–44)

Jonson's clowns are not only verbally comic, as here. He displays, too,
a very marked ability to create comic business, and an active awareness
of what looks ridiculous on stage. On a simple level he gives us his
clowns engaged in mock fighting, practising court manners, or
parading their finery when they come by the miser's gold, and try to
turn themselves into great men. A more complex effect is achieved at
the introduction of the miser: Jonson portrays him as running madly
on and off stage while other characters are trying to hold conversations
with him, in an ungovernable frenzy of apprehension that his gold
will be stolen from him while he talks (this piece of stage business is
borrowed from Plautus, but Jonson both extends and exaggerates it to
make it funnier). This early capacity of the budding craftsman to
manage stage space is evident in other ways, too; an interesting comic
moment occurs when one of the clowns, like Berowne in *Love's
Labour's Lost*, climbs up a 'tree' on stage, and contributes to the action
from this vantage point.

As this suggests, *The Case Is Altered* illustrates throughout that
Jonson can think and write in a mode that is intrinsically dramatic. It
never strikes us, as so many plays do, as a narrative or poem in the
wrong form. Towards the end Jonson succeeds in combining the
disparate strands of the action into some telling examples of dramatic
parallelism. In three successive scenes of Act IV (ix, x and xi) he brings
on the count grieving for the loss of his son, another old man
bewailing the loss of Rachel whom he has been duped into thinking
would marry him, and the old miser raving over the theft of his gold:

COUNT: Ay me, my son, my son.

SCENE X

Enter Christophero.

CHRISTOPHERO: O my dear love, what is become of thee? . . .
I shall run frantic, O my love, my love.

SCENE XI

Enter Jaques the miser.

JAQUES: My gold, my gold, my life, my soul, my heaven.
What is become of thee? See, I'll impart
My miserable loss to my good lord.
Let me have search, my lord, my gold is gone.

(V.ix.29; V.x.1–6; V.xi.1–4)

With the comic repetition of the tender enquiry 'What is become of thee?', Jonson highlights the absurdity of any self-deceiving and foolish affection in a vein that clearly points forward to the humour plays.

Weaknesses and strengths together, this play is nothing if not thoroughly Jonsonian. Despite the inevitable preoccupation with the complex plot, there is throughout an overflowing delight in language, and an abundance of characteristic words and phrases. Jonson's relish of linguistic pretension is spiritedly displayed in Juniper's blend of colloquial vulgarity with Latinate nonsense: 'Away, scoundrel! dost thou fear a little elocution? shall we be confiscate now? shall we droop now? shall we be now in helogabalus?' (V.xiii.29–31). Note here the origin of Jonson's deep and perennial conviction that irresponsibility of language is linked to moral irresponsibility: language is simply too important to be left to fools. Juniper and Onion are handled fairly lightly, but they are stylistic prototypes for the legion of gulls and fops who are subsequently arraigned for their verbal affectations throughout the work of Jonson.

The Case Is Altered contains many such examples of the early appearance of the traits associated with the mature Jonson. He was, from the start, a master of comic invective; characters are condemned as 'drones', 'motley brains' and 'a nest of rooks', all within the same speech (I.vii.3–30). And the irrepressible Jonsonian rhythm of ascending comic hyperbole is to be heard in this attack of the miser on the foolish Juniper:

JAQUES: Soft, sir, you are not yet gone, shake your legs, come, and your arms, be brief, stay, let me see these drums, these kilderkins, these bombard slops, what is it crams them so?
JUNIPER: Nothing but hair.
JAQUES: That's true, I had almost forgot this rug, this hedgehog's nest, this haymow, this bear's skin, this heath, this furzebush.

JUNIPER: O let me go, you tear my hair, you revolve my brains
and understanding.

(IV.viii.33—41)

Of all these adumbrations of Jonson's later work, the most significant in view of Jonson's immediate development as a dramatist was
the emergence of satire in the play. As originally conceived, *The Case
Is Altered* was a conventional romantic comedy of mistaken identity
and true love crossed, of the kind that was already rather old-fashioned
in 1597. Yet the text that has survived incorporates a later addition by
Jonson in the form of a satiric attack upon his contemporary Anthony
Munday.[2] Under the name of 'Antonio Balladino', the 'pageant poet
of the city of Milan', Munday is caricatured as an out-of-date hack who
is stupidly satisfied with the inferior shows that he creates for
London's festivals: 'I do use as much stale stuff, though I say it myself,
as any man does in that kind, I am sure. Did you see the last pageant I
set forth?' (I.ii.48—50).

Balladino is further shown to be completely out of touch with the
theatre of his day. All modern developments in the drama he
scornfully stigmatizes as 'new tricks' and 'toys', vowing that 'if they
give me twenty pounds a play, I'll not raise my vein'. He is in fact
made to expose his own limitations even as he boasts of his own
superiority:

Why look you now, I write so plain, and keep that old decorum
that you must of necessity like it; marry, you shall have some
now (as for example in plays) that will have every day new tricks,
and write you nothing but humours. Indeed, this pleases the
gentlemen, but the common sort, they care not for it; they know
not what to make of it. They look for good matter, they; and are
not edified with such toys.

(I.ii.58—65)

Most interesting of all, however, is the satirical introduction by
Jonson of the compliment that Francis Meres had paid to Munday in
Palladis Tamia (1598) as 'the best plotter' among contemporary
dramatists. Munday himself is made to assert the importance of the
plot above all else in drama — 'the plot shall carry it.' Jonson himself
evidently devoted great care to the plotting of *The Case Is Altered*. Yet
when he came to pen this satirical insert, his views had changed
radically, along with his dramatic practice. The new humour plays
had usurped the older style of romantic comedy which placed great

25

reliance upon mechanism and structure; and *The Case Is Altered* is the work of an Elizabethan which the Jacobean Jonson had come to despise.

The satirical insert represents the moment when the direction in which Jonson had progressed breaks free of the surface of the level of his achievement at that earlier stage. It points forward to a maturer dramatic practice and a developed dramatic theory which sit uneasily with the older style. This in itself led to one specific difficulty. As a burlesque of the old-style hack playwright turning out romantic comedy for the uncritical popular repertory, the character of Balladino simply could not be incorporated into a play of the very type that he is supposedly attacking. Jonson had the sense to see this, and Balladino makes no further appearance in the play after this one early scene.

Yet even within *The Case Is Altered* as originally conceived there is ample evidence of Jonson's sardonic, and increasingly satirical vision. The opening of the play, where Juniper warbles an old song of romance while Onion tries to break in on him with such mouth-filling oaths as 'A pox of God on you!', establishes the characteristically Jonsonian contrast between the world of love, fairy-tale and illusion, and the sordid reality of everyday life. In a lighter vein but with no less seriousness Jonson introduced an otherwise redundant French page, in order to create a scene which satirizes French affectation and English dullness in equal measure:

> PACUE: Monsieur Onion? Is it not *fort bien*?
> ONION: Bean, quoth he? Would I were in debt of a pottle of beans I could do so much.
>
> (IV.iii.32–4)

Linked with Jonson's developing interest in satire are the choice and characterization of his miser figure. This Jaques is introduced and developed in such a way that he can fairly be regarded as an embryonic Jonsonian 'humour' character. From his first distracted appearance, when he is described as looking like one who has seen a ghost 'in an unsavoury sheet', he is established as a man in the grip of a ruling passion. His devotion to his gold is such that any imagined threat to it brings him out in palpitations and feverish sweating fits, while his neurotic suspicion of visitors trembles on the brink of a full-blown paranoia. Jaques's 'humour', and Jonson's view of it, are brilliantly encapsulated in the irresistible stage-direction to Act III, scene v: *'Enter Jaques with his gold and a scuttle full of horse-dung.'* As the miser proceeds to cover his gold with the horse-dung as a means of ensuring that no one could suspect its hiding-place and so steal it, Jonson savagely characterizes his perverted mental processes and symbolizes the disgusting nature of his obsession with 'filthy lucre':

> And if the devil that envies all goodness
> Have told them of my gold, and where I keep it,
> I'll set this burning nose once more a-work,
> To smell where I removed it . . .
> Who will suppose that such a precious nest
> Is crowned with such a dunghill excrement?
> . . . Sleep sweetly, my dear child . . .
> . . . Rot all hands that come near thee,
> Except mine own. Burn out all eyes that see thee,
> Except mine own. All thoughts of thee be poison
> To their enamoured hearts, except mine own . . .
>
> (III.v.9–21)

It is worth remarking that all this is Jonson's invention, and not found in his Plautine source. Finally, when Jaques is lured out of his nest and trapped into betraying himself through following a false trail of gold coins, this plot motif anticipates Jonson's later devices for 'purging' and thus curing humorous characters in plays yet to come.

In one key respect, the character of Jaques looks even farther ahead than the humour plays. As a man in love with his gold, he clearly served as an early study for Volpone. Jaques is not simply a conventional stage miser; he is obsessionally, besottedly attached to his treasure. From the first it is his 'sweet companion kind and true', 'better than any brother, or friend, or wife'. In the horse-dung scene, his mania is fully revealed, and he worships at the shrine of his idolatry in a manner irresistibly reminiscent of the opening lines of *Volpone*:

> I'll take no leave of thee, sweet Prince, great Emperor,
> But see thee every minute. King of Kings,
> I'll not be rude to thee, and turn my back
> In going from thee, but go backward out,
> With my face toward thee, with humble curtsies.
>
> (III.v.22–6)

Like Volpone again, Jaques's every action is determined by his love of gold, even to the point of self-destruction: he too chooses to betray his secret rather than allow another to take his hoard. *Volpone* naturally affords the more sophisticated study of this obsession with gold; where Jaques simply adores the thing, Volpone loves it also as an instrument of power and gratification. Yet as this suggests, Jonson learned through the experience of writing *The Case Is Altered* that character is vastly superior to plot as a source of interest, tension and humour. From this time forward he never again relied upon the construction and manipulation of an ingenious plot mechanism as the primary factor in the making of a play. Jonson was never to discount plot. But he slowly evolved the knack of plotting the kind of comedy that would give the fullest expression to his developing satiric vision of human affairs. As a play, then, *The Case Is Altered* shows Jonson working towards his own highly idiosyncratic form of dramatic comedy through the modification of the standard contemporary dramatic forms, reaching for something that evaded him for now, but which he clearly saw lay within his future grasp.

Also yet to evolve was that special relationship between the playwright and his audience that Jonson came to feel was so important and, as he found it, so unsatisfactory. It is in the nature of romantic comedy that it purports to unfold of itself, and hence allows no room for any authorial presence in the play. The fiction is that the fiction is real; the success of the illusion lies in its convincing approximation to an uncriticized 'reality'. This type of play belongs to another order of experience entirely from that demanded and offered in Jonson's mature art, in which the writer is ever-present to elicit, shape and check audience response as the play is in progress.

Only in small matters do we have the sense of Jonson's shaping consciousness. Underlying the whole piece is his muted distaste for the world of romance and the literature of escapism; this makes itself felt in his inability to commit himself to the love-business of the play. As Herford and Simpson drily observe, 'there is a prodigious amount of love-making, but little or no convincing love' (I, 326). We are informed that Rachel is beloved by one and all, but we are never shown anything lovable in this chilly and undeveloped girl, nor convinced by the love frigidly or bombastically declared by her suitors. As a romantic comedy, *The Case Is Altered* was rendered absolutely defective by Jonson's inability to satisfy this crucial aspect of audience expectation; and related to it is Jonson's inability at this stage to create any warm, genuine, disinterested relationships. He simply was not interested in creating normal people.

The later additions to *The Case Is Altered* show much more clearly Jonson's awakening desire to control and instruct his audiences, in short to have them in the palm of his hand. This proceeded from his

low opinion of the contemporary taste as it operated when left to its
own devices:

> The sport at a new play is to observe the sway and variety of
> opinion that passeth it. A man shall have such a confused
> mixture of judgement, poured out in the throng there, as
> ridiculous as laughter itself. One says he likes not the writing,
> another likes not the plot, another not the playing . . . the
> rankest stinkard of them all will take upon himself as peremp-
> tory, as if he had writ himself *in artibus magister* [M.A.].
>
> (II.vii.40–58)

Jonson later rejected *The Case Is Altered*, presumably because of its
inherent tensions and unresolved contradictions. *Every Man in his
Humour* thus became the first of his comedies that Jonson chose to
preserve. Both he and posterity have agreed with Aubrey's statement
that this was the first success of his early writing career, the play in
which he 'did hit it admirably well' (HS I, 179). The play was not quite
the runaway theatrical triumph of subsequent mythologizing. But it
was sufficiently well received to encourage Jonson to proceed along
these lines. Jonson was later to identify *Every Man in his Humour* as the
origin of his career as a writer of satirical comedy, and of his literary
practice; in his Induction to *The Magnetic Lady* more than thirty years
later he referred to himself as 'beginning his studies of this kind with
Every Man in his Humour'.

Jonson's was a natural desire to restructure his dramatic progress in
a sweeping retrospective that joined all his comedies in one unbroken
chain of achievement. To that end he extensively revised the play for
the 1616 Folio, and the existence of the later version has tended to
eclipse the earlier work. Jonson's own lead, so firmly given, has caused
critics to link *Every Man in his Humour* forward to the other 'humour'
plays and the comical satires that were soon to follow it. To the
audience of 1598, however, the play's correspondences with *The Case
Is Altered* would have been far more evident than they are now.

Most immediately obvious is the same reliance upon authority of
the yet-fledgling dramatist. As with *The Case Is Altered*, once again the
off-stage presences are those of the old Roman comedians. Plautus
provided Jonson this time not with plot-structures but character-
types: the elderly kill-joy father, his fun-and-poetry-loving son, the
braggart soldier and the wily servant are all familiar denizens of the
Plautine world. The influence of Terence also appears more clearly

29

here, in the carefully created five-act structure modelled on the precepts of Roman comedy.

In wider terms, too, Jonson is evidently finding support from the theoreticians, as well as the practitioners, of the comic art. There is a dutiful observance of the unities of classical comedy as they had been interpreted by Renaissance critics. The strictures of Sidney, in particular, expressed in the *Apology for Poetry* (1595), Jonson had taken to heart. *Every Man in his Humour* is a more confident and assured performance than *The Case Is Altered* in almost every way. But throughout it Jonson is to be seen conscientiously adopting serviceable models, rather than adapting them freely and creatively as he was later to do.

Other elements reworked from *The Case Is Altered* would also be familiar to the audience of 1598. Jonson was too much of an Elizabethan to avoid all the cherished conventions of his age; and prominent among those deployed in the construction of this play is the favourite technique of disguise. The serving-man Musco, Jonson's version of the wily slave of Plautus, proves himself to be a virtuoso in this field, transforming himself into a decayed soldier, a lawyer's clerk and a 'common varlet' with equal speed and success. Similarly Elizabethan and equally reminiscent of *The Case Is Altered* is Jonson's handling of that mainstay of the contemporary comedy, the theme of 'crabbed age and youth'; his young Lorenzo and Prospero are fresh versions of a common type, young men whose spirits are as high as their ideals, and who are thus inevitably brought into conflict with their cantankerous if not crackpot elders.

Jonson's depiction of the old men in *Every Man in his Humour* again lies in direct line of descent from *The Case Is Altered*. Narrow, irritable and suspicious, focused on totally different objects from those of the young people, they are agitated with fears of imaginary evils, while blindly missing what goes on under their noses. Old Lorenzo and Thorello, tormented respectively with anxieties about the trustworthiness of a son and a wife, are brothers in spirit to Count Ferneze and Jaques. And once more the audience pays the price for Jonson's absorption with these elderly eccentrics, in an imbalance of masculine and feminine within the play. Here again the women are colourless, too slightly realized to provide an adequate counterpoise for the men, or to justify the action they are supposed to support within the plot.

Every Man in his Humour is in fact remarkable for the extent to which it shows Jonson repeating and redeploying his own previously successful dramatic creations. The water-bearer Cob, for instance, is clearly from the same mould as Juniper and Onion, even down to his highly-coloured comic patter – 'Helter skelter, hang sorrow; care will kill a cat, uptails all and a pox upon the hangman!' (I.iii.83–4). Yet the finished result is very much a new and strong dramatic entity in its own right. There is nothing tentative or apologetic about it – Jonson comes before his public this time not as a 'young beginner in his trade', but as an assured playwright and contemporary critic who has something to say, the skill with which to say it, and the confidence that it will be received. Abandoning the problematic double-plot structure of the earlier play, he devised a rich plot of his own invention, displaying a new command both in the selection of his material, and his mastery over it.

The confidence that Jonson displays in the artful complications of his plot emerges fully at the play's conclusion. In place of the hurried ending of *The Case Is Altered*, Jonson supplies a full resolution of the issues under the supervision of the genial Justice Clement, whose name indicates his merciful nature as a judge, while the quasi-judicial nature of the proceedings ensures a fair hearing for all parties. Finally Clement, in a clear adumbration of Justice Overdo in *Bartholomew Fair*, is used to bring about a warm finale in which all the characters are united and tensions dissolved in the festive manner of the old comedy:

CLEMENT: Well then I conjure you all here to put off all
    discontentment – first you, Signior Lorenzo, your cares; you
    and you, your jealousy; you your anger, and you your wit,
    sir. . . . Say, do you approve my motion?
PROSPERO: We do, I'll be mouth for them all.
CLEMENT: Why then, I wish them all joy, and now to make our
    evening happiness more full, this night you shall be my
    guests, where we'll enjoy the very spirit of mirth.

                             (V.iii.435–42)

The well-rounded conclusion is only one of many examples of Jonson's ability to write in greater depth than in the previous play. Stagecraft in general is more efficient and economical, so that characters are got on and off, established and withdrawn, more speedily and convincingly throughout. They are, too, drawn in greater depth and more consistently; Cob, for instance, with his comic misprisions and grumbling ordinariness, maintains his sturdy reality throughout. He does not, like Juniper and Onion in *The Case Is Altered*, come in and out of focus, fading whenever the dramatist's grip on character and material falters. Equally, the overworked disguise convention receives at Jonson's hands a fresh and vigorous treatment, which both advances the plot whenever it is employed, and provides an unfailing source of humour in itself on each occasion. Here Jonson represents Musco's exuberant portrayal of a whining beggar:

> MUSCO: I protest to you, a man I have been, a man I may be, by your sweet bounty.
> LORENZO: I pray thee, good friend, be satisfied.
> MUSCO: Good signior, by Jesu you may do the part of a kind gentleman in lending a poor soldier the price of two cans of beer, a matter of small value; the King of Heaven shall pay you, and I shall rest thankful, sweet signior.
> LORENZO: Nay, if you be importunate –
> MUSCO: O Lord, sir, need will have his course.

(II.ii.44–53)

Jonson's union of a vivid vernacular with the zestful depiction of character is nowhere more successful than in the creation of the play's fools and knaves; the first fully realized examples of the distinctively Jonsonian breed that was to be one of his major contributions to drama. The braggart soldier Bobadilla, his foolish side-kick Matheo and the country cousin Stephano are rendered with loving attention to the minutest gradations of their folly. Bobadilla escapes any whiff of the staleness of a familiar character-type; his military reminiscences and the sham glory he derives from them, his social pretensions unblushingly combined with shameless free-loading, his status as a self-styled expert duellist and leader of fashion, each and every one of these affectations is unfolded and pinned down by Jonson in a characterization which blends severity with a strong undercurrent of reluctant admiration for this marvellous monster.

Matheo and Stephano are not quite so clearly realized as Bobadilla – there is indeed a degree of overlapping between them, since each is essentially the same character, that of the simpleton abroad – but the distinction is made through the contrast between the urban aspirations of Matheo and the bucolic dimness of Stephano. Matheo wishes to swear and swagger like a town gallant; Stephano simply wishes to be more, and other, than the clown he is. Matheo also incorporates a theme which was already dear to Jonson's heart, and was to become even dearer in the next year or two, that of the ignorant poetaster who admires false styles and churns out his own rubbish under the claim to be considered a true poet alongside the greatest of that name.

What links all three of these characters is their picturesque speech and Jonson's evident delight in creating and elaborating it. Bobadilla is the wellspring of linguistic eccentricity in the play, which Matheo enthusiastically emulates as far as he can. But Bobadilla's speech operates on a level of superlative and hyperbole which is beyond the reach of lesser mortals. Not only his set-pieces, like the summary of how twenty men could dispatch an army of forty thousand if the other nineteen were men of his mettle (IV.ii.67–86), but even his mildest oaths – 'by the life of Pharaoh!' – have a megalomaniac assurance and bizarre fruitiness that render them inimitable by any except their creator himself.

Most of the great moments in *Every Man in his Humour*, like those of Bobadilla, take place in prose. Not that Jonson was neglecting verse as a dramatic form; but his sense of the appropriateness of each, at distinct moments, and of the point at which to effect the transition between the two, was developing rapidly. Lorenzo senior naturally unfolds the anxieties of his 'troubled soul' in verse, which as naturally gives way to the gabbling prose of the mendicant soldier:

LORENZO: So doth that mind, whose fair affections ranged
> By reason's rules, stand constant and unchanged.
> Else, if the power of reason be not such,
> Why do we attribute to him so much?
> Or why are we obsequious to his law,
> If he want spirit our effects to awe?
> Oh no, I argue weakly, he is strong,
> Albeit my son have done him too much wrong.
MUSCO: My master; nay, faith, have at you – I am fleshed now I
> have sped so well – gentleman, I beseech you respect the state
> of a poor soldier.

(II.ii.29–39)

Prose is, in short, becoming the comic norm of Jonsonian drama. But it is never indulged in simply for its own sake. As much as Jonson clearly relished heaping up the absurd locutions of Bobadilla, for example, with his mixture of classical references with duelling terms, mock-genteel phrasing and bombastic oaths, yet the spirit of Jonson the censor lurks only just below the surface. Through Bobadilla and his emulators, Jonson asserts the importance of keeping the well of English undefiled. These characters are identified and stigmatized as

33

foolish self-interested debasers of all standards, social, moral and literary. 'Wantonness of language' is firmly linked to all forms of falsehood, affectation and slackness – the abandoning, in short, of all civilized standards. Jonson's passionate concern for these matters, expressed by the literary critics of his day but ignored completely by the contemporary drama, accounts for the severity of the final punishment inflicted upon Bobadilla and Matheo, which displays a harsher accent of reproof than has seemed merited by their offence.

Ultimately, of course, like any comedy of quality, *Every Man in his Humour* is remarkably vital and dramatically so, very actable and very funny, with excellent parts for actors, as Dickens discovered in his amateur theatricals, and as the highly successful revival by the Royal Shakespeare Company of the Swan Theatre in 1986 amply demonstrated. The play moves along at a brisk and hearty pace, yet it is not devoid of moments of quietness and pathos; its subtle and complex episodes are alternated with broader, simpler strokes. The plot is fertile in amusement, while the richly varied prose dialogue is among the best in Elizabethan drama. Yet to the enjoyment of witnessing Jonson's display of an assured comic and dramatic technique may be added that of sharing his experience of exploration and discovery. For in writing *Every Man in his Humour* Jonson found his way through to a new and rich dramatic vein, that of the so-called 'comedy of humours'.

The concept of humours was known to every Elizabethan in some degree, as part of the bedrock of medieval thought. But the original use as a term of physiology to denote the four essential fluids which combined to produce a perfect balanced whole in human beings – phlegm, blood, choler (yellow bile) and melancholy (black bile) – had already shown itself capable of a psychological rather than a strictly physical application. From the humours, the theory ran, arose vapours which ascending to the brain affected the mind. An imbalance of humours was accepted as both cause and explanation of any eccentricity in human behaviour. A person's 'humour' was that element in his or her character which predominated over the rest; and a commonly acknowledged extension of the original meaning of 'humour' was 'whim' or 'affectation', something essentially foolish and frivolous.

What Jonson contributed to this was a fresh slant on a familiar idea, and a distinctive reworking of the traditional emphasis. He was, however, drawing on and working within a far more diverse field than the concept of 'humour theory' would allow. Fenton's *Tragical*

Discourses, for instance, published twenty years or more earlier in 1576 as a collection of stories from Bandello via Belleforrest, constantly employs the term 'humour' in various shades of attitude not unlike those of Jonson, but with this critical difference, that Fenton restricts the meaning to love. A more immediate and incontrovertible source for Jonson was the performance, on many occasions during the spring and summer of 1597, of Chapman's play *An Humorous Day's Mirth*. With what can only be regarded as an access of prophetic vision, Chapman made one of his characters observe at the beginning of the play:

> The sky hangs full of humours . . . but the day is likely to prove fair . . . for we shall spend it with so humorous acquaintance as rains nothing but humour all their life-time.

Other streams also fed Jonson's 'comedy of humours', although they do not employ the term and would not be recognized as such. The technique of constructing a character around one dominant characteristic, or ruling passion – his 'humour', in short – has a long medieval pedigree tracing back to the character sketch of Theophrastus with its device of selecting one adjective to convey the unifying idea. The majority of Plautus' characters similarly are used to illustrate one quality, and are not drawn in the round. The Renaissance movement towards verisimilitude, with its stress upon the poet's duty to study from life, did not succeed in humanizing and individualizing the creation of character across the board. Shakespeare's tragic heroes or the heroines of his comedies effortlessly outclass their prototypes in earlier plays. But examples of the older techniques of rigid character delineation nevertheless continued to survive as pockets of resistance throughout the rest of the contemporary drama.

Jonson was drawing on medieval precedent, then, in his employment of 'humours' to embody one central idea or principle. But in the writing of *Every Man in his Humour* he is to be seen moving towards a much harsher definition of the term. He began to apply it according to a strictly psychological view of human nature and conduct; whoever was not in harmonious balance within themselves had a damaged personality, rather than simply a silly mannerism or two. Jonson's characterization of 'humorous' characters does not neglect the inclusion of fads and follies – but these are presented as affectations that have hardened into a personality deformity, resulting in a permanent warp or bent in nature. So Thorello's mistrust of his wife's fidelity and his consequent fear of all masculine visitors to his house are not merely foolish habits; they are the product of a deeply ingrained neurosis, or even a psychopathological disorder whose effect is to render him less than human and a profound nuisance, if not a danger, to those around him.

Naturally Jonson's thinking on this subject did not proceed in quite the linear way that he, with his talk of 'his studies in that kind', would have us believe. His development of humour theory came experientially, and remained empirical and pragmatic, however much he dressed it up in classical precedent and Renaissance commentary. For this reason the full and final definition of 'humour' never entirely superseded the simpler, older meanings of 'bodily element' and 'whimsical trait'. Again, as a practising dramatist Jonson knew the value of allowing himself the maximum artistic freedom, rather than wilfully limiting himself by too strict and narrow an interpretation of the rules.

Hence Jonson's use of 'humours', both as a descriptive noun in his work and as a body of thought underpinning much of his comedy writing is always flexible and inclusive. Macilente in *Every Man out of his Humour* may on one level exemplify Envy, while Carlo Buffone personifies Detraction. But Jonson's programme of his 'studies' of the humours does not only include qualities of character; he gives his attention to topics as varied as social distinctions, the Seven Deadly Sins, modish follies and contemporary manias, ignorance and pretension and the manners and dress indicative of any of these. Another medieval inheritance, from such pieces as *The Ship of Fools* (1509), is Jonson's method of handling his fools and knaves in a group, to be disposed of wholesale at the end of the play. No matter how strongly developed the humour may be, it cannot promote its owner-victim to the status of being treated as an individual human being – the reverse in fact.

Nevertheless, as was clearly recognized at the time, Jonson achieved with his humour plays something new and avant-garde. The more judicious of his admirers were quick to compliment him upon his radical vision of

> The strange new follies of this idle age,
> In strange new forms presented on the stage
> By thy quick muse.

> (HS XI, 320)

One innovation of *Every Man in his Humour* was the employment of humours not merely to characterize or ornament the play's personnel, but to form the plot foundation of the whole; old Lorenzo's humour, his suspicion of his son, provides the initial impulse for the action, while Thorello's jealousy, Musco's trickiness and Bobadilla's pretension all contribute in their way to propelling it along. Even the conclusion is arrived at in this way — it is the humour of Justice Clement to be humorous.

This functional, structural treatment of humours allowed for a far fuller consideration of them, and consequently raised their status as a subject for intellectual enquiry. It paved the way, too, for the evolution of the newer, 'plotless' style of dramatic construction described by Balladino in the first scene of *The Case Is Altered*; humours succeeded the complicated stories of old romance, with its love tangles, mistaken identity, and match-making climaxes as the source and basis of comedy, making them look irredeemably old-fashioned. 'Beginning his studies in this kind' the prentice craftsman had effectively worked his way through the pre-existing structures. Nothing now lay ahead but the challenging labour of hacking out new forms for his brand-new meanings.

3

TO SPEAK THE VICE

Of his fourteen extant plays 'of the comic thread', Jonson designated only three as 'comical satires', *Every Man out of his Humour, Cynthia's Revels* and *Poetaster*. The others he referred to simply as comedies. Through the mouth of Cordatus in the Induction to *Every Man out of his Humour*, Jonson tried to establish that this play was 'strange, and of a particular kind by itself, somewhat like Old Comedy': the Aristophanic prototype of formal Roman satire, in other words. This in itself sets the play apart from its predecessor *Every Man in his Humour*, which has none of the distinctive marks of formal satire. In fact the links between these two dramas are purely extrinsic, resulting from two of Jonson's classic *post hoc* decisions, first to give *Every Man in his Humour* a special and spurious status as his first 'real' play, and, second, to capitalize on the interest aroused by *Every Man in his Humour* by closely echoing its title in the subsequent work. In reality, then, although the similarity of the two titles has led to the plays being taken as a pair there is the strongest possible break between them. Jonson's initial experiments with the comedy of humours had alerted him to their potential as agents of comic and satiric enquiry. In refining and extending the concept of humours while sacrificing none of its flexibility, Jonson wrote himself into a new and distinctively different phase of his career. In the first of these two plays he glimpsed the link between humours and satire; in the second, he forged the humours into an unprecedentedly effective satiric weapon.

For the experience of writing *Every Man in his Humour* had left Jonson with the conviction that as far as humours went, he had hardly begun to scratch the surface of a crucial contemporary issue with this play. It was an important part of Jonson's concept of the poet's function that he should use the form of the drama to discuss serious issues of contemporary relevance. On this principle, the Induction to

38

Every Man out of his Humour was devised by Jonson to formulate and propound the development of his theories. The subject which filled the bill for him and engrossed a considerable amount of his attention in this opening phase of his dramatic career was the ongoing re-examination of the application of the humours. Jonson worked his way through the theory of humours, examining it for its conceptual value, extracting from it whatever it held in the way of dramatic or explanatory power, and finally abandoning it in favour of other avenues of approach. Jonson's interest in the subject is observable as early as *The Case Is Altered* but humour had then held for him no more than its primary traditional meaning of 'mood' or 'whim', a trivial and passing phase of temper. This is the definition which holds good during the early part of *Every Man in his Humour*, where Jonson manufactures a lot of his comedy from the essentially frivolous and fleeting nature of the humour seizures that his characters undergo.

Yet already Jonson was working his way towards a more serious use of the term than his original plan for the drama implied. The ignorant Cob, enquiring the meaning of the word, is flatly told that a humour is 'a monster bred in a man by self-love and affectation, and fed by folly' (II.iii.157–8). Later Justice Clement, who embodies the voice of wisdom, is made to declare that rational discrimination, among those who should know better, 'is now governed entirely by the influence of humour, which instead of those bold flames that should direct and light the soul to eternity, hurls forth nothing but smoke and congested vapours, that stifle her up, and bereave her of all sight and motion' (V.iii.344–8).

This more serious and substantial definition of humours is continued and carried further in *Every Man out of his Humour*. In the Induction to this play, among the complex psychological, literary and dramatic ideas that Jonson was wrestling with, the humours were critically important; and Jonson devotes a good deal of time to trying to locate, contextualize and explore the 'poor innocent word' which was daily 'racked and tortured' in 'these ignorant well-spoken days'. During the course of the play, the casual or passing uses of the term which in *The Case Is Altered* and *Every Man in his Humour* had held the slighter meanings of 'mood', 'affectation', or 'mannerism', now take on the characteristically Jonsonian inflection of 'personality-type', 'predisposition', or even 'the shape a character decides to adopt'.

These more interesting meanings do not of course supersede the lesser, which continued to exist side by side; and it is these lesser meanings which carry on while the newer definition fairly soon faded

39

from view. *Every Man out of his Humour* represents the peak of Jonson's 'humours' study, and his most intensive investigation. In *Cynthia's Revels* Jonson may be seen reverting to the simpler usage; humour here means 'desire', or 'fashionable folly'. By the time that Jonson came to write *Poetaster*, with his attention fixed firmly on those who were enemies both to him personally and to his muse of poetry in general, 'humours' theory as an investigative tool had been outstripped in importance by other considerations. Other attitudes, values, vices and follies began to crowd his canvas, insisting on other forms of expression. The humours, although vital to an understanding of Jonson's early critical theory and literary practice, belong to this phase properly, and do not outlive it. Henceforth they are absorbed and disseminated; they sink to the bedrock of Jonson's thought and writing, where they continue to underpin almost all later characterization; but they were never again to surface in anything like their original, unmodified form.

With the opening up of the moral dimension, however, Jonson was able to give added depth and weight to the concept of humours. He also made possible an unforeseen connection which he then proceeded to bring to its highest achievement, the link between humours and satire. Other dramatists continued to use the term in its lighter sense; Jonson, having once come to perceive the humorous man as a disease both to himself and to the society he inhabited, spared neither the identification nor the correction. The linking of humours theory with satire brought forth the harsh and censorious elements of Jonson's artistic armoury; these in turn aroused others, and led to a series of dramatic and literary developments that Jonson himself could hardly have foreseen.

Satire holds this advantage for a writer, that it provides both material and the stance from which to handle it; it prescribes what to say and how to say it. It further offers the possibility of artistic expression, justification even, to a certain ruthlessly critical cast of mind such as Jonson not only possessed but rejoiced in; it was this that had attracted him to Nashe's unfinished play *The Isle of Dogs*. Satire is intellectually attractive, too, in its paradoxical reconciliation of two absolutes, being both anarchic and yet also conducted by ancient and well-known rules; simultaneously capable of being both exquisitely complex and brutally simple.

Jonson began from the hallowed satiric standpoint that the number of fools in the world is infinite; as he was later to make one of his prize idiots observe, 'they all come out of our house, the La Fooles of the

North, the La Fooles of the West, the La Fooles of the East and the South – we are as ancient a family as any is in Europe' (*Epicene*, I.iv.34–6). He also knew that he was the man to proclaim them; in the country of his mind, Jonson was lawgiver, priest and king. In so doing he drew on a variety of available traditions and techniques. Most consciously, of course, he harked back to the classics. Dryden was to say that 'the meat of Horace is more nourishing, but the cookery of Juvenal is more exquisite'.

Jonson strove to keep alive in his work, then, the weightier, more reflective Horatian stance, with its broad and firm moral base, without losing touch with the venom and vigour of Juvenal's attack. The Juvenalian capacity for inspired invective, vicious abuse and rampant pessimism had previously re-emerged in Nashe, and was to become, increasingly, Jonson's tone. In addition Jonson was, and remained, deeply interested in both private morality and public behaviour, the contrast between which was the staple of classical satire.

Overlaid upon this basis, and perhaps more deeply rooted in his mind and heart than Jonson cared to acknowledge, was the far less self-conscious English tradition of satire. This, in the Middle Ages, had been a thoroughly rambunctious business of zestful vilification, energetic rebuke, or pointed burlesque, often grounded on personal instances drawn from real life. Two central elements in the native tradition were the twin preoccupation with social class and with religion. Public behaviour was interpreted as the duty to marry the moral with the social. Jonson's work rarely lost the opportunity to stress this obligation.

As this suggests, the earlier satire was not always funny. On the contrary, it could be a matter of such high religious seriousness or earnest bitterness that it could quite fail of its purported reformatory effect. Jonson's satire never falls into this trap of deadly humourlessness. But he retained throughout his career a prejudice against ready mirth, and a feeling that it was somehow a descent on the part of the dramatist to raise a laugh among the spectators. Among other disadvantages or limitations of the form which Jonson either came to terms with or turned to advantage, the chief was the ephemerality of much of satire's material. If topical, it threatened always to be transient and insubstantial. Jonson overcame this by sticking to the Renaissance prescription of 'truth to nature' in a general rather than in a narrowly personal interpretation. He tried to achieve moral generalities, rather than particular instances, and to make the foul appear ludicrous, as well as disgusting, in every occurrence or application. This it was that lifted the level of Jonson's satire and gave it such lasting value as it possesses. When, at the end of his career, he abandoned this principle in the direct personal attack upon Inigo Jones, the play not only involved him in a good deal of obloquy, but worse, it patently failed as satire. To keep a separation between the personal and universal was not easy, and more than once Jonson's claim to be disinterested was called into question, or was seen to falter.

For Jonson embraced with equal enthusiasm the three divergent roles of the satirist: detached moralizer, committed reformer, and pitiless scourge. The assumption of the satirist's task in itself reveals a deep idealizing conviction that humanity is capable of so much more than it achieves; and this faith is sustained by a touching nostalgia for the golden world of former times, the vanished age of simplicity and truth. Yet the service of these noble ideals provides the opportunity for the exercise of Jonson's whole repertory of moral and intellectual scorn, endlessly reworked with a new inflection and relentless emphasis.

For whatever the elements that went into the composition, the final product and the tone in which it was delivered were all Jonson's own. Jonson seized on the essence of satire, that it is dialectical, an ongoing, unresolvable argument. While other writers manage some impressive satiric moments in the course of a play, or sustain a satiric tone, it fell to Jonson in his time to handle satire in an intrinsically dramatic way. His characters are not simply types paraded before us and finally exposed in one simple *peripeteia*; they vividly embody qualities and forces brought into the conflict that is the stuff of drama.

External circumstances combined to direct Jonson's gift for satire into the form in which it could find its true expression and expansion. From the publication of Thomas Lodge's *A Fig for Momus* in 1595, the first formal satire in English, an interest in the form had developed with unprecedented speed. Within a few years the upsurge of satirical expression as poets and pamphleteers energetically castigated various social classes, religions, customs and trades and the representatives of all these, had so alarmed the authorities of church and state as to arouse the fiercest opposition. In June of 1599 two leading prelates struck back. By order of the Archbishop of Canterbury and the Bishop of London, several volumes of satirical writings, including those of Marston, were burned at Stationers Hall, and the publication of any more 'satires or epigrams' was forbidden.

Denied a literary outlet, satire found a new channel for expression through the drama. Jonson's personal contribution to the circumventing of the edict was the creation of 'comical satire', whereby the satirist's concerns could find their statement in a theatrical vocabulary. He did not, however, regard this as an ideal solution. From the very start of his use of this new form, Jonson displayed a clear awareness both of its potential and its pitfalls. In each of his three subsequent 'comical satires' he made a distinct and different effort to find a satisfactory way of handling the conflict between the two personae, that of the sane reasonable author interested only in the correction of vice, and the unbalanced, intemperate railer who inevitably became his theatrical *alter ego* and mouthpiece. He did not exclude from his satiric scrutiny his own endeavours; he used satire to discredit comical satire and the new satirists, and attacked the form from within.

Jonson's decision to launch himself on the writing of comical satire in 1599 involved him in a good deal of this sort of self-scrutiny and critical reworking of his own concepts and methods. One development which outlived this immediate phase of Jonson's writing career, and influenced heavily his non-dramatic poetry too, was the question of the audience. A new form, in the hands of a new dramatist, once again raised the question of a new type of auditor; or at the least, of creating new attitudes in the old ones. As he wrote his way into his satiric dramas Jonson found himself involved not simply in educating his audience according to the time-honoured mandate of satire, but in creating an entirely new relationship between dramatist and spectators. What he sought was something like the interplay, the degree of mutual commitment, which existed between the satirical poet and his educated reader. This semi-accidental occurrence, whereby the expectations of the study were translated to the very different conditions of the public playhouse, became, for Jonson, over the course of a long writing career, something of an obsession. He was, as it proved, chasing a will o' the wisp – an ideal to him, but in its implication that audiences were, in their natural state, ignorant and inadequate, an insult to others. But no contemporary dramatist tried so hard and so sincerely for this special relationship with his audience, or felt so betrayed by his audience's failure to respond.

Every Man out of his Humour, then, was Jonson's first fully developed 'humours' comedy, his first 'comical satire', and his first experience, though not his last, of biting off more than he could chew. There is every evidence of his keen awareness that in attempting to link these two elements in dramatic form, he was embarking on a totally different kind of play from that which he had attempted before, or with which his audience was familiar; the composite Latin motto, for instance, explicitly asserts that the play is of a new kind. So from his first explosive entrance, Asper proclaims himself an unflinching satiric corrector, exceptional and unique. Driven by the moral 'evils and prodigies' around him, and temperamentally unable 'to flatter vice and daub iniquity', Asper delivers his famous satiric pledge:

> . . . with an armed and resolved hand
> I'll strip the ragged follies of the time,
> Naked, as at their birth . . .
>   . . . and with a whip of
>   steel
> Print wounding lashes in their iron ribs.
> I fear no mood stamped in a private brow
> When I am moved to unmask a public vice. . . .
> No brokers', usurers' or lawyers' gripe
> Were I disposed to say, they're all corrupt.
>   (Induction, lines 16–26)

A comparison between this bitter character and the parallel figure in *Every Man in his Humour* who ultimately controls the action and censures the fools and knaves, the humorous Justice Clement, readily illustrates that Jonson has leaped, at a bound, into a new world entirely. Jonson makes the savage, bitter Asper turn into a schoolmaster for the nonce, as he lectures the audience with a boiled-down version of medieval humours theory by way of a preliminary to the action, concluding with Jonson's often-quoted statement of the later modifications:

> Now, thus far,
> It may, by metaphor, apply itself
> Unto the general disposition,
> As when some one peculiar quality
> Doth so possess a man, that it doth draw
> All his affects, his spirits and his powers
> In their confluctions, all to run one way;
> This may be truly said to be a Humour.
> But that a rook, in wearing a pied feather,
> The cable hat-band, or the three-piled ruff,

A yard of shoe-tye, or the Switzer's knot
On his French garters, should affect a Humour!
O, 'tis more than most ridiculous.
                                    (Induction, lines 102–14)

'Humours' interpreted in this way, in and through the techniques
of satire, form the bridge between Jonson's old-style Elizabethan
comedy and the great comic masterpieces of his mature art.

The incorporation of these new themes and concepts in a new form
inevitably demanded new methods, and an abandonment of the old.
The use of an Induction, for example, is a marked technical departure
for Jonson. Nor was this the only innovation. Even in its own time,
Every Man out of his Humour caused comment through its lack of
conventional plotting. Jonson begins the play proper only after the
Induction, when Asper and two friends orate at length to frame the
play for the audience. Thereafter, although Asper steps inside the
frame of the drama by adopting the character of Macilente, the others
remain outside the action, where they can only interrupt the dramatic
flow by a constant stream of interjection and comment. The main
plot, subjected to this strategy of discontinuity, can hardly live up to
the name, resolving itself as it does into a series of episodes, each one a
vignette only loosely related to the others, and none firmly linked to
any central narrative thread.

Lacking the discipline of the tight, clockwork plot structure that
he had created for *Every Man in his Humour*, Jonson was hard put to it
to give his 'new form' any sense of forward movement. Within its
loose dramatic construction the characters float free of the action
neither governed nor propelled by any requirements of plot, and
forming as a result rather a procession or pageant than a play. Jonson's
attempts to interweave them with one another through the external
links of blood, marriage, or obligation, fail to produce any real
involvement or coherence, which could be produced in performance
only by the continued contrivance of visual and pictorial effect.

None of this, however, was accidental. Jonson was highly aware of
the play's formal deficiencies, and was drawn into an aggressive
defensiveness as he tried to explain its effects and thereby control the
audience's response. For the apparent weakness or failure of the play
was the result of a deliberate artistic policy to craft it just so, while the
running commentary of the two bystanders Mitis and Cordatus
indicates Jonson's sense that this decision and its fruits needed
constant elucidation. In his efforts to ensure that *Every Man out of his*

Humour was interpreted according to his requirements, Jonson engaged in a bewildering and distracting series of forward skirmishes and rearguard actions both with his real-life audiences, and with the critics in the theatre of his mind. Yet nowhere is there any sense that the still inexperienced author might have made any misjudgement, either of his drama or of his audience. Consider Jonson's method here of disposing of any possible objections:

> MITIS: Methinks Cordatus, he dwelt somewhat too long on this scene; it hung in the hand.
>
> CORDATUS: I see not where he could have insisted less, and t'have made the humours perspicuous enough.
>
> MITIS: True, as his subject lies; but he might have altered the shape of his argument, and explicated them better in single scenes.
>
> CORDATUS: That had been single indeed; why? be they not the same persons in this, that they would have been in those? . . .
>
> MITIS: Marry, you shall give me leave to make objections.
>
> CORDATUS: Oh, what else? it's the special intent of the author you should do so; for thereby others that are present may as well be satisfied, who happily would object the same you do. [1]
>
> (II.iii.288–308)

Despite the note of confidence here, Jonson's self-imposed plot problems were not so easily dealt with as this implies. They are nowhere more evident than in the play's conclusion. The old-style plot mechanism, if properly wound up, will go off like clockwork at the crisis of the action under its own momentum, as Jonson joyously demonstrated with *Every Man in his Humour.* But an unarticulated gallery of grotesques, whatever the satiric charge of each as an individual, cannot supply the dramatic impulsion necessary for a satisfying denouement. At the end of the play, Jonson's difficulty in finding a conclusion is evidenced by his original inspiration: Queen Elizabeth was to be personated on stage, in order that 'the very wonder of her presence' would strike Macilente dumb, and cure his envious humour. What Jonson was reaching for here is an essentially undramatic solution to a dramatic problem; he is offering a masque-like *coup d'oeil* instead of plausible plotting. And the introduction of the queen as a divine personification of all the abstract virtues, despite its link with the rather more up-to-date technique of using the royal personage to resolve the action in play-pageants like Sidney's *Lady of May* and Peele's *Arraignment of Paris*, still smells rather too much of the clumsy old device of the *deus ex machina* than of any new discovery of the new 'satirical comedy'.

In any case, the introduction of the queen did not please; either as a blatant piece of flattery devised as a bid for court favour or as a formal evasion of the issues raised within the play. At the first performance 'many seemed not to relish it', as Jonson stated in a note added to the text when he published it in 1600. But the chance to find a more convincing conclusion which the forced rewriting afforded was not taken up. In place of the dazzling conversion of Macilente, Jonson substituted a lame declaration of Asper/Macilente that the final verdict on the play rested only with those who could 'with discerning thoughts measure the pace / Of our strange Muse in this her maze of humour' (revised conclusion, lines 3–4). The Epilogue goes on to restate Jonson's by now laboured claims to be writing a new form, for a new audience. It is in no sense a dramatic or satisfactory conclusion.

Difficulties of plotting which result from the adoption of a literary rather than dramatic form are echoed in difficulties of characterization. One essential requirement of satire is the poet-commentator, half author and half critic, who will identify the objects of satiric scorn and undertake their correction with no holds barred. This figure is easily created in formal literary satire; he positively leaps from the pages of Marston in his Satire II, *Difficile est satyram non scribere* ('It is difficult not to write satire'):

> My soul is vexed, what power will'th desist,
> Or dares to stop the sharp fang'd Satirist?
> Who'll cool my rage? Who'll stay my itching fist,
> But I will plague and torture whom I list?
> (*Poems of John Marston*, ed. Arnold Davenport,
> Liverpool, 1961, lines 6–9)

Jonson's determination to translate this character into the drama, presenting him as an actor on stage while retaining the flexibility of his literary usage, involved him in some interesting manoeuvres. First, evidently, came the discovery that one persona was not enough to incorporate both his satirical and his 'humours' programme of investigation; so Asper was created simply to get the play off to a cracking start, after which he steps into the play as one of the participants, transmogrified into Macilente. Jonson clearly felt the need to have one satiric commentator inside the play, and one outside.

Yet even this proved not to be adequate. Within the play Jonson was forced to develop yet another satirist in the character of Buffone, to carry out the coarse railing which Macilente's austere and repressed personality makes inappropriate for him. Buffone is a jester of unrestrained detraction; he has no reforming zeal, but is heir to a long *commedia* tradition of loutish clowning and physical farce. His is the speech of vulgar scurrility, which does not deride the folly, but serves only to wound the fool.

This division of the satiric responsibility weakens Macilente's position at the centre of the drama, a position already somewhat confused by Jonson's desire to represent him both as an agent of satiric correction and as one in need of such correction himself (if this latter point is not the result of confusion on Jonson's part, but an attempt to create another deliberate and meaningful layer of irony, then we can only regret the absence of yet another satiric commentator to make this clear to us). In fact Jonson seems accurately to have foreseen the danger of making Macilente too far removed from the sinful and stupid 'humours' around him – he had to be implicated in their action somehow – but the gain in interest and complexity achieved by giving Macilente a 'lean and envious' humour of his own is paid for with a loss of clarity and control.

Nor can Jonson so easily dismantle the conditioned tendency of any audience to accept a character in a play as another human being like themselves. In human terms, Macilente is repellently vicious as he lurks on the fringes of the action of others; in dramatic terms the character cannot 'gel', nor cause others to do so. His ferocious frustration causes a kind of whirlpool effect, as Jonson sees to it that all the action is sucked around him, and in the last analysis goes down with him. All Jonson's preliminary decisions about this play mean that the audience has to accept the paradox of an unattractive character attracting all the action and interest. In subsequent 'comical satires' Jonson took pains to see that his satirists were imbued with better qualities. The intensity of Macilente's humour was, finally, another contributory factor to the failure of the play's original conclusion. A humour, as Jonson himself had laboured to establish, was a deeply psychological warp in nature, and as such to be cured only by an equally deep psychological stress, rather than by a trick of the theatre.

The use of the character of Macilente primarily to develop and to demonstrate 'humours theory' involves Jonson in formal and conventional difficulties of dramatic construction that are shared with the other characters. Jonson's devotion to his literary and intellectual purpose blunts his interest in characterization *per se*; it further ensures that the characters are trimmed to conform to the schema, and never develop the exuberant off-the-page life that Jonson shows himself capable of elsewhere. And as each character is conceived of in terms of its dominant 'humour', they all remain so, each one strongly individualized, but sealed within his or her own bubble of identity and isolated from any common flow of action; whirled around by Jonson simultaneously, but apart.

As in Jonson's previous plays, the *dramatis personae* particularly victimized by this method are the female characters. The indifference to women displayed by the young dramatist of *Every Man in his Humour* has, in the satiric vein, hardened into outright contempt. *Every Man out of his Humour* displays that strenuous anti-feminism which from henceforth was to be among Jonson's most characteristic and wildest wood-notes. Of the two female characters in the play, Fallace is characterized by her creator as 'a proud mincing peat' who 'only wants the face to be dishonest', while Saviolina is 'a court lady, whose weightiest praise is a light wit, admired by herself' (HS III, 425). These and other attacks upon the two women are pure Jonson, having no immediate classical source, though ample precedent in Juvenal, for example.

Indeed Jonson's anti-feminism in *Every Man out of his Humour* strikes a new and strident note. More recognizable, even at this early stage of Jonson's career, are the gulls, fools and knaves of the play, in whose creation we see Jonson both exercising his recently acquired skills and extending his range. Critics have pointed to the similarities between the 'Captain' Shift of this play, and Bobadilla of *Every Man in his Humour*, similarities which this speech of Shift amply illustrates:

> Sell my rapier? Gods lid! Nay, sir (for mine own part) as I am a man that has served in causes, or so, so I am not apt to injure any gentleman in the degree of falling foul, but sell my rapier? I will tell you, sir, I have served with this foolish rapier where some of us dare not appear in haste – I name no man – but let that pass. Sell my rapier? Death to my lungs! This rapier, sir, has travelled by my side, sir, the best part of France and the low country; I have seen Flushing, Brill and the Hague with this rapier, sir, in my Lord of Leicester's time; and by God's will, he that should offer to disrapier me now, I would – look you, sir . . .
>
> (III.vi.48–58)

Yet these characters are no mere rehashing of old forms. Shift is a lower creature altogether than Bobadilla, a far more shameless and egregious hustler. In addition, Jonson employs a dramatic technique new to him, Shakespeare's favourite device of doubling to intensify the effect, so that while the churl Sordido is 'a wretched hobnailed chuff' pure and simple, his brother Sogliardo, though no less of 'an essential clown', compounds his stupidity with gentlemanly pretensions. Similarly the 'neat, spruce, affecting courtier' Fastidius Brisk is satirized both in himself and by Jonson's technique of giving him a foolish shadow, Fungoso, whose vain attempts to imitate and keep up with his idol provide an interesting echo-effect and a biting commentary at the same time.

In a piece in which the author's main attention is given to the 'satirical humours', it comes as no surprise that these humours are its most successful aspect, being frequently very amusing, and realized with a genuine sense of stagecraft. The device by which Fungoso repeatedly appears on stage in an exact imitation of Brisk's costume, only to realize that his model has already changed into something new, provides one of many true moments of comic theatre. Similarly the running gag about Puntarvolo's dog, with the other characters enquiring solicitously after its health and its owner uttering bombastic threats – 'if thou losest my dog, thou shalt die a dog's death; I will hang thee' (III.ii.498) – is sustained throughout in both a comic and dramatic way.

Yet still, the play as a whole suffers from being over-controlled. Jonson is afraid to allow his 'humours' their head, so that local bursts of dramatic energy are soon trimmed back to keep them within the overarching framework of the whole. Jonson's obsession with his satiric purpose leads to an ever-present self-consciousness, as he seeks throughout to explain, justify and describe what he is doing. The attempts to give his play this perspective, and hence to control the audience's response, begin immediately it opens, with the often quoted passage in which Jonson expounds the relation of his play to classical forms of drama as defined by the authoritative critics of the Renaissance. In reviewing the available precedents Jonson hopes to establish the authenticity of his own proceedings; but he is clearly also trying to bully the spectators out of raising any objections, by massing the intellectual heavyweights of ancient authority against them.

This heavy didacticism dominates all aspects of *Every Man out of his Humour*, particularly its structure and tone. The search for a new comic form to replace the rambling romances or knockabout farces so popular on the Elizabethan stage had resolved itself into the need, in Jonson's eyes, to re-educate the contemporary audience. Hence the creation of Mitis and Cordatus, whose very existence is something of an anomaly since they are neither characters nor chorus, but a hybrid of Jonson's own devising in between. And having created them, Jonson clearly found them something of a liability; not only does their habit of interjection between scenes quite disrupt the dramatic flow, but Jonson is hard put to it to find something pertinent and penetrating for them to say on each appearance. Too often they are reduced to banalities like 'See who presents himself here!' and 'You understand where the scene is?' (III.ix.150–5).

Nevertheless the creation of these two characters is foremost among the factors which lend *Every Man out of his Humour* its strange and undeniable power. Jonson's underlying purpose, to shatter the comforting illusion that what the spectator is watching is a 'real' action, was a radically revisionary concept in the theatre of his time. The soaring confidence with which Jonson carried out his revolutionary undertaking sustained him through to the end, and the interjections remain as interesting as the play proper, despite the absence of 'character' as such in Mitis and Cordatus. Even with this, Jonson was not satisfied that the audience was sufficiently distanced from the action to maintain the required critical perspective. Accordingly he created an interlocking set of openings, or rather pseudo-openings, for the play. The original Induction, with Asper, Mitis and Cordatus, gives way to a duologue between Mitis and Cordatus; this is superseded by a Prologue, who amusingly disclaims his duty in that respect, on the grounds that Mitis has done his part for him, and who in turn is succeeded by Buffone, who in his own coarse and naturalistic fashion carries out the Prologue's traditional tasks of welcoming the audience and introducing the play proper. Even now, more short exchanges between Mitis and Cordatus, and a 32-line soliloquy, have to take place before the real action of the drama is allowed to begin.

Every Man out of his Humour, then, can in no sense be regarded as the work of a 'learner' dramatist. It is with the confidence of an established practitioner that Jonson sets himself to overthrow the conventional intrigue formulas of the comedy of his day, in favour of something that he himself was discovering only as he went along. This play in fact marks a critical moment in Jonson's evolution both as a dramatist-craftsman, and as an artist in the wider sense. It enabled him to practise those skills which he had already developed, most notably of language; the texture of the prose has a crackling intensity, and energy and tension, which at its height equals the best dialogue that Jonson was ever to produce. 'Wantonness of speech' is vividly dramatized through every variety of linguistic exhibitionism, and firmly geared to the moral and personal slipperiness that underlies and produces it.

In wider terms, too, the exploration of this theme in this form offered Jonson certain clear intellectual opportunities. Through and in *Every Man in his Humour* Jonson was able to examine and develop his theory of humours, his ideas about satire, his vision of the poet's artistic status and ideal relationship with the audience. Almost every item on this agenda was a new undertaking in drama; and this spills over in the undoubted sense of intellectual excitement which the play conveys, a certain intellectual flashiness, even. The play has enormous local vitality. Both its texture and its sense of purpose are electric.

These themes are, however, not in themselves intrinsically dramatic. *Every Man out of his Humour* in the last resort fails, at the simplest level, as a play. Yet its value to Jonson was enormous in the stage it marks in his evolution as a dramatist. To judge it alongside the plays of Jonson or his contemporaries is to miss its significance; it may not succeed as a play, but remains a powerful, memorable dramatic experiment whose value was to be felt much later on in Jonson's career.

Cynthia's Revels, or The Fountain of Self-Love, Jonson's second adventure in the new form of 'comical satire', nevertheless had certain crucial differences from his first.[2] *Every Man out of his Humour*, whether intentionally or not, seems to have inaugurated that curious sequence of events known to historians as the Stage Quarrel, or 'War of the Theatres', with the character of Clove intended as some sort of reflection upon John Marston. When Marston retaliated with *Jack Drum's Entertainment* in the first half of 1600, Jonson devoted the remainder of that year to working up his revenge.[3] When the new play, *Cynthia's Revels*, was staged by the Children of the Chapel at the Blackfriars around the turn of the year, he had the satisfaction of having created two offensive but highly recognizable portraits of his antagonists. Marston was pilloried as Hedon ('Pleasure'), a shallow voluptuary, while Dekker appeared as his foul-mouthed, down-at-heel side-kick Anaides. These are not of course the only characters or satirical targets in the play. But they are rendered with vigour, and even today can still attract attention; while in their own day they made exactly the impact that Jonson desired.

Jonson had other aims in view, too. This was the first occasion that he had worked for the re-formed boys' company, and the move to the private theatre had certain definite advantages for him. In the public theatre, the writer traditionally held a subordinate role in the company, and in the production of the play. Among the boys, there was the opportunity for the dramatist to be actively engaged in the presentation and direction of his work. Jonson's lifelong struggle for creative autonomy was more satisfied by this greater artistic freedom and control; his relish of the situation emerges clearly from the Induction to *Cynthia's Revels*, where he makes two of the boy players quarrel over who shall speak the Prologue:

> BOY 2: I think I have the most right to it, I am sure I studied it first.
> BOY 3: That's all one, if the author think I can speak it better.
>
> (lines 5—8)

As this suggests, the boy players took their work seriously, and achieved a notably high standard of performance. Their quality is attested not only by the famous reference in *Hamlet* (II.ii.338—43), but also by the playwright Middleton's advice to a London gallant, to 'call in at the Blackfriars, where he should see a nest of boys able to ravish a man'.[4] Two of the young players in particular attracted Jonson's attention and won his regard. Salomon Pavy had the task of playing one of the main characters, Anaides, in *Cynthia's Revels*; although he was only 11 when Jonson met him, he had been on the stage for some time, and his speciality lay in playing old men. Another 'leading man' of the boys' company was Nathan Field, later described by Jonson as the 'best actor' (*Bartholomew Fair*, V.iii.88).

To work with this talented and interesting company also answered another of Jonson's long-term aims, his desire to raise the status of the poet. The audiences of the Blackfriars, both more selected and selective, held out greater promise in this regard than the public of the Globe. Jonson could address himself there to the university wits, the Inns of Court men, the fashionable and sophisticated elements of London life. He could thereby hope to escape some of the odium which attached to writing for the theatres of the common people, and appeal directly to a more elevated society which would respect his role as poet within it.

Dramatically, however, the fact that *Cynthia's Revels* was written for a company of boy players rather than for adult actors made for some important modification; a more simplified, mannered technique of characterization, for instance, with plenty of opportunity for the parody acting for which the boys were celebrated. As an ex-actor himself, Jonson knew better than to overtax youthful performers, however talented; hence no part is unduly long or demanding, and the high spots are written to be conducted rather as arias, as an exchange of set-pieces, than as complex, rapid, or fluid emotional experiences.

More significant yet was the choice of a mythological setting for the play. Jonson's previous work on humours – Macilente as Envy, Buffone as Detraction – had tended towards the symbolic and the abstract. But *Cynthia's Revels* is the most determined expression of Jonson's allegorical tendency in this period. Jonson ambitiously sought to create a timeless world, composed of acknowledged eternal verities, yet with enough topical bite to give it a purchase on his audience's contemporary experience and expectation. To do so he combined several quite disparate elements; and if the result is questionable, the wonder is that he succeeded in his purposed synthesis of contradictory elements as well as he did.

The first of these, and the element most accessible to Jonson, was the mythology of Greece and Rome that supplied the framework; the choice of the two boy gods Mercury and Cupid as choric commentators being particularly appropriate to the capacities of the boy players. Closely connected with this were classical types, such as the foolish Asotus, who could have stepped straight out of the pages of Plautus. Another strand is composed of those characters who although given classical names are in fact old-fashioned English morality figures; their Greek names are Englished to 'Money' and 'Self-Love'. In strong contrast with these venerable literary and dramatic techniques was the continuance of Jonson's programme of 'humours study'. Not only are certain characters like the courtier Hedon produced by Jonson's newly perfected techniques, but whole areas, such as court pastimes and conduct, are surveyed and censured according to his sharpest satirical criteria.

It is to Jonson's credit that he succeeds in holding these potentially conflicting elements in tension rather than in open collision. They are not, of course, handled as separate lines of treatment; there is some overlapping, and with it some inevitable loss of definition. Cupid and Mercury, for instance, suffer the disadvantage of their mythological divinity, with a consequent loss of warmth and immediacy. Yet because of the overriding perspective of 'comical satire', Jonson cannot make too much of their godlike power and splendour. In the event the pair end up as merely commonplace – Cupid talks like a bootboy, and Mercury threatens to box his ears. It is perhaps noteworthy that Jonson had the best of all classical precedents, Horace, for treating Mercury like a 'rascal boy' (see *Odes* I, x); but

Horace was careful to restore the glory and grandeur of the godhead, too.[5]

More critical to the success of the play overall was the problem of combining all these elements into a persuasive and forward-moving drama. *Cynthia's Revels* has laboured under the stigma of being ponderous, formless, incoherent and undramatic, and cannot escape the charge of fundamental confusion in the structure of the plot. The double focus of the play emerges clearly from the opposition between title and subtitle, neither of which succeeds in catching up the main business of the plot – 'Cynthia's Revels' do not occur until the sixth scene of the fifth act in a masque-like series of episodes which bear no relation to what has gone before, while the 'Fountain of Self-Love' is introduced with a flourish at the beginning of the play, but soon drops out of sight into the background of the action.

This scene, of the introduction of the fountain (I.ii), neatly encapsulates many of Jonson's primary difficulties with his material. As a means of establishing the fountain and its properties, the lengthy and involved scene between Echo and Mercury can only be regarded as unwieldy and self-indulgent. Jonson, in the throes of a good *literary* idea, does not stop to question whether or not it can be made viable in dramatic terms. The scene reads well, but lacks the necessary tension and impulsion to make it work on stage. This is despite moments of evident lyrical power and pathos, like Echo's song, 'Slow, slow, fresh fount'. And as a dramatist Jonson is both throwing away the early opportunity to establish something of importance to the drama as a whole, and labouring to create something that he will not use again – the plays of his maturity are distinguished by a more careful husbandry than this wastefulness of the still experimental dramatist.

Throughout the play there is ample evidence of such slight dramatic situations, interlarded with heavy moments of tendentious set-pieces, where Jonson's recurrent fondness for baroque elaboration has its head. Jonson's preoccupation with his schema stifles his instinctive feeling for movement in the theatre, and an arid intellectualization converts intrinsically good comic ideas into static set-pieces, as Jonson deliberately side-steps the theatrical possibilities in favour of formal satiric comment. Typical is this address of Amorphus:

> I will now give you the particular, and distinct face of every your most noted species of persons, as, your merchant, your scholar, your soldier, your lawyer, courtier, etc, and each of these so

truly, as you would swear, but that your eye shall see the variation of the lineament, it were my most proper and genuine aspect. First, for your merchant or city-face, 'tis thus, a dull plodding face, still looking in a direct line, forward . . . then have you your student's, or academic face, which is here, an honest, simple, methodical face . . .

(II.iii.21–5)

And so on for fifty lines, while the other characters on stage are frozen into false attitudes of earnest attention. Numerous episodes like this clog the flow of the plot with essentially undramatic material, and Jonson's difficulties reach new heights as the play draws to its conclusion. Having committed himself to assigning the play's centrality to Cynthia, Jonson had to provide something appropriate to the play's *raison d'être* by way of allegorical or mythological contrivance. But he was labouring under one severe constraint, since his use of Queen Elizabeth in person at the end of *Every Man out of his Humour* had been so badly received. For this occasion then, in bringing on Cynthia, the 'Queen and Huntress, chaste and fair', Jonson offered a shameless reworking of the same motif of the divine and regal apparition that had failed at the end of the earlier play; this time, however, it was represented with all the allegorical and mythological contrivance that his ingenuity could summon up.

The last act of *Cynthia's Revels* therefore depends for its success upon the audience's readiness to accept the hardening of an already stiff and inflexible play into the overt formality of masque. The elaborate, cold and conventional flattery of the queen thrusts to the forefront of the dramatic business, while the humours recede into the background. Undeniably these long passages, so many dead expanses on the page, would be relieved in performance by spectacle, movement and music, the spectators' attention caught and nourished by other aspects of the theatrical art. But whatever allowances are made for it in the theatre of the mind, *Cynthia's Revels* in framework and design remains an intractable and over-schematized piece.

This is not to say, though, that the play is devoid of interest or merit. Once again Jonson's unfolding of his 'satirical humours' makes its own oblique comment on his earlier versions, techniques and solutions. The figure of Crites, for instance, represents a decisively different attempt on the figure of the satirical commentator; he holds his place at 'Cynthia's Court' as a sort of Moral Laureate, 'a creature of most perfect and divine temper':

56

one in whom the humours and elements are most peaceably met, without emulation or precedency; he is neither too fantastically melancholy, too slowly phlegmatic, too lightly sanguine, or too rashly choleric, but so composed and ordered as it is clear Nature went about some full work – she did more than make a man when she made him.

(II.iii.123–30)

Not for Crites the poisonous venom of the 'lean raw-boned anatomy', Macilente. Crites is judicious and restrained, a good-natured critic who in I.iv would rather simply flap the 'brace of butterflies', Asotus and Amorphus, than break them on the wheel of his rage. His moral position is established through general reflection in soliloquy rather than through direct attack upon the other characters as in the preceding play, and his comments come more in sorrow than in anger:

> O vanity,
> How are thy pained beauties doted on,
> By light and empty idiots! How pursued
> With open and extended appetite! . . .
> O how despised and base a thing is man
> If he not strive t'erect his grovelling thoughts
> Above the strain of flesh . . .
>
> (I.v.24–35)

Johnson is careful to keep Crites elevated above the satirical hurly-burly of the rest of the play by making him profess his indifference to any hostile comment:

> Do, good detraction, do! And I the while
> Shall shake thy spite off with a careless smile.
> Poor piteous gallants! What lean idle slights
> Their thoughts suggest to flatter their starved hopes
> As if I knew not how to entertain
> These straw-devices . . .
>
> (III.iii.1–6)

Despite this softening of the satirical commentator, however, the satire itself does not lack bite. Throughout the play social and moral follies are brought to the higher bar of ethical satire, and court foibles in particular come in for more serious censure than in the earlier plays. Jonson's production of fools, knaves and gulls is not inexhaustibly inventive – some of the characters in *Cynthia's Revels* strike notes sounded before – but in the procession of offenders none of these truants from sense and morality will escape the severest castigation. Jonson's main satiric focus is on the court and on the 'two essential parts of the courtier, pride and ignorance'. In a series of speeches in III.iv, Crites attacks the 'proud and spangled sir', attended by his 'mimics, jesters, panders, parasites'; the powerful thrusting verse here anticipates the portrait of Volpone. Other court-types, and their pastimes, are censured – Jonson later makes a particular satiric point of the silly wordgames and other shallow occupations with which the courtiers while away the time – in a comprehensive satiric survey which leaves none out (see IV.iii).

Yet again Jonson is careful to elevate his satire above the purely destructive, insisting that his attack upon court follies springs entirely from his concern that the court should be a mirror of virtue, leading in moral rather than worldly fashion and habits. As the individual 'humorist' betrays his humanity by failing to live up to its highest standards ('How far beneath the dignity of man / Their serious and most practised actions are!') so the corrupted court on a larger scale mimics the same action. This obvious truth, Jonson asserts, will be recognized by the true courtier, who will welcome the prospect of correction and reform:

> The better race in court
> That have the true nobility called virtue
> Will apprehend it as a grateful right
> Done to their separate merit; and approve
> The fit rebuke of so ridiculous heads
> Who with their apish customs and forced garbs
> Will bring the name of courtier in contempt . . .
> (V.i.30–6)

In addition to the sharper concentration upon the court as a satiric target, two further elements distinguish *Cynthia's Revels* as a key stage in Jonson's development of his craft. One is the emergence of personal satire in the attacks upon Marston and Dekker under the characters of Hedon and Anaides. These two former colleagues of Jonson were soon to be his bitterest enemies in the so-called Stage Quarrel. Such traces as there are of personal satire here, though, are slight – Jonson was still, as he so often and so virtuously claimed, interested in the type rather than the individual. Yet he came near enough for the two men to accept the caricatures as intended, in a move that clearly paved the way for the far more sharply individualized satiric portraits in his next play, *Poetaster*.

A second important element of Jonson's satire in *Cynthia's Revels* lies in its intensified anti-feminism, this time with the addition of an unmistakably Jonsonian grossness. Jonson's satirical models of the classical period, most notably Juvenal, slander women consistently and do not spare the lash. Jonson's attitudes to his female characters have also, however, another base and one closer to home, the 'realism' of medieval satire combined with the unquestioned 'common-sense' folk beliefs presenting women as shrews, sluts, witches, coarse-fibred, lubricious, garrulous and uncontrolled. Even Jonson's court 'ladies' are tarred with this brush. Here one is made to outline her fantasy vision of pruriently peering into others' secrets:

> There should not a nymph, or a widow, be got with child i'the verge, but I would guess, within one or two, who was the right father, and in what month it was gotten, with what words, and which way. I would tell you which Madame loved a Monsieur, which a player, which a page; who slept with her husband, who with her friend, who with her gentleman usher, who with her horse-keeper, who with her monkey, and who with all. Yes, and who jigged the cock, too.
>
> (IV.i.149–57)

In Jonson's scornful vision of womankind there is no counterbalance to these vulgar, foul-mouthed harpies; the bloodless Arete, a character of unreal excellence, exists rather as a moral example than as an individual. Arete clearly illustrates a prime weakness of Jonson's developing technique, and one that was to prove a lasting handicap, Jonson's inability to draw a warm, convincing, good woman. His virtuous female characters are invariably shallow and painfully thinly drawn; quite patently the work of a man who does not believe a word of what he is writing.

What then are the strengths of this odd and uneven production? One obvious advance for the still-budding dramatist is the increasing mastery over the distinction between verse and prose. In *Cynthia's Revels* Jonson moves decisively towards the establishing of prose as the appropriate vehicle for his form of comedy, avoiding the scenes of verse and prose mixed of the earlier works. Now verse is consistently used to signal a higher mode, employed by the characters who have a monopoly of truth and virtue in the play. Prose, in well-marked dramatic contrast, is the speech of the world of folly and affectation; as such it is common to all inhabitants whether fools or not; thus Crites speaks prose with the foolish then later rises to verse for his speeches of moral assertion or reproof. This use of the verse/prose contrast to denote a moral universe rather than as a device of individual characterization, is far simpler and more dramatically effective than anything Jonson had previously achieved.

Other elements, too, suggest Jonson's growing confidence in his powers. Many small touches denote Jonson's developing stage-craft, the ability to realize events and characters in this medium. Arete's simple black gown, for instance, amid the brilliantly plumaged courtiers makes a dramatic point in visual terms, clearly antedating the use of the same device in *Hamlet*. Similarly the scene in which Amorphus endeavours to instruct Asotus in the art of impressing a court lady (III.v) is a small masterpiece of comedy stagecraft, in which the lines are clearly written to be bodied out with comical movement and stage business:

> AMORPHUS: First, you present yourself, thus; and spying her, you fall off, and walk two turns, in which time it is to be supposed your passion hath sufficiently whited your face. Then, stifling a sigh or two, and closing your lips, with a trembling boldness and bold terror you advance yourself forward. Prove thus much, I pray you.
>
> ASOTUS: . . . Here I come in, you say, and present myself?
>
> AMORPHUS: Good.
>
> ASOTUS: And then I spy her, and walk off?
>
> AMORPHUS: Very good.
>
> ASOTUS: Now sir, I stifle and advance forward?
>
> AMORPHUS: Trembling.
>
> (III.v.7–20)

The scene reaches ever-increasing heights of absurdity as Amorphus, in a scene which anticipated Orlando's wooing of Rosalind in *As You Like It*, decides to stand in for the absent mistress and as such receives Asotus' laborious attentions:

> ASOTUS: I protest, you are the only, and absolute, unapparelled –
>
> AMORPHUS: Unparalleled.
>
> ASOTUS: Unparalleled creature I do adore and admire and respect and reverence in this court, corner of the world, or Kingdom.
>
> (III.v.66–71)

For the student of Jonson's career as a whole, however, the main interest of *Cynthia's Revels* lies in the place it holds in the evolution of Jonson's relations with his audience. As the Folio Prologue makes clear, Jonson was still hoping that his new form would find, or create, a new response. To that end, as in *Every Man out of his Humour*, he took pains from the opening lines of the play to shatter the dramatic illusion; we have again the repetition of the insistence that actors are only actors, and some are better than others. The same point, with illustrative examples, is also made about the spectators; Jonson vigorously condemns those who go to the play in selfishness, ignorance, or fashionable inanity.

What is emerging ever more clearly is that Jonson is demanding a new relationship between poet and audience. He seeks to redefine the nature of the dramatic relationship into one rather resembling that between the poet and his discerning reader, than that between the contemporary 'playwright' and his uncritical consumers. Outlining the qualifications of the ideal audience ('gracious silence, sweet attention / Quick sight and quicker apprehension') Jonson explicitly distinguishes between the 'vulgar and adulterate brain' and the 'learned ears' of discriminating spectators. To this, the highest type of audience, Jonson offers himself in his most elevated garb, that of 'poet'; which in itself attempts to construct, or reconstruct, the spectators as readers rather than as auditors.

In *Cynthia's Revels* Jonson is still only reaching towards this theory; yet it is sufficiently present throughout to prevent the work from being fully developed as a play. It remains a thin production, its characters little more than an animated set of gilded twittering insects. It floats in a never-never land somewhere between its mythological fantasy and the real world of court and city. Other shortcomings lie in the uneven nature of the work (like *The Case Is Altered*, it gets better as it goes along, showing that the dramatist had to write himself into it) and in the structural mismanagement which results in long unwieldy scenes following one another at critical stages of the action. Essentially it is over-written, and dedicated to non-dramatic purposes; as the Prologue boasts, the dramatist's aim was to offer 'words above action, matter above words'. Had action figured higher on the list of priorities, the result would have been more like a play. But the single major impediment to this was Jonson's own self-confidence, defiantly asserted in the Epilogue:

By God, 'tis good, and if you like't, you may.

61

Poetaster, Jonson's final flourish in the vein of 'comical satire', represents the culmination of this crucial phase of his 'self-perfection' as a working poet. As such the play looks both forward and back, while still remaining very much *sui generis*. Clearly Jonson did not learn easily from his mistakes. Once again he was driven to attempt the same type of conclusion that had already now twice proved unsatisfactory, the epiphany device of the sudden appearance of a character whose rank and moral quality combine to rebuke all fools and knaves. Undeterred by the difficulties he had brought on himself with the appearance of Queen Elizabeth at the end of *Every Man in his Humour* and Cynthia's in *Cynthia's Revels*, Jonson yet again chose to build his dramatic climax and denouement around the intervention of Augustus Caesar, whose court proceedings in the last act combine both the regal and the legal senses of the term.

This use of Augustus is part of a wider technique again reminiscent of *Cynthia's Revels*, the creation of a world based on classical history, myth and allegory. Working yet again within the necessarily circumscribed range of the boy players, Jonson went for slight characterization, stylized and shallow, as in the Act IV farewell of Ovid and Julia: 'Ovid, my love?' 'Here, heavenly Julia . . .' (line 1 ff). In some ways, however, Jonson's dramatic technique in *Poetaster* is much more clearly a throw-back as far as *Every Man in his Humour*. The early scenes especially, in which Jonson introduces a high-spirited young man whose devotion to poetry and worldly pastimes sets him at odds with his crusty old father, are irresistibly reminiscent of the earlier play. And when we see Jonson's plotting of the play's opening moves in terms of the older style of intrigue comedy, the reversion seems complete. This is in part attributable to the known speed with which Jonson finished this play, not more than four or five months after the production of *Cynthia's Revels*, in an uncharacteristic fifteen-week burst of productivity – there simply would not have been time for the notoriously slow-working dramatist to devise more 'new ways' of handling his 'comical satire', and what more natural than that he should fall back on his 'first good one', as Aubrey styled *Every Man in his Humour*?

Yet as the play unfolds, Jonson's maturer purposes begin to emerge. Dominant overall is a firmer and darker satiric intent; this is reflected also in *Poetaster*'s heightened moral intensity and more complex ethical situation. Jonson's satire in *Poetaster* is multi-faceted, taking in a wider range of subjects and concerns than is implied by its conventional location as the climactic skirmish in the personal battle of the 'War of the Theatres'.

Much critical attention has been devoted to the personal satire on Marston and Dekker in the characters of Crispinus and Demetrius Fannius. The former in particular is a harsh portrait of a ridiculous man, fulsome, vain, garrulous and clinging. Demetrius is possessed of the even more unattractive quality of being 'nitty', and together both are made to represent all that is intellectually shabby and contemptible. Clearly these are not entirely personalized character sketches – Jonson adapted previously established humours types as the frames for his satiric portraits of Marston and Dekker. There are many non-Marstonian traits in Crispinus, and the envious slanderer Demetrius, only lightly individualized, does not bear any close relation to the man revealed in Dekker's works. But the overarching identification remained to indict these two men. The crisis of this strand of the action is designed to bring humiliation upon their respective characters; in the final proceeding in Caesar's court, Marston-Crispinus is paid out in a cruel, coarse vomiting sequence during which he violently spews up all the long words and affected utterances that have so offended Jonson (V.iii.466–528).

Other victims of the satirist's scorn are not served so harshly. As a lampoon either upon an individual or on the breed of vainglorious soldier, Captain Tucca is a markedly affectionate characterization, and the caricatured actors, too, are very lightly sketched in. As a result, although they may very well glance at known members of the Lord Chamberlain's Company, or other members of the theatrical profession whom Jonson had worked with, the evidence is far too slender to permit of any firm identification of a precise satiric victim. The same is true of Jonson's satire on lawyers.

For as Jonson constantly insists, the impersonal mode is his chosen satiric purpose and method:

> I used no name. My books have still been taught
> To spare the person, and to speak the vice.
> (*Apologetical Dialogue*, lines 84–5)

As this claims, the players are not attacked individually in *Poetaster*. And where they are generally censured, the attack is often double-edged. Here, for instance, a pompous worthy criticizes the actors in terms that reveal his own shortcomings as much as those he condemns:

These players are an idle generation, and do much harm in a state, corrupt young gentry very much, I know it. I have not been a tribune thus long, and observed nothing. Besides, they will rob us, us that are magistrates, of our respect; bring us upon their stages and make us ridiculous to the plebeians. They will play you, or me, the wisest men they can come by, still . . . only to bring us into contempt with the vulgar, and make us cheap.

(I.ii.36–44)

Jonson goes to considerable lengths throughout *Poetaster* to try to keep his satirical comment upon this generalized level. Despite the inclusion of the personal element, essentially he wishes his auditors to accept that this is not a personal quarrel. Jonson uses his satire as an instrument of prescription as well as of proscription, and *Poetaster* is to be seen ultimately not as an attack upon any one individual or group, but as a dramatized defence of the sacred right of play-making itself; 'poetry', in Jonson's term. The elevation of poetry above her currently degraded usage involved Jonson in this critique of poetry's enemies. These include all those who impede the true poet in his work; those who are false pretenders to be poets themselves; and those who as educated people ought to be upholding true art against debasers of the standard.

Poetaster ridicules all these assorted enemies of the literary art in turn. The poetasters themselves are prominent here as types of incompetence and fraud as well as examples of Jonson's personal enemies: 'poet-apes . . . whose forked tongues / Are steeped in venom as their hearts in gall'. Such men 'wrest, pervert, and poison all they see' (Induction, 35–9), and must be identified and resisted as a moral duty. The running satiric theme is the prevalence of 'that common spawn of ignorance' of which these are only instances.

Even without the known background to this play of the personal bitterness which provoked the dramatic infighting later known as the 'War of the Theatres', it would be wise to take Jonson's moral protestations with a pinch of salt. Jonson certainly considered it beneath the dignity of a poet to indulge in highly personal invective, but he was not above giving the vicious or foolish traits of his enemies and acquaintances to some of his stage characters. Yet however closely grounded his satire was in personal experience or classical precedent, Jonson continued to sound the note of general moral outrage. This is coupled with an examination of the history and function of satire in such a way as to lend support for Jonson's own satiric targets and practices.

Among these, one of the most interesting is his creation of the old Roman poet Horace as his own dramatic persona in the play. With the choice of this character, the off-stage presence of a key classical author as deployed in the earlier plays (Plautus, for instance) now comes on stage. Jonson's presentation of Horace seeks to vindicate and to elevate his own endeavours by associating them with one of the greatest writers of the classical world. So we are told of Horace–Jonson that 'they say he's an excellent poet' (III.i.3–4); and Jonson also tries to cast over his own activities, both within the play and outside it, the well-known Horatian veil of urbane toleration of the follies of lesser men.

Horace offered an attractive model for Jonson in terms both of his life and art. As an author Horace never tried to deny his humble origins, and remained devoid of social pretension, despising equally court society and political intrigue. He was an exacting craftsman, who throughout his career cared little about pleasing the average reader, but sought the approval of the discriminating few. There is an element of pathos in Jonson's self-projection, since Horace attained a level of artistic excellence which Jonson was as yet striving for, and with it commanded the respect of his contemporaries which Jonson long wished for in vain. There is, however, nothing but humour in Jonson's adaptation of his Horace character to work in his own boasts. 'Horace is a man of the sword,' we are told, 'they say he's valiant' (IV.vii.17–18). Jonson is here reworking for telling comic effect the familiar fact that Horace was a small weakly man, who on his own admission fled ingloriously from his one military engagement.

Despite such touches of humour, however, the device rebounded on Jonson's head within the play, as well as offering his antagonists a heaven-sent satiric handle for their riposte. In view of Horace's stature, the identification seemed purely overweening: none too accurate, either, as the Horatian pose of calm restraint and human tolerance cracks under Crispinus' provocation into an unmistakably Jonsonian irritability. Jonson's attempt to use Horace as the satiric commentator and also as his own mouthpiece within the play very soon breaks down under the strain of these opposing demands.

Equally problematic is Jonson's other primary use of the Horace figure, as the symbol and standard of literary merit against which the poetasters are measured and found wanting. This involves Jonson–Horace in writing his own specious self-justification. In the course of the characterization, Jonson incorporated considerable amounts of Horace's poetry, closely and vigorously rendered into Jonson's own English, in order to demonstrate the classical standard from which the contemporary practitioners were deviating. One entire scene (III.v) is devoted to a debate, in 140 lines of rhymed couplets, whose sole purpose is to allow 'Horace' to discuss satire in general, and to proceed from there to a defence of his own practices. Even worse, however, is the introduction of Virgil to add his voice to the chorus admiring Horace–Jonson. In a long speech Virgil is made to attack the 'brainless creatures' or 'malicious, ignorant and base' misinterpreters of Jonson (V.iii.135–44). The whole device leads to an embarrassing climax in which Jonson's integrity is shamelessly vindicated and exalted.

As in this episode, so throughout. Jonson allows the satiric purpose of the play to determine its framework and movement. From the first *Poetaster* suffers from the lack of any firm plot structure that will lend conviction to its narrative. The early scenes are unpersuasively articulated, and the focus of interest is dissipated as characters like Hermogenes, Gallus and Albius are introduced who carry no significance for the rest of the play. In the third act Jonson loses his way as he complicates the thread of the plot with a plethora of minor characters; while major characters like Horace and Crispinus are involved in scenes of over-indulgent writing and inordinate length, like III.i, where the single joke of Horace's desire to escape from Crispinus' fatuous company is hammered into the ground.

Objections to the plot of *Poetaster* cluster thick and fast as the end of the play comes into view. Where does the play's emotional centre lie, and what are we to make of the parting of the two lovers, Ovid and Julia? Critics have disagreed over whether Jonson intends an affecting scene of true love thwarted, attended with pathos, or whether this scene too contributes to the play's overall satiric structure, and as such ironizes the lovers heavily. Only if we accept that the satiric task of the play is to deflate the pseudo-poets can we discover any kind of meaning in the play's structure; any attempt to follow certain characters through to the climax is doomed to frustration. *Poetaster* has some vital and amusing episodes, but it is, overall, thin on plot, a deficiency which is not compensated for by long dense speeches and scenes.

As this suggests, like the earlier 'comical satires', the moving spirit at work within *Poetaster* is, in the last resort, undramatic; and despite moments of local vivacity, the piece does not ultimately convince as a play. The high moments are supplied, predictably enough, by Jonson's ever-extending skills with language and dialogue. His Captain Tucca, for instance, in a play that nowhere else rises to this level of idiosyncratic brilliance, is a work of genius, a genuinely exhilarating comic creation. One of Jonson's great successes in the technique of using speech to define character, Tucca is given more extraordinary linguistic variations than any other Jonson character. His energetic, eccentric, jerky style is based on a series of aggressive questions:

> A player? Call him, call the lousy slave hither. What, will he sail by, and not once strike, or vail to a man of war? Ha? do you hear? you, player, rogue, stalker, come back here – no respect to a man of worship, you slave? What, you are proud, you rascal, are you proud? ha? you grow rich, do you? and purchase, you twopenny tear-mouth? you have fortune and the good year on your side, you stinkard? you have? you have?
>
> (III.iv.120–7)

The split between verse and prose is once again articulated in terms of the opposing worlds of the play, the virtuous and the vicious – the good speak verse, and the bad, prose. But the central area in which the two interact is all uncertainty. The play is a stylistic hiatus in a line of development which leads to all-verse plays like *Sejanus* and *Catiline*, and all-prose plays like *Epicene* and *Bartholomew Fair*. Lesser characters too, like the affected Crispinus or the besotted Albius, occasionally catch the spark of Jonson's imagination. But Jonson's own defiant and defensive tone in the speech of the armed Prologue indicates his awareness that his play needs a good measure of sabre-rattling to get it off the ground:

> Here now, put case our author should once more
> Swear that his play were good; he doth implore
> You would not argue him of arrogance . . .
>
> (lines 15–17)

Either as a symbolically represented world of the dramatist and his professional adversaries, or as a scholarly and imaginative revival of life in Ancient Rome, Jonson cannot knit together his undramatic and untheatrical materials into a convincing play.

Yet for this very reason *Poetaster* marks a critical moment in Jonson's career as an artist. Many of its elements, like those of *Cynthia's Revels* and the finale of *Every Man out of his Humour*, look forward not in the direction of the plays soon to come, but towards the form Jonson was yet to take up, that of the masque. Notably masque-like devices and conventions include the choice of a mythological setting, with its adaptability to an allegorical interpretation; the abundance of static, non-dramatic set-pieces and speeches; the use of music and formalized movement; and the discussion of the function of royalty with the assertion of the supereminence of the monarch as the cynosure of all hopes.

All these elements were to become much more familiar in the years ahead. But the over-laboured journeyman playwright had for the time being gone as far as he could go with the form of 'comical satire'. Stung with the venom of the personal attacks upon him, Jonson published his intention to 'leave the loathed stage', not without a lengthy, anguished and still-defiant burst of self-vindication:

> I, that spend half my nights and all my days,
> Here in a cell, to get a dark pale face
> To come forth worth the ivy, or the bays
> And in this age can hope no other grace —
> Leave me! There's something come into my thought
> That must, and shall, be sung high and aloof,
> Safe from the wolf's black jaw, and the dull ass's hoof.
>
> (*Apologetical Dialogue*, lines 223–9)

Jonson had learned much of his professed craft, and his early work has much that it can teach us. Many Jonsonians hasten past these plays, seeing them at best as a preparation for the greater glories that were yet to come. But Jonson in 1603 had no cause to see his own work in this light. One avenue had proved a dead end – so be it. There was a world elsewhere.

4

SUNG HIGH AND ALOOF

Every Man out of his Humour had been designed to elevate Jonson's claim to high seriousness as both writer and thinker. But received by his fellow dramatists on an altogether more personal level, it had triggered off the sequence of satiric assault and retaliation which literary historians have come to call the 'War of the Theatres' or the 'Stage Quarrel'.[1] In the blast and counter-blast of insulting dramatic caricatures, Jonson found himself isolated and quite literally out-played. His defeat in the 'War' was therefore nothing less than a stinging humiliation. But it was not experienced as an artistic rebuff. On the contrary it intensified his determination, expressed in the *Apologetical Dialogue*, 'to come forth worth the ivy, or the bays', to rise like the phoenix and confound his scoffing enemies and unappreci-ative public with the skill of his craft and the might of his art. For Jonson continued to see himself both as the guardian of the highest traditional standards, and as a pioneer of all that was new in the drama, unaware or unheedful of the inherent contradictions between these two positions. But he accepted that he had taken his programme of reform as far as it could proceed through 'comical satire'. The withdrawal from the public stage to sing 'high and aloof' after the completion of *Poetaster* ushered in a sabbatical of rest and retrench-ment – apart from the play *Richard Crookback*, proposed to Henslowe in 1602 but otherwise unknown and either lost, unfinished, or unwritten, Jonson wrote nothing of substance for upwards of two years.

What he produced at the end of this time, however, clearly demonstrates his conviction that he could and must elevate his craft into art. This phase of Jonson's career was one of new departures; it yielded Jonson's first masque, his first sustained production of non-dramatic poetry, but above all the first tragedy that Jonson thought fit to preserve for posterity, and arguably his first great play. *The Tragedy of Sejanus*, a piece of strange and brooding power, is not least remarkable as the first example of the fusion of satire and dark intrigue that was to prove so fruitful for *Volpone* and *The Alchemist*.

Jonson's ruthlessness with his own prentice and hack work has placed *Sejanus* upon a false eminence. Jonson was in fact no stranger to the form of tragedy. His debut in the theatre had been as an actor in the most famous tragedy of the age, Kyd's *Spanish Tragedy*; he had also worked on this play under commission to refurbish it for newer audiences. As early as 1598 Francis Meres in *Palladis Tamia* had cited 'Benjamin Johnson' as 'among our best for tragedy'; among his lost works are several that, like *Robert II King of Scots* (1599), point to an interest both in history and in doomed rulers of other countries. Henslowe's accounts also make mention of an outline by Jonson for the plot of a tragedy that was finished by Chapman.

It is not surprising, then, that *Sejanus* has little of the feel of the novice tragedian about it. Nevertheless there was much about the writing of this play that was new for Jonson, or designed to accomplish a newer object than the plays noticed by Meres. This was, for Jonson, a conscious departure from the earlier modes both of citizen comedy and 'comical satire'. It was to be the inauguration of a grander vision, more ambitious in scope and scale; it was to incorporate Jonson's artistic and literary theories; and by doing all these, it was to chastise and reform the vulgar. In the service of these lofty objectives, Jonson moved into the only predominantly verse phase of his writing career; tragedy, masque and epigram alike avoid the prose medium which he had previously been developing with such skill and verve.

But Jonson's well-flourished launch in a fresh direction has obscured the extent to which some key factors of his thought and style pull through quite consistently from the earlier work. Chief among these is the continued reliance upon classical sources for material and inflection; the satiric colouring too carries over from comedy to tragedy with a very distinctive effect. Nor has Jonson abandoned his battle with the audience; rebuffed in one assault, he had regrouped his forces for another onslaught upon the only enemy of art, ignorance. Nothing had shaken his conviction that the way to reshape the theatregoer's preference was through the establishing of new standards by main force both of precept and of example. Finally *Sejanus* discusses in a darker guise some familiar Jonsonian themes: the corruption of manners, the time's decay, and the centrality of the court as the *fons et origo* of personal and public standards of conduct.

Jonson's use of his classical knowledge in the construction of *Sejanus* provides some interesting insights both into his dramatic purpose and his method of working. Wide-ranging source materials here include Books IV and V of the *Annals* of Tacitus, and Dio Cassius' *History of the Romans* (this last a Greek, not a Latin text), while copious footnotes prepared by Jonson for the play's later publication make reference also to Juvenal, Seneca, Suetonius, Pliny, Horace and Plautus – Jonson took a keen pleasure in loading the printed text with documentation. He also made it a point of pride to follow his sources with great fidelity. Not for him Shakespeare's conspirators against Julius Caesar with their hats plucked about their ears (II.i.73); he aimed for a scholarly reconstruction of life in Ancient Rome, correct in every detail from forms of address to religious rituals. Act V, scene iii. for instance, introduces at a critical moment of the action an extended piece of stage business of this authentic sort:

> The Flamen [priest] takes of the honey with his finger, and tastes, then ministers to all the rest; so of the milk in an earthen vessel he deals about; which done, he sprinkleth upon the altar milk, then imposeth the honey, and kindleth his gums, and after censing about the altar placeth his censer thereon, into which they put several branches of poppy, and the music ceasing, proceed.

At this and many other moments of *Sejanus*, a whiff of the study evokes Jonson at work with his pile of authorities at his elbow, the relevant passage in the text open upon the table before him. In dialogue, too, the correspondence is often so close that Jonson's wording is virtually a translation of his original. Such passages of translated or closely paraphrased material amount to upwards of a quarter of the finished text. [2]

Yet *Sejanus* is not simply a pedantic assembly of classical matter. Jonson felt quite free to rework these elements into a more appropriate form; he denied the need for a formal chorus, for instance, but incorporated some kind of choric performance at the end of the first four acts. For his aim was to make a drama, not a history, and although he was scrupulous to employ the best authorities available to him, he took a brisk way with historical events, compressing action from years into minutes to heighten dramatic tension or to create a sense of menace. He welcomed, too, the chance to body out the historical narrative and to fill in the gaps that history had left blank. At various points, therefore, characters are introduced into situations where history has not recorded their presence, and the order of events is reversed, as when Jonson makes Sejanus begin his seduction of Drusus' wife before Drusus has shamed him publicly, rather than after, as in Tacitus. This change intensifies Sejanus' calculation and malignity, and increases pity for his victim. As Sejanus himself cynically observes, the whole business has no connection at all with love: 'Venus hath the smallest share in it' (I.384).

And Jonson's historical realism operates at a deeper level than that of surface verisimilitude. His saturation in the writings of the period enabled him to recapture some of the feel of Tiberius' Rome, and the emotional attitudes of the time that combined to form the widely famed Roman temperament. Sejanus, however himself despised by the nobility of Rome, still expresses the contempt felt by every freeborn Roman for 'Egyptian slaves, Parthians and barefoot Hebrews'. Again, Silius, wound about by Sejanus' treacheries and at bay against his enemies, bursts out with 'I am a Roman'; the simple but unassailable declaration of faith with which the Romans fortified their world-wide sense of mission in law, government, art and literature, 'Romanus sum'.

Jonson's use of classical writers in Sejanus is, also, as much a matter of tone and colouring as of sheer information. As with the comical satires, the influence of Juvenal is pervasive and strong; his import-ance to the composition of the whole is freely acknowledged by Jonson in the footnotes to the 1605 edition. From Juvenal Jonson derived such information as he had of the climax and catastrophe of Sejanus' story, Tacitus' original narrative having perished. Juvenal supplied, too, many of Jonson's most telling phrases and images – 'Cut / Men's throats with whisperings' (I.30–1), for example.

In addition to the wealth of arresting detail, Juvenal provided a sardonic perspective which Jonson found peculiarly compatible with this theme and material. Through the eyes of the few good characters who survive in the corruption of Rome, Jonson presents an attack upon the evil consequences of untrammelled ambition in a vein of dark and savage satire. To rail upon the degraded state of things is the only course open to the virtuous; and the speeches of Arruntius in particular demonstrate his Juvenalian pedigree throughout. Arruntius is Jonson's invention – he is not mentioned in Tacitus, Dio Cassius, or Suetonius, Jonson's other principal sources. Jonson gives him first an interest in scurrilous personal gossip like this recalling of Sejanus' origins:

> I knew him at Caius' trencher, when for hire
> He prostituted his abused body
> To that great gourmand, fat Apicius,
> And was the noted pathic [sodomite] of the time.
>
> (I.213–16)

Equally strongly present is the venomous personal involvement of the satiric commentator – 'I'd hurl his panting brain about the air' – with the ability to progress from the immediate to a magisterial analysis of the state of the nation at large:

> No place, no day, no hour we see is free,
> Not our religious and most sacred times
> From some one kind of cruelty; all matter,
> Nay, all occasion pleaseth. Madmen's rage,
> The idleness of drunkards, women's nothing,
> Jester's simplicity, all, all is good
> That can be catched at. Nor is now the event
> Of any person, or for any crime
> To be expected, for 'tis always one –
> Death, with some little difference
> Of place, or time . . .
>
> (IV.300–21)

This declaration and the profound moral sense that it displays trace back directly to Juvenal's satiric stance, and in particular to his moral aversion to the life of the Roman Empire in decay.

Yet Jonson did not come to his ancient authors directly, but through the Renaissance scholars and editors who prepared the texts upon which he depended. Nor did Jonson confine his reading to the productions of the classical world, but took a lively interest in contemporary writings both from England and Europe, resulting in a substantial Renaissance colouring of the whole. In composing such a play at all, Jonson was obeying the contemporary humanist impulse to make history, and history plays, an instrument of moral education. More specifically, critics have pointed out Jonson's dependence on his editor of Tacitus, the great Belgian Justus Lipsius. Another helpful figure was the scholar described by Jonson as 'Rhodig', Lodovico Ricchieri Rhodiginus, the author of *Sixteen Books of Old Authors* (1516).[3]

The single most important Renaissance influence on *Sejanus*, however, came from the well-thumbed pages of Machiavelli.[4] Jonson's reading of Machiavelli's *Discourses on Livy* and his major work *The Prince*, had the effect of altering the balance and tone of the Roman originals that he used. Machiavellian philosophical importations include the detailed examination of statecraft, and the discussion of the duty of the prince to protect himself from the ambitions of those around him. The contribution of Machiavelli's thought to Jonson in the making of *Sejanus* goes across many lines of theme and plot; the desire to preserve the lawful rule and to ensure the true succession, for instance, was purely a Renaissance, never a classical notion.

To what purpose, then, did Jonson attempt to put these blended elements of classicism, satire and Renaissance theory? *Sejanus* was intended as a weighty and instructive examination of both personal and public corruption; from the evil centre of the 'noted pathic', 'minion of Fortune', and opportunistic manipulator Sejanus, a tide of rottenness washes out to engulf the good and bear up only those light enough to go with the current. Sejanus' ruthless exploitation of his position as the emperor's trusted adviser does not only flow downwards to corrupt his subordinates, and lower-placed colleagues; it flows upward, too, to compromise the ruler by the nearness of a tainted deputy. Yet the tainted deputy could only spring up in the shadow of a corrupted principal like Tiberius. From this it follows that the state itself is sick – it is noteworthy that metaphors of disease and death recur in the play – so that only a violent convulsion like the fall of Sejanus can purge it. Jonson's analysis of these important themes remains dark, even despairing, throughout. There is no suggestion, for instance, that the removal of Sejanus will extirpate the vice, rather the ominous implication that by using Macro to dislodge Sejanus, Tiberius is merely taking another viper to his bosom.

Within this thematic framework the examination of the corruption of the court has much in common with that undertaken in a lighter vein in the comical satires. Jonson begins the play by fiercely stigmatizing the skills needed for success in this world of wickedness; the social climber has to be able to 'Lie / Flatter and swear, forswear, deprave, inform, / Smile, and betray' (I.23–5). From there he hacks away at the tentacles of parasitism and the 'flatteries that do corrupt the times'; as more and more dependants, servants and minions are drawn into the activities of the 'great ones', the evil spreads in ever-widening circles. Sejanus' career occurs as much through the weakness, self-seeking, and moral vacuity of those who lack the conviction to oppose him, as it does through his own energies.

And like the comical satires again, underlying Jonson's stern depiction of the decay of Rome is the ideal of the good society, the healthy commonwealth. The moral base of his political theory is always the ordered, organic Renaissance cosmos with God at the head, while all things below 'observe degree, priority and place'. When any member neglects his responsibilities, from the ruler (God's deputy) downwards, sinking his duty to others in blind self-seeking, then all suffer, good and evil alike. Jonson's inability to make the appearances of Elizabeth, Cynthia and Augustus work dramatically as the manifestation of 'lawful rule and right supremacy' at the end of the 'comical satires' had done nothing to undermine his faith that this was still the ruler's obligation and prerogative: his concept of the ruler remained the same, whether in the context of 'comical satire', or of tragedy. *Sejanus* is by far the most subtle and penetrating of these attempts to dramatize this view, being simultaneously an essay on the theme that 'a prince's power makes all his actions virtue' (III. ii. 713) and a harshly ironic gloss upon it, through the vicious actions of Tiberius and Sejanus.

This conviction of Jonson's, tying in as it does with his general moral schema, lends *Sejanus* its undeniable thrust and sombre power. From the first entry of the dissidents, contrasted with that of the spies and sycophants immediately following, to the appearance of the 'court-god' Sejanus himself, Jonson holds our attention through to the climax of the tragedy. Both the Act III turning-point, when Sejanus overreaches himself, and the intermittent climaxes like the death of Silius are carefully sited to generate maximum tension and dramatic thrust. Within this confident and forward-moving structure, short scenes are artfully varied with longer episodes, private fortunes are set against the business of the state, and *tête-à-têtes* superseded by full public occasions.

Jonson's maturing stagecraft indeed is everywhere evident, as also are the benefits that come from the longer period of more careful composition. Despite the large number of characters in the play – thirty men and two women, excluding extras – Jonson establishes them all firmly, if briefly, as individuals, and supplies all that the audience will need to follow them throughout the play. To his previous command of the duologue Jonson has now added the ability to handle characters in groups, so that the climactic senate sequence, where the all-powerful Sejanus is at last pulled down, is realized visually as a stunning piece of theatre, with the senatorial rats deserting Sejanus one by one and slipping away to the other side of the stage as they begin to get wind of his impending fall.

Another remarkable feature of *Sejanus* lies in Jonson's new mastery of verse. The comical satires, where Jonson's verbal inventiveness had been directed towards the development of a naturalistic dramatic prose, hardly seem adequate preparation for this effortless, naturalistic and vigorous verse. The play abounds in examples of exchanges in which, through a bold and flexible use of the caesura, endstopping and enjambment Jonson creates a medium which echoes the rhythms of everyday speech while still retaining the special effect and distinction of verse:

> HATERIUS: How well his lordship looks today!
> TRIO: As if
>   He had been born or made for this hour's state.
> COTTA: Your fellow-consul's come about, methinks?
> TRIO: Ay, he is wise.
> SANQUINIUS: Sejanus trusts him well.
> TRIO: Sejanus is a noble, bounteous lord.
> HATERIUS: He is so, and most valiant.
> LATIARIS: And most wise.
> SENATOR: He's everything.
> LATIARIS: Worthy of all, and more
>   Than bounty can bestow.
>
> (V.480–7)

Impressive too is the facility with which Jonson succeeds in combining his individually well-crafted iambic pentameters into lengthy speeches which unroll with a massive driving force. Generations of critics have admired Sejanus' megalomaniac rhapsody at the start of Act V, 'Swell, swell, my joys . . .' Here Jonson exploits to the full the anti-realistic and hyperbolic nature of his verse, and its potential as a more incantatory medium than prose. But almost every scene of the play demonstrates Jonson's skill in creating a fluid, pulsing verse which at its best has the unmistakable quality of pure dramatic power:

> O, you equal gods,
> Whose justice not a world of wolf-turned men
> Shall make me to accuse, how e'er provoke[d],
> Have I for this so oft engaged myself,

Stood in the heat and fervour of the fight,
When Phoebus sooner hath forsook the day
Than I the field? Against the blue-eyed Gauls
And crisped Germans, when our Roman eagles
Have fanned the fire with their labouring wings
And no blow dealt that left not death behind it?
When I have charged alone into the troops
Of curled Sicambrians, routed them and came
Not off, with backward ensigns of a slave
But forward marks, wounds on my breast and face
Were meant to thee, O Caesar, and thy Rome.
And have I this return?

(III.i.250–65)

In Silius' restrained yet passionate rebuke of the degenerate Senate as he faces his death, Jonson shows his capability of a flowing and 'mighty line' comparable with the best that any of his contemporaries were capable of producing.

Yet with all its acknowledged qualities, the play has never won the regard that it so clearly merits. In its own time it recovered from its first inauspicious staging to make its way into 'the love of good men', and later was successfully revived for the stage both before and after the Restoration. But since the eighteenth century the play has largely survived in the study, where it has also generally failed to please. Criticism has settled upon Jonson's heavy and explicit use of the classics as a pedantic method producing an indigestible result. Sejanus himself has also been faulted as a tragic hero, seen as too petty for tragic status and too vicious to arouse pity for his fall; and the piece overall has been found defective in its lack of a moral resolution of the great issues raised.

So to argue betrays a refusal to grasp what Jonson was trying to achieve in *Sejanus*. The implied standard here is that of Shakespearean tragedy, the triumph of the rival poet against whom Jonson is always judged and found wanting. The 'true soul's tragedy', with its suffering and failure, the haunting sense of emotional loss, inner torment and the final dignity in defeat, these play no part in Jonson's purpose. But as with the comical satires, Jonson's difficulty has lain in conveying to his audiences through the medium of the play itself, rather than through his extra-dramatic comments and instructions, what he wished to accomplish.

The problems that Jonson encountered in the transmission of his original conception to audiences and readers stem from his initial choices at the onset of construction. The selection of the vicious Sejanus, at the court of the degraded, even psychopathological Tiberius, aptly emblemizes his pre-selected themes, but he is too specialized a character to be universalized as a tragic hero. By deciding to exploit the educative function of Sejanus' story and deploying him throughout as an *exemplum*, Jonson denied the possibility of unravelling the wider applicability of his story.

Again, by moving from a thematic starting-point, Jonson ensures that the finished play lacks one clear constructional centre, either Sejanus, Tiberius, or even Rome itself. Jonson determinedly clung to the two pillars of his earlier creative process, the classics as source and standard, and the centrality of the didactic function of drama. This means that his play is too schematized, too firmly controlled within a predetermined framework, to give it that lift into the free realm of the imagination. The classical detail can clot and impede the action, the classical design produces a marmoreal monolith as a tribute to Jonson's scholarship rather than to his dramatic powers, and the didactic purpose ultimately makes for an effect of material unpenetrated by the imagination: Jonson is demonstrating his convictions all the time, rather than illuminating his themes from within and through the interaction of character in a way that could have been more emotionally palatable to those not as highly intellectualized in their response as Jonson was.

If *Sejanus* then falls short of the compelling success of an acknowledged masterpiece, Jonson must take the responsibility for his unblinking fixation on his own goals, literary and moral, to the exclusion of other considerations. But even if flawed, the nobility of *The Tragedy of Sejanus* cannot be denied. In this play Jonson contrived to examine and discuss matters of central importance to the writing of contemporary drama, or indeed of any form of literature. He took on large questions of morality and government, of individual and public conduct; he resurrected and assessed an interesting historical episode and cast it in a form which his re-creation did not disgrace. It is not too high a claim to make for *Sejanus* that it was Jonson's first fully developed, fully focused play.

Without a doubt Jonson was trying in a variety of ways to extend and perfect his technical command at this time. An interesting parallel activity, and one that was to become increasingly important to Jonson as time went on, was the practice of his non-dramatic verse. Indubitably Jonson's writing of poetry went back to his schooldays; he told Drummond 'that he wrote all his [verses] first in prose, for so his master Camden had learned him' (HS I, 143). Jonson did not publish any of his poetry until about twenty years after he left school, in the 1616 Folio. Yet a number of these pieces can be firmly located in this period of composition, either by internal, or external evidence, or both; some twenty in all (Epigrams 40, 45, 60; *Forest* 12; *Underwood* 25; *Ungathered Verse* 1, 2, 3, 4, 5, 6, 7; Songs 1, 2, 3, 4, 5, 6, 7, 8).

As with Jonson's first masque, *Of Blackness*, the experience of reading these early pieces is to sense the later and fuller development of issues and personages who are to come into much greater prominence. There is, too, the pleasure of witnessing Jonson saluting various members of his acquaintance, welcoming new friends and paying his last dues of mourning to those departed. Greetings and last tributes are made with equal intensity; and the 'hail and farewell' note which classicists would derive from Catullus and which is inalienably associated with Jonson's poetry makes itself heard from the very beginning.

Undeniably, though, the jewel of the early years is Jonson's epitaph on his son Benjamin, who had died in 1603 at the age of 7:

> Farewell, thou child of my right hand, and joy,
> My sin was too much hope of thee, loved boy.
>> Seven years thou wert lent to me, and I thee pay,
>> Exacted by thy fate, on the just day.
> Oh, could I lose all father now! For why
>> Will man lament the state he should envy?
> To have so soon 'scaped world's and flesh's rage,
>> And if no other misery, yet age?
> Rest in soft peace, and, asked, say here doth lie
>> Ben Jonson his best piece of poetry.
> For whose sake, henceforth, all his vows be such
>> As what he loves may never like too much.
>
> (Epigram 45)

This piece, agonizingly self-aware without being in the least self-conscious, expresses through its every taut rhythm the sense of pain held in check; and in its tortured ratiocination, experienced as the stumbling attempts of a hurt mind to make some sense of its sufferings, it conveys the very essence of an unlooked-for bereavement.

Of another sort entirely is the epitaph upon Margaret Ratcliffe (also

Radcliffe), which must have been written shortly after her death in 1599. The poem is cast in the form of an acrostic, a device which, if Drummond is to be believed, Jonson later came to despise. At this stage, however, Jonson is to be seen conscientiously experimenting with different forms in the struggle to extend his range by working at his craft. The demands of this ingenious but intransigent poetic form meant that Jonson's lines are here and there less than perfectly shaped. Yet given the tyranny of the acrostic, Jonson undoubtedly succeeded in contriving a formal yet graceful tribute to this unfortunate young woman, who had died of grief at the deaths of four of her brothers within a month of each other:

> M arble weep, for thou dost cover
> A dead beauty under thee,
> R ich as nature could bequeath thee;
> G rant that no rude hands remove her.
> A ll the gazers on the skies
> R ead not in fair heaven's story
> E xpresser truth or truer glory
> T han they might in her bright eyes.
>
> R are as wonder was her wit,
> A nd like nectar ever flowing;
> T ill time, strong by her bestowing,
> C onquered hath both life and it.
> L ife whose grief was out of fashion
> I n these times; few have so rued
> F ate, in a brother. To conclude,
> F or wit, feature and true passion,
> E arth, thou hast not such another.
>
> (Epigram 40)

The funerary was only one of Jonson's singing-coats, however. In strongly contrasted veins among the other early productions are the elaborate classical ode to James, the Irish Earl of Desmond, the verse epistle to the Countess of Rutland, and the dedicatory verses contributed to the publications of various members of Jonson's early literary circle. There could hardly be more marked distinctions, social, sexual and literary, than between these individuals and groups. For the student of Jonson, the most interesting is the long verse epistle, on several different grounds. It is one of the handful of poems ever addressed by Jonson to a woman; it denotes the improved social level on which Jonson found himself through the patronage of members of the nobility; and it incorporates some of Jonson's more cherished and long-lived themes.

For behind the whole genre of the verse epistle lay the ever-active spirit of Jonson's beloved Horace. Horace's verse epistles are crucial to an understanding of his thought and his art; yet they are in themselves unpretentious and unassuming, seldom rising much above the level of conversational prose. Within them Horace reckoned up unflinchingly his own weaknesses and shortcomings, the strength of his self-irony rendering his analysis of others' deficiencies morally plausible and unflinchingly authentic. While Jonson never slavishly followed any of his classical sources, many features of Horace's verse epistles served as a model for him: the perfect candour, the warm common sense, the shrewdness, humour and truth of perception. As Jonson was abundantly to do in his own time, Horace tells us more about himself and his way of life than any other poet of antiquity. But these writings were never simply untransmuted autobiography; Horace saw himself as a bee flitting from flower to flower in the conversion of his own experience into poems that could only hope to hold their own for posterity by an absolute and unwearied aspiration to perfection of thought and phrase.

Horace's, of course, is a benign off-stage presence; Jonson does not wear his erudition so lightly throughout. A noticeable feature of the earliest examples of Jonson's verse is the way that the classical knowledge is not assimilated as philosophy, but heftily ladled in, as a consequence lying clotted upon the surface of the poem:

> He showed him first the hoof-cleft spring
> Near which the Thespiades sing,
> The clear Dircean fount
> Where Pindar swam,
> The pale Pyrene and the forked mount;
> And when they came
> To brooks and broader streams
> From Zephyr's rape would close him with his beams.
> (from *Panchyris*, 1603; *Ungathered Verse* 6, stanza 3)

Even in its own time, this would have required a dictionary of classical topography to elucidate all the references that Jonson so carefully works in.

Equally familiar even at this early stage of Jonson's literary career are some characteristically Jonsonian themes. To his noble patroness

81

Jonson dedicated not the silken flattery of a servant pen but a lecture
on the importance of poetry, and of the poet in particular, as against
the contemptibility of gold and worldly rewards. Another commonplace of Jonson's early writing was that central preoccupation of
humanist thought, the mutability of life, with a corresponding stress
on the importance of honour in the face of time's slow ruin. Jonsonians
will recognize already the twin tendencies to moralize and to dogma-
tize, along with the throbbing refrain of the certainty of his own work
to survive its own age:

> Lo, what my country should have done – have raised
>   An obelisk or monument to thy name,
> Or if she would but modestly have praised
>   Thy fact, in brass or marble writ the same –
> I, that am proud of thy great chance, here do!
> And, proud my work should outlast common deeds,
>   Durst think it great, and worthy wonder, too:
> But thine, for which I do it, so much exceeds!
> My country's parents have I many known.
> But saver of my country, thee alone.

(Epigram 60)

Familiar the themes may be, but the enormous experimentalism of
this verse remains fresh and impressive throughout. Almost every one
of these poems displays some new approach in form, structure, or line
length. The acrostic, for instance, cleverly copes with the fact that the
lady had thirteen letters in her name – hardly a propitious number –
by developing the poem as four distinct quatrains, with one concluding line, which is adroitly tied in to the overall structure by Jonson's
happy device of rhyming the last line with the first. In keeping with
its profounder feeling, the epitaph on his son consists simply of six
pairs of rhymed couplets, while the eulogy to Mounteagle (Epigram
60, quoted above) takes the form of a mini-sonnet, with two a-b-a-b
quatrains instead of the conventional three, capped with the clinching
final couplet (for an example of a 'real' sonnet, see the prefatory verse
to Thomas Wright's 1607 book in *Ungathered Verse* 7).

Jonson had already by this point so mastered the rhymed couplet
that he could turn out one hundred lines of them 'in haste' for the
Countess of Rutland. But considering how much Jonson is associated
with this form, and how steadily literary historians have built on this
to trace a direct line of descent through to the Augustans and to Pope
in particular, the variety of Jonson's metrical experimentation in these

early years argues a wider range than this neat piece of literary historiography might suggest. The earliest piece of all, for example, the 'Ode to the Earl of Desmond' (*Underwood* 25), comprises five stanzas of a tortuously intricate thirteen-line format bedevilled with an ingenious rhyme scheme that the youthful poet might almost have devised on purpose to set himself the most daunting poetical challenge he could conceive of.

In terms of diction, too, the Jonson of this phase is clearly evolving the skills that the later Jonson will exploit to the full. Particularly remarkable is Jonson's gift for rhyme, stemming from his preference for firm, chiming monosyllables. Some flourishes with feminine rhymes ('flowers/powers', 'passion/fashion') in the very earliest pieces soon give way to the authoritative and indisputable rhymes that give Jonson's lines their magisterial effect:

> Beauty I know is good, and blood is more;
> Riches thought most. But madam, think what store
> The world hath seen which all these had in trust,
> And now lie lost in their forgotten dust.
>
> (*Forest* 12, lines 37–40)

And as this shows, Jonson had already found the colloquial flow, the unforced rhythms, with which he so successfully imitated in poetry the natural speech of everyday life.

Non-dramatic poetry was always very dear to Jonson as part of his wider plan to raise his status and claim the rank and rights of a poet in the ancient mould. The importance of this may be gauged from Jonson's efforts to grasp any opportunity to further these aims and vindicate his position. The failure of *Sejanus* on stage hardened rather than undermined Jonson's sense of vocation; and after the dust of the *dégringolade* had settled, he took advantage of the publication of his cherished 'poem', as he called the play, to prefix a summary of his aims and a counterblast to his critics.

The preface to the 1605 quarto of *Sejanus* begins, touchingly enough, with Jonson's defence against the charge that it is 'no true poem'. Objections had been made that the play was not classically authentic, since it did not conform to the first of the dramatic unities, that of time; it lacked, too, according to its detractors, a proper chorus. Jonson's rebuttal of these charges consisted of the by now familiar theme of the inadequacy of contemporary audiences; strict rigour, so Jonson argued, was out of the question, faced as the playwright was with the lowness of his theatre and of its spectators.

Nevertheless he claimed to have 'discharged the other offices of a tragic writer' in more important particulars — 'truth of argument, dignity of persons, gravity and height of elocution, fullness and frequency of sentences [moral reflections]' (HS IV, 350). Content, he declared, was more important than 'forms' and empty structural gestures. There was some advance in Jonson's critical position in that he recognized here, for the first time, the entertainment needs of the audience. But ever-present too was the by now established defensive/ aggressive response to the audience, against whom Jonson deployed his classical learning like a shield, 'to show [his] integrity in the story, and to save [himself] in those common torturers that bring all wit to the rack'. He refused to 'plant his felicity' in the hope of general approbation, condemning this as a weakness that could only bring him into contempt.

Critics have noted, and condemned, the strain of special pleading in this. But with this attempt to sum up his critical stance and artistic attitude, Jonson terminated this mixed and experimental stage of his career. From now on he was to move forward with confidence unalloyed, not only in the direction of his greatest plays, but into areas previously untried and indeed unthought.

5

ROYAL AND MAGNIFICENT ENTERTAINMENT

After the unrewarded venture into high tragedy with *Sejanus*, Jonson received an unlooked-for opportunity to display his craftsmanship and to promote his status as an artist in a quite different mode. In 1604 he received a commission to write the queen's masque for the first full season of Christmas revelry since James VI acceded to the throne, the court still having observed the mourning dues to Queen Elizabeth in the winter of 1603–4. Jonson's debut was accorded the signal honour of being placed last in the twelve days of the court's continuous revelry, a mark of favour all the more remarkable for being accorded to a novice masque-maker. The masque, that strange and vanished form of entertainment now seeming remoter than the drama of the ancient Greeks, was at that time not only new to Jonson, but new in itself. The court of Elizabeth had seen over the years a variety of dances, displays and 'mummeries', and Britain's best-loved queen was no stranger to loyal pageants and country compliments such as the 'Princely Pleasures of Kenilworth', the great show with which Leicester declared his welcome to her in 1575. But it was only under the aegis of an improvident king ever hungry for adulation, and a queen whose love of 'masking and balling' had seemed to the grim Scots to outrun her judgement, that these extravagant, costly and difficult productions enjoyed the conditions which could permit of their full growth. It was an unprecedented artistic opportunity; and Jonson had the good fortune to be present from the beginning.

Jonson had of course served an apprenticeship of sorts with the four formal welcomes and royal entertainments written between the summers of 1603 and 1604. *The Entertainment at Althorp* in June 1603, later known as *The Satyr*, had been Jonson's first ceremonial show, but its assurance belies any suggestion of novitiate. Commissioned by Sir Robert Spencer to welcome the new queen, Anne of

Denmark, and her son the heir apparent Prince Henry when they rested at his Northamptonshire seat on their progress to London, this simple pastoral welcome is thoroughly conventional, leaning both upon classical precedent and native example. The separate elements, though, are put together with confidence and charm, while the cheeky satyr who pops in and out of the action, teasing the fairies and disordering their fairy ring, is thoroughly Jonsonian. Through the use of this character, who despite his classical name is none other than an old folk-tale Puck, Jonson uncovers a rich vein of English fantasy which both complements and contradicts his image as a stern classicist. The satyr, Queen Mab and her attendant elves draw the spectators into a world of housewives and hobgoblins, where dirty sluts are pinched black and blue in their sleep, and deserving maidens are rewarded with dreams of their future husbands on 'sweet St Anne's night'.

This little piece, less than 200 lines in all, is managed with a gaiety and grace that obscure the inherent difficulties of the project. This was in fact a tricky assignment. Jonson was required to link a number of different elements: the formal welcome; a celebration of the event in music and dance; a gift-giving as a rich jewel was donated to the queen; and finally the presentation of the Spencers' eldest son. All this had to lead into woodland sports – the finale of the show took the form of a staged hunt in which two deer were killed 'as they were meant to be, even in the sight of Her Majesty' (compare this with Act IV, scene i of *Love's Labour's Lost* where the Princess of France takes part in a very similar episode). While the pastoral setting afforded Jonson his framework, only his own skill could effect the fusion of these disparate elements, their harmonization into a whole, and the smooth transitions between the different phases. The unifying medium in this case is the verse, which alternates easy quatrains with rhymed couplets, all of four beats to the line, with subtler rhythms reserved for the exaltation of song:

> *ELF.*
> Mistress, this is only spite
> For you would not yesternight
> Kiss him in the cockshoot light.
>
> *SATYR.*
> By Pan, and thou hast hit it right
>
> *There they laid hold upon him and nipped him.*

FAIRY [QUEEN MAB].
Fairies, pinch him black and blue.
Now you have him, make him rue.

SATYR.
O hold Mab, I sue.

ELF.
Nay, the devil shall have his due.

*There he ran quite away and left them in a confusion, while the Fairy
began again.*

FAIRY.
Pardon, lady, this wild strain,
Common with the sylvan train,
That do skip about this plain;
Elves, apply your gyre again.
And while some do hop the ring,
Some shall play and some shall sing,
We'll express in everything
Oriana's welcoming.

SONG.

This is she,
   This is she,
In whose world of grace
Every season, person, place
   That receive her, happy be . . .
                    (lines 88–116)

Jonson's other royal commission of the summer of 1603, although
not performed until 1604, was on a grander scale. But paradoxically,
it did not afford him so much scope. The 'Royal and Magnificent
Entertainment' of King James 'through his honourable city of London', or as Jonson later entitled it for the 1616 Folio, *The King's
Entertainment on Passing to his Coronation*, however stately a city
pageant, denied the writer the chance to work in the humour, song,
games and dances with which he had varied the tone and increased the
delight of the Althorp piece. Yet Jonson clearly determined to make
the most of the opportunity that the form afforded him. As he
explained in his description of 'the complemental part' of the first

stage, in it he 'not only laboured the expression of state and magnificence, as proper to a triumphal arch, but the very site, fabric, strength, policy, dignity and affections of the city were all laid down to life'.

To Jonson then, this was no hollow exercise but a historic occasion, and one incorporating all that he and others held true about their city and its king. For the triumphal arches for which he was responsible, he devised a carefully worked-out emblem of which the purely literary parts, the speeches, were only one element. For here Jonson was as much designer, and director, in modern terms, as he was simply writer; in the fullest sense of the words, he was 'the author of the whole'. In working out his allegories, and carefully multiplying their levels of meaning, Jonson leaned heavily and determinedly on classical precedent, once again as in *Sejanus* taking ancient authority as the only mode appropriate to high ceremonial occasion. So Jonson's 'Londinium' is both 'according to Tacitus', and also 'taken out of Martial', while in addition 'alluding to those verses in Seneca'. As in its underpinnings, so in its framing device Jonson's conception was heavily classical; this is a 'golden age' piece, in which the new reign is pictured as inaugurating a return to the primal age of peace, purity and plenty that had already vanished from the despairing gaze of the Greek pastoral poets of the seventh century BC.

Both this and other notes in *The King's Entertainment* foreshadow themes that Jonson was to develop more fully in the court masques. Central to these was his new concept of the golden monarchy as the source of light and power, warmth and sustenance to its subjects, contrasted with the darkness of evil:

> Let ignorance know, great king, this day is thine . . .
> That no offensive mist, or cloudy stain
> May mix with splendour of thy golden reign.
>
> (lines 724–31)

This show has, too, Jonson's first use of a simple 'revelation' motif, by which one speaker is ignorant of what is going on and has to have everything outlined by another obliging participant. Primitive and antiquated though this device was, it was invaluable to Jonson in his masque-making career. Yet the finished result is not as contrived as this may suggest. Jonson was not merely interested in the verbal and intellectual aspects of the work; colour and show were very important in his overall vision, and are prescribed accordingly, in minute detail. Here, for example, is 'Monarchia Britannica', the Spirit of Britain:

She was a woman, richly attired, in cloth of gold and tissue; a rich mantle; over her state two crowns hanging, with pensile [hanging] shields through them; the one limed with the particular coat of England, the other of Scotland. . . . In her hand she holds a sceptre; on her head a fillet of gold, interwoven with palm and laurel; her hair bound into four several points, descending from her crowns, and in her lap a little globe, inscribed upon [it] ORBIS BRITANNICUS . . .

(lines 33–43)

In Jonson's perception, the minutiae of the symbolism added to and enriched rather than detracted from the splendour of the full scene, providing a worthy case for the expression of the compliments to the king which were the *raison d'être* of the whole proceeding. As Jonson earnestly explains in his description of the representation of London, 'Though this city, for the state and magnificence, might by hyperbole be said to touch the stars, and reach up to heaven, yet was it far inferior to the master thereof, who was His Majesty; and in that respect unworthy to receive him'. Yet though Jonson's praise of James is consistently elevated, even exaggerated, it was of a piece with the hysterical adulation of King James common at this time to both court and country. As Jonson expressed it in *The King's Entertainment*:

I tender thee the heartiest welcome yet
That ever king had to his empire's seat;
Never came man more longed for, more desired:
And being come, more reverenced, loved, admired.

(lines 334–7)

This is no vain eulogy but an accurate description of England's response to James's accession. The Stuarts inherited all the Tudor goodwill towards the monarchy, enhanced by the general relief at the ease of the succession. It was no mean achievement of James and his son to convert this feeling into a regicidal frenzy within the space of forty years.

As this extract suggests, Jonson had a gift for stately occasional utterances, when his favourite form of the rhymed couplet could come into its own, its potential stiffness varied by his subtle and flexible use of the caesura. The same skills came into play in the *Panegyre*, the outburst of joy written by Jonson to herald the triumphal opening of James's first Parliament. Here, in the brief space of 162 lines, Jonson restates his favourite theme of the contrast between the light and glory

89

of James, and the darkness of sin and ignorance. Another concept that Jonson was to rework extensively in the masques is that of the 'rich chain / That fasteneth heavenly power to earthly reign' (lines 21–2). As this shows, although his model was the classical panegyric in honour of the Roman Emperor, Jonson's version was very much his own, and his *Panegyre*, paradoxically, is much less heavily Latinate than *The King's Entertainment*. What is significant is Jonson's seizing the occasion as a means of instructing the king: this is the first emergence of the Jonson who was more and more strenuously to assert the poet's right of prescription, and 'would not flatter, though he saw death'. Had James been able to absorb and to apply Jonson's sound comments upon ruling with wisdom and honesty, respecting the laws of England and her subjects' rights, in the knowledge that

> men do more obey
> When they are led, than when they are compelled

then the course of English history would have been very different.

In marked contrast with this formal ceremonial occasion was the last of Jonson's entertainments of 1604, a private occasion at High-gate outside London, when Sir William Cornwallis entertained the king and queen. This little piece, only 260 lines long, adopts the same format as that of the Althorp entertainment, and maintains the same spirit of playfulness. As the king and queen entered the gates of the house, they were welcomed by the household tutelary spirits, the Penates, in linked pairs of sprightly and elegant stanzas:

> Welcome, monarch of this isle,
> Europe's envy, and her mirror;
> Great in each part of thy style,
> England's wish and Scotland's bliss,
> Both France and Ireland's terror.

> Welcome are you; and no less
> Your admired queen; the glory
> Both of state, and comeliness.
> Every line of her divine
> Form, is a beauteous story.
> (lines 11–20)

Jonson's careful contrivance once more produced what seemed to him the appropriate metaphor for the occasion: Maia presides, in honour of the May-day on which the visit took place, over Aurora, Zephyrus and

Flora, signifying the rural delights of Highgate's situation at this time when London was only a distant prospect:

> Where now behold my mother Maia, sitting in the pride of her plenty gladding the air with her breath and cheering the spring with her smiles. At her feet the blushing Aurora, who with her rosy hand casteth her honey dews on those sweeter herbs, accompanied with that gentle wind Favonius, whose subtle spirit in the breathing forth Flora makes into flowers, and stick them in the grass as if she contended to have the embroidery of the earth richer than the cope of the sky. Here, for her month, the yearly delicate May keeps state.
>
> (lines 66–75)

Classicists will recognize here not only familiar phrases, but the origins of the various images; yet the work is anything but derivative. It progresses with confidence and ease through various careful modulations of tone; its variety, within the short space of 150 lines, is remarkable and impressive. A further development took place in the second part of the entertainment, 'after dinner', when Jonson must have calculated that the administration of food and drink would have loosened the stays of the occasion. As the royal couple re-entered the garden, they were introduced to Pan, with the promise that he would be both 'rude' and 'salty'. Again Jonson employs the device of the ignorant participant; Pan is unaware of the majesty of the visitors, and fools around the king, assuring him of the same treatment 'were he a king or his mistress a queen'. Jonson pushes this device to the limits of familiarity, making Pan discuss with Mercury whether or not James had an eye for a woman (here vulgarly rendered as 'a smock'). The conclusion, that from the look of him James 'should love both a horse and a hound', does not prevent the gossipy advice to Queen Anne, 'Well, look to him, Dame'; this is proffered in true 'over the garden wall style', with a sly crack both at the queen's Danish ancestry and her personal habits in the line 'By my hand, I believe you were born a good drinker' (lines 220–6). With a king whose intolerance of formal speeches was as well known as his fondness for coarse humour, this entertainment went down very well. That the queen, too, took pleasure not offence from the show is amply demonstrated by her choice of Jonson a few months later to write her own first masque as queen of England.

These early royal entertainments had given Jonson vital experience in the area of formal ceremonial. Yet the entertainment was so different in kind from the masque that these shows have to be regarded as a preparation for the forthcoming demands on Jonson's professional skills, rather than as mini-versions of the same thing. In simple terms, the entertainments were much shorter than the masques; more significantly they all took place outside, in daylight, in settings which minimized rather than maximized their theatrical potential. Of the four, two were entirely public statements for Londoners at large, *The King's Entertainment* and the *Panegyre*, and two were for great households where the nobility, gentry, servants and local residents assembled to share the occasion. None partook of that extraordinary blend of the private and the public that marked out the masque as the court's ceremonial for the court. At bottom, Jonson's early works were traditional welcomes, not extended celebrations. All these factors combined to ensure that the entertainments, despite some elaborate trappings, were vastly more informal and less special than the masques. They were written for different performers, and to a much smaller budget. They did not afford the opportunity for developed allegorical conceptualization that Jonson was able to deploy in the new and still emerging form.

As Jonson found it, the masque held no special promise of the heights to which he would raise it. Deriving originally from a primitive folk ritual featuring the arrival of guests in disguise bearing gifts to royalty or nobility, masking or 'disguising', even under Queen Elizabeth who delighted in such flatteries, had not progressed much beyond the level of the kind of country mumming mocked by Shakespeare in *Love's Labour's Lost*. But with his perennial capacity for dignifying his own endeavours, Jonson was just the man to elevate its claim to high seriousness, and exploit its undiscovered potential. In so doing he developed an exalted view of the masque as a form, much as he had done with the plays of the public theatre that he had converted into 'poetry'. The ephemerality of the masque, for instance, he capitalized upon as one of its major attractions. His masques recognize and exploit the transience of beauty and the fragility of grace, drawing their central conceits from the notion of the rare and unrepeatable occurrence. Each was consciously created to offer a moment of experience in which a visionary ideal is briefly and gloriously brought before the spectator; and the knowledge, repeatedly stressed, that the moment must pass, sounds a poignant elegiac note, but also intensifies the delight. Jonson saw into the heart of the intrinsic pathos of the masque, and made it flourish as a glittering flash against the darkness of eternity.

For Jonson's craft was essentially a shaping faculty, and the masque provided the opportunity for him to use his skills to develop a literary form out of a number of non-literary elements; to impose a verbal framework that would overarch and include music, dance, occasion, setting and spectacle. In addition to the formal was the thematic challenge; the task was to deal with the audience's expectations in as fresh and striking a way as possible, while still satisfying these not inconsiderable demands. The pseudo-mythological fables that some critics have seen as forced upon Jonson by the subclassical taste of the court in fact offered Jonson a series of fantasy worlds, one opening off another like a series of Chinese boxes. He readily embraced the chance to have one illusion dissolve into another, relishing the expression of the visual side of his art, that it too should be a 'revel' in colour, movement and imagery.

Within these fantasy worlds, Jonson moved confidently between the purely classical figures like Pan, and the abstractions of Elizabethan didacticism like Reason, with personifications like Father Thames and the River Niger dreamed up at need. Jonson grasped at the chance of writing the kind of speech that mythological creatures and deities might be thought to use to one another, in a vein strongly contrasted with his mastery of the demotic elsewhere. The masques further illustrate aspects of Jonson's genius not employed in the satiric comedies: a delicate grace and lyrical fantasy, with a rural impulse quite alien to the urban laureate of citizen London. The idealization at the heart of the masque is far removed from the concentration on vice and folly that had been Jonson's stock-in-trade both as a comedy writer and a tragedian.

Another feature of masque-making that must have appealed strongly to Jonson was the unique opportunity it provided to obtain the king's ear. Of the twenty-five masques that Jonson wrote between 1605 and 1631, only three were not for James; two for James's son Charles, and one for the French ambassador, the Baron de la Tour. Even in those which notice the rising star of the heir apparent Prince Henry, the focus is always on James, his rule, and his family. And the masques were always given before the king, in one of his own banqueting halls in London, with the exception of *The Masque of the Gypsies Metamorphosed* in 1621, and possibly *Pan's Anniversary* (1620).

To Jonson therefore the masque was not a frivolous diversion for the idle rich, but an educative instrument of great potential; under what other circumstances could a bricklayer's stepson enjoy the privilege of speaking directly to the reigning monarch in his own hall?

The masque was a chance to instruct and inform great ones – to offer precepts and to demonstrate virtue. That this was a real and no fleeting impulse is evidenced by the fact that fifteen years later Jonson told Drummond that 'he hath a mind to be a churchman, and so he might make one sermon to the King, he careth not what thereafter should befall him' (HS I, 141). All Jonson's masques were in some form or another fables based on the image of the perfect monarchy, in which hierarchy is asserted as the prerequisite of harmony. And Jonson had the further gratification that this king to whom he directed his efforts was sufficiently interested in masques to have written one himself, fifteen years before he came into England; James's own *Epithalamion* of 1588 is the only Scottish example of the masque form extant.

The rest of the audience besides James also held its attractions for Jonson is his struggle to 'raise his art' and sing 'high and aloof'. After the rough ride of the public theatre, the more civilized and educated spectators of the court provided a welcome change. To be the masque-maker in a situation where masques were so carefully wrought and so highly valued was in itself congenial to Jonson; in addition it brought him noble friends and patrons, with an enhanced social position and literary prestige. As an indication of what these changes meant to him, Jonson's preoccupation with the ignorance of his audiences vanished as soon as he could count on a different sort of spectator. Finally, but not insignificantly, came one practical consideration. Jonson's efforts in producing some hundreds of lines for a masque were much better rewarded than the hundreds more that he had to write for a play – James paid him five times as much for a masque as he obtained from the producers of a new drama.

Jonson in fact seized on and relished every difference between the masque and the drama of the popular stage. Where that was substantially word-based, with occasional interruptions for a song or dance, the text for a masque had to be in the nature of a scenario or libretto, an outline to be fulfilled with the arts of choreography, music and design. Jonson's invention was fully stimulated by the greater lavishness, care and preparation that went into the creation of a masque, in contrast with the hurried staging of contemporary plays. The stage and scenic technique of masque-making, too, was enormously in advance of that available in the public theatre. The Jonson who mocked crude stage effects revelled in the chance to create swift and breathtakingly convincing dramatic illusion. In our limited knowledge of the contemporary technology, there is little agreement on the means by which Inigo Jones's spectacular effects were achieved. Sceptics have noted the stage directions calling for loud music at the point of scene changes, as a means of covering up any clanking, grinding, or thumping that could be going on. But with this aural blanket, it must have been wonderful to see rocks split open, globes descend, or new worlds reveal themselves; and Jonson's freedom of creation shows how much he rose to the splendid and unprecedented possibilities now open to him.

What Jonson did, in short, was to substitute a substantial dramatic, visual and emotional experience in place of empty compliment. He firmed up the story-line element of the masque (always potentially a weak link) without losing sight of the masque objective of drawing together masquers and audience in united homage to the throne. He tried to combine both concept and function of the masque; and drawing on his own relentlessly verbal and literary training he succeeded in promoting the words, in this basically non-literary and never text-based form, to a remarkable and impressive extent.

Jonson was fortunate to be at hand at a moment when this fresh and hybrid species was evolving. Coming together as a blend of text, music, dance, sound, song and stage spectacle, it offered a wider scope for his innovative faculty and sense of performance. Although Jonson's approach was never highly experimental, he decisively imposed on the masque his own view of its appropriate structure and content. Through his controlling concept and his high skills in execution, Jonson became the true creator of the Jacobean masque, and the undisputed master of the genre.

Jonson's success was won in the teeth of the difficulties and disadvantages inherent in the form itself. Both in its origins and development, the masque could never be other than intrinsically undramatic, its fragile world held together only tenuously by the delicate links of song and dance. As the contemporary records amply illustrate, the spectators were always more impressed by the brilliance of the visual effects than by the power of the words. Despite all Jonson's efforts, the music and spectacle – later bitterly derided by him as 'shows! shows! mighty shows!' – remained the most potent element of the ceremony for those involved.

For the masque owed its growing popularity every bit as much to the efforts of the designer as to those of the writer. Jonson's controversial *Masque of Blackness* had held the place of honour, the Twelfth Night and final ceremonial of the 1604–5 Christmas season at court. Its predecessor, Samuel Daniel's masque, *The Vision of the Twelve*

Goddesses given on 6 January 1604, had been staged on the old medieval principle of dispersed settings; a cave and a temple were erected at one end of the hall, a mountain at the other, and all three settings were visible to the spectators at the same time. For Jonson's debut as a masque-maker with *The Masque of Blackness* in 1605, the designer Inigo Jones boldly dispensed with the time-honoured practice of multiple settings, and one stage only was used. The effect of focusing the action, however, was so stunning that the old system went overnight out of fashion.

Inigo Jones's revolutionary new masque setting consisted of a cleverly painted backcloth with properties arranged in perspective in front of it. This created an unprecedented effect of depth through the illusory evocation of the third dimension. Jones had borrowed the concept from the Italian theatre-worker Sebastiano Serlio, who had published his *Architettura* in Paris in 1545, but he was also familiar with other Italian sources. The whole thing, however, was new and sensational in England – the court was ravished by the landscape of 'small woods', with 'an artificial sea . . . which seemed to move'. The masquers appeared seated in a great shell, also 'curiously made to move on those waters', as Jonson describes it. Here was a level of sophistication previously unattained in English ceremonial performance.

Not unnaturally, Jonson was initially delighted with the work of a collaborator who so magnificently 'bodied out' his conception, that central idea which was 'the soul of the masque'. But in the parallel of importance of the designer with the writer lay the seeds of future discord. Neither as man nor as artist was Jonson temperamentally suited to second place. The history of Jonson's involvement with the masque form, his jostling with designers, painters, musicians, dancing masters, singing teachers, dressmakers and tailors, is the history of his unswerving but ultimately unsuccessful determination to establish the supremacy of 'the poet's' contribution over that of 'the master of the shows'.

Equally unforeseen or disregarded by Jonson in his bid to raise his art by craft, was the expendability of the masque. Months of strenuous exertion and phenomenal expense (in an era when Shakespeare could buy the best house in Stratford for £60, the cost of a 'gallant masque' was £3,000) went into a production that occupied only an hour or two of a single night's entertainment at court, with the infrequent possibility of one other evening's revival. Essentially the masque was the most frivolous of occasional pieces, and not at all the enduring literary monument that Jonson spent so much of his professional energies in trying to create. Because of its collaborative nature and blend of artistic media, each masque could live only in its unique performance. Consequently Jonson's later publication of his masque texts must be seen, first, as a last-ditch attempt to assert the literary value of the libretto as the 'soul' of the masque and, second, as a gesture of defiance of the triviality and ephemerality of masque performance by memorializing the once-in-a-lifetime moment of realization.

Related to its essential nature as a court event were the main artistic problems that the masque presented. The formal outline, with the compliment to the king and the celebration of the gathering in his honour, was fixed and established. The monarch was always the structural and thematic focus; and the masque's emotional climax was pre-designated in the entry of the masquers, with the revelation of the central conceit. The masque was in fact designed to lead up to the point at which the players and audience mingled in dance, the dramatic spectacle forming a mimetic prelude to the main business of the evening, the revels. There was thus an intimate bond between the performers and the audience, and the final movement was always to unite performers and spectators in one communal celebration, the very opposite of the theatre with its final message from actors to audience of 'You that way; we this way'. As with the form of the masque, so with its function; masques were always required to be revels in themselves, in which the shared universal joy was expressed physically rather than verbally, through the long intricate dances in which James (rather pathetically in view of his rickety legs) so delighted.

Not only was this always the predetermined order of events, with an immutable audience expectation of its key elements, but by definition, in what was designed as a complimentary celebration, there could be no real thematic tension. No conflict was possible within this stylized and decorous form; no apparent room for the low-life vigour which was one of the strongest weapons in Jonson's professional armoury. None of the masque features in fact could be drawn from life; characters were emblematic where not allegorical, language was elevated and formal, themes were lofty and encomiastic. As masquers did not speak dialogue, their speeches could not interlock, as in the drama; they do not exchange views, argue, swear, or curse. According to his own central and cherished artistic principle of decorum, there was too much here that Jonson could not do. The masque shared very little with the world of the drama – masques remained, despite all efforts, metaphors.

Yet with only a slight shift of perspective, and with an intellectual effort that Jonson was certainly prepared to make, some of these drawbacks could be converted into advantages. For his first masque, *Of Blackness*, Jonson was pre-empted to some degree by Queen Anne's choice of the central conceit; the queen insisted that she and her ladies were to appear as 'Blackamoors', and Jonson's task was to devise a dramatic development around this. With a characteristically Jonsonian imaginative boldness, he came to the notion of personifying blackness itself as Niger (Latin *niger*, 'black'). From this initial flash Jonson evolved a full-blooded allegory. His 'Niger' embodies the soul of the great African river, 'in form and person of an Ethiop'. This conceit also enabled Jonson to introduce Niger's father, the 'King of Floods', 'divine Oceanus' himself, and Niger's daughters. These Ethiopian nymphs have become dissatisfied with their dark skins, and seek a land which is ruled by a greater sun than they have known: 'whose beams shine day and night, and are of force / To blanch an Ethiop, and revive a corpse' (lines 253–4). In Jonson's simple but strong dramatic outline, the great River Niger and the princesses his daughters all combine to grace 'Albion', which serves as a conflation of England, her people and her ruler:

> Call forth they honoured daughters then,
> And let them, 'fore the Britain men
> Indent the land, with those pure traces
> They flow with, in their native graces.
> Invite them boldly to the shore.
> Their beauties shall be scorched no more:
> This sun is temperate, and refines
> All things on which his radiance shines.
>
> (lines 258–65)

Saddled as he was with a potentially restrictive commandment to accommodate the queen's eccentric fancy to appear as a black woman, Jonson displayed considerable ingenuity in playing with, and expanding upon, the central motif.

In this task, Jonson's classical knowledge came naturally to the fore; it is more easily and plausibly incorporated into a masque fable than into the drama of the earlier phase. Although there is a heavy panoply of learning, it is largely to be found in the footnotes, underlying the text rather than being superimposed upon it. A reference to Phaeton, for instance, in line 161, is self-evidently clear; the spectator would not need to be assured that the reference comes from Ovid. Nor, as with his plays, were the classical writers Jonson's only source of fact and inspiration. Amongst other contemporary sources, Jonson drew on an Italian authority on classical mythology, Nathale Conti, whose *Mythologiae* was a key text in the complex process by which knowledge of the gods of Greece and Rome had been transmitted from late antiquity through the Middle Ages to the Renaissance. But Jonson's use of his sources was commanding and eclectic; he picked out what would enable him to structure his fiction, and never bound himself to unnecessary detail.

Jonson's invention, then, was grounded upon his knowlege of antiquity both directly, and through his learned reading of the secondary sources of Renaissance humanism. It finds its expression through a verse style of such polish, grace and assurance that it is hard to recall that *The Masque of Blackness* was Jonson's debut in this strange and demanding form. The majority of the masque is developed through stately rhymed couplets whose mannered grace is never allowed to weigh down the forward drive of the piece:

> Be silent, now the ceremony's done,
> And Niger say, how comes it, lovely son,
> That thou, the Ethiop's river, so far East
> Art seen to fall into th' extremest West
> Of me, the King of Floods, Oceanus,
> And in mine Empire's heart, salute me thus?
> My ceaseless current now amazed stands!
> To see thy labour through so many lands
> Mix thy fresh billow with my brackish stream
> And, in thy sweetness, stretch thy diadem
> To these far distant and unequalled skies,
> This squared circle of celestial bodies.
>
> (lines 109–21)

The same metrical confidence is evinced in the shorter lines employed by Jonson both in the songs expressing the high moments of the action, and the transitional verses establishing a change of tone or pace within the body of the masque. Consider, for example, this delicate and varied exchange; as the nymphs are about to choose their partners, 'one from the sea was heard to call them with this charm, sung by a tenor voice':

99

SONG

Come away, come away,
　We grow jealous of your stay:
If you do not stop your ear,
We shall have more cause to fear
Sirens of the land, than they
To doubt the sirens of the sea.

*Here they danced with their men, several measures and corantos; all which
ended, they were again [summoned] to sea, with a song of two trebles, whose
cadences were iterated by a double echo, from several parts of the land.*

SONG

　Daughters of the subtle flood.
Do not let earth longer entertain you;
1 ECHO: Let earth longer entertain you.
2 ECHO: Longer entertain you.

　'Tis to them enough of good.
That you give this little hope to gain you.
1 ECHO: Give this little hope to gain you.
2 ECHO: Little hope to gain you.

　If they love,
　　You shall quickly see;
　For when to flight you move.
They'll follow you, the more you flee.
　1 ECHO: Follow you, the more you flee.
　2 ECHO:　　The more you flee.

If not, impute it each to other's matter:
They are but earth ⎫   and what you vowed was water.
1 ECHO: But earth ⎪   1 ECHO: And what you vowed
                    ⎬   was water.
                    ⎪
2 ECHO:　　Earth. ⎭   2 ECHO: You vowed was water.

(lines 294–323)

As this shows, Jonson was obviously enjoying the chance to handle
his themes and figures lightly and allusively. With emblematic
figures rather than human beings, Jonson could also bring into play
his powers of symbolic generalization and illustration. This elevated

and idealizing mode may be the obverse of his gift for the vulgar, but his artistic temperament delighted in crafting these extremes. It submitted, too, very readily to the miniaturization that the masque implied; this little libretto has 238 lines of text, only about the length of one longish scene in a play.

From successful practice, Jonson developed his theory of the masque. From what he discovered as he inherited, examined and developed the masque form, he built up a considerable theoretical backbone to these flimsy structures. In an earlier note to *The King's Entertainment* he had summed up his underlying concept of the unity of the piece:

> The nature and property of these devices is to present always some one body or figure, consisting of distinct members, and each of these expressing itself in its own active sphere, yet all with that general harmony so connexed and disposed, as no one little part can be missing to the illustration of the whole.

Jonson's whole-hearted adoption of the masque as a legitimate and noble literary form led him to refine this view into renewed statements of the masque's importance. He firmly separated the 'invention', to which he gave primacy, from the production elements which he dimissed in casual aside: 'so much for the bodily part'. He was so far from accepting any view of masques as glittering bubbles that he stated that court masques should be 'the mirror of man's life', which 'ought always to carry a mixture of profit with them, no less than delight'. This fairly and squarely makes the claim of the masque to be rated by the same criteria, and productive of the same effects, as the two ancient and primary forms of comedy and tragedy. In view of the later disappearance of the masque as a form, Jonson was clearly overstraining a genre whose literary sinews were never strong or well developed. Yet as a new-born masquer Jonson not only articulated this suprising claim; he made every effort within his power to sustain his masques on the level to which he had promoted them.

It should not be forgotten, though, that from its inception Jonson's masque-making was closely tied in with his dramatic development. The one was a supplement to, not a substitution for, the other. We have seen that Jonson believed from the start that the masque's separate elements had to be harmonized by the central device. The training which masque-writing afforded Jonson in the centralization and logical working-out of one dominant concept inevitably spilled over into his thinking about dramatic construction. From the masque he learned how to hang on to and work through the medium of one unifying idea, how to create an overriding and unifying centre which could draw all the other elements to it. The tendency of inexperience, seen throughout the earlier plays, to scatter and diffuse his forces over too many areas, gives way to the much-admired ability to create plays with a truly centrifugal force. When Jonson resumed serious play-making with *Volpone*, the structural maturity is one of its most striking features.

Before this great leap forward, however, there occurred a strange warp in Jonson's writing career. In 1605 he collaborated with Chapman and Marston in the writing of *Eastward Ho!* The play is in two separate ways something of a throw-back for Jonson; first, in the reversion to the old Henslowe days of collaborative authorship, when through his court commissions he had seemed to be raising himself above the ruck of Elizabethan hack work; and second in the subject-matter, which with its lively citizen comedy format recalls *Every Man in his Humour* rather than any of Jonson's later, maturer writing. Possibly this was a belated production of an earlier piece, one of 'the half of his comedies' that were not 'in print'. It is equally likely, however, that under pressure, financial or otherwise, Jonson found himself re-using characters, themes and devices that he preferred to think he had left behind; Jonson's own inveterate tendency to stress the upward and forward movement of his career inevitably obscures any backslidings or regressions.

Another problem lies in ascertaining how much of the finished whole Jonson was actually responsible for.[1] In the absence of any external evidence, the authorship of the various sections has been extensively disputed, but Jonson's contribution, it is generally agreed, was small; he had little, if anything, to do with shaping the plot or devising the characters, and his part seems to have consisted in furnishing satirical dialogue to what is, on the surface of it, a conventional comedy of Jacobean city life. These Jonsonian inserts, however, give the play its bite, and encapsulate whatever interest the play now holds for us, whether literary or historical. For they contain some satire against the Scots and satirical reflections upon King James's decision to raise money for an exchequer depleted by extra-vagances like masquing by selling honours to any parvenu who had money to buy. James was not amused. When word of the play reached the king's ears, as with the *Isle of Dogs* affair seven years previously, Jonson found his dramatic career interrupted by a swift and savage incarceration.

In this emergency Jonson made no attempt to minimize his part in the play. But in his letters of self-defence to various powerful lords, including the king's right-hand man, the Earl of Salisbury, he stoutly refused to accept all the blame for the offending phrases: 'If others have transgressed, let me not be entitled to their follies', he wrote (HS I, 190–200). Chapman, imprisoned with Jonson, was less reticent, throwing the blame squarely on to Marston, who had providentially made his escape. Both men succeeded in satisfying the authorities, since they were eventually released without charge or punishment. But if Jonson did not write this satire, it is hard to see where his part in *Eastward Ho!* lay, and his contribution to it must remain one of literature's minor mysteries.

For ultimately, the play is of limited importance in the story of Jonson's development as a writer, even when its send-up of citizen virtue is taken to anticipate the fuller and more successful ironizing of 'good' characters in *Volpone* and *Bartholomew Fair*. Undercrafted, of erratic artistry, it is 'no true poem'. Jonson's own opinion of it provides all the guidance we need – he never acknowledged it, nor sought to preserve it. Posterity can only agree with this implied assessment of its worth. For Jonson was on the brink of much greater things; the greatest, even, that he was to achieve. Despite his sudden and unexpected success at court, Jonson was drawn back to the public stage; his triumph with the masque had not quenched his interest in the drama, and the plays he now produced were for the first time of that level of craftsmanship that ensured their eternal survival as his highest art: *Volpone*, *Epicene* and *The Alchemist*.

6

QUICK COMEDY REFINED

In the writing of *Volpone*, Jonson's genius found its home. Not only was this play his first undisputed dramatic masterpiece; it also inaugurated a new wave of Jonson's creative career. In three years he produced three triumphs of his art, a feat never equalled by him at any other stage. At this point, for the first time, Jonson was able to build on previous experiments and achievements, efforts that may have appeared only partially successful at the time, but which now revealed the contribution they had made to the fuller realization of his artistic vision and dramatic powers. *Volpone*, *Epicene* and *The Alchemist* form in effect another trio of comical satires echoing *Every Man out of his Humour*, *Cynthia's Revels* and *Poetaster*; not under any generic title nor given classical settings and trappings like the earlier plays, but undoubtedly works in which Jonson's previous formal and thematic essays into comedy and satire have their mature expression.

At the same time, Jonson found his own voice. From the time of writing *The Case Is Altered*, he had altered his dramatic technique in every one of the comedies surviving from this period. The earlier plays, as they are constantly experimental, are only intermittently successful. Here Jonson has discarded all his former theoretical supports and experimental devices; *Volpone* has no chorus, no commentary, no historical detail to confuse the issue, no overt allegory nor obvious Latin comedy elements. Because Jonson is no longer constantly shifting his ground, the plays manifest the authorial assurance that too often before sounded like bullying or bluster. In these three Jonson discovered what was for him the most serviceable dramatic structure. Each piece is based upon a house to which greedy gulls and simple innocents are attracted alike, and in which the owner-occupier, who seems to have the whip hand in terms of control or cash, is subject to sudden and unforeseen reversals.

This device provided the perfect framework for Jonson to develop his own satirical, even Machiavellian, brand of comedy. It offered what Jonson had long been seeking, a viable alternative to his bugbear, Shakespearean romantic comedy. Shakespeare, commanding as he does the middle ground of human hopes and fears, convictions and aspirations, is the paradigm of the consensus dramatist; Jonson needed a dramatic method with which he could lead, instruct and influence the audience not from within, but from outside its circle. Where Shakespeare was content to irradiate the great clichés of life, to rediscover the eternal platitudes, Jonson's compulsion was to provoke, not to console; to stimulate thought and a critical response; and to pierce the complacency that inhibits improvement.

And never in his career did Jonson write with a sounder basis of formal technique. He had thoroughly assimilated the indigestible classical material that had previously tended to clog both his dramatic structures and the texture of his verse and prose alike. The soul and body of his classical sources had passed into his mind as a set of internal values, colouring his characteristic viewpoint; they were no longer externally applied every five minutes as an indispensable yardstick of excellence and appropriateness. Now he was able to apply the fruits of his 'wonted studies' to his own world, where he saw enough material for comical satire in contemporary life. The manic excesses of individuals and groups in the rapidly burgeoning capitalist economy of Stuart London, with the concurrent strains of the associated challenge to traditional life and thought, afforded Jonson a world of lurid amorality and imposture more intense than he had previously been able to realize. From the essential sillinesses of the earlier comical satires, Jonson turned now to more profound forms of greed and speculation, and to the commercialized, professionalized exploitation of the weaker members of the human jungle.

Volpone brilliantly exemplifies Jonson's unique jungle vision, with its self-contained world composed entirely of predators and prey. His contempt for mercenary motivation and capitalistic enterprise is blistering; the commanding indictment of the vicious habits of the new acquisitive society shows Jonson's forward leap in terms of intellectual and analytical maturity. The play demonstrates throughout Jonson's new-found ability to use the grim stuff of human wickedness and weakness, material not of a comic nature in itself, as the basis of satiric comedy. Obsessional greed, lust, the savage disregard of all other human beings and even eventually of personal survival – these are hardly funny, but Jonson makes them so. Yet never does he diminish the power of his portrayal of these ruthless materialists who embody 'Appetite, the universal wolf'.

Jonson's success in this is due to the fact that his maturing analysis has shifted the satiric focus from the individual offender to the corruption of the world at large. There is now an increased social impetus to Jonson's satire; he stresses the scene rather than the anger of the satirist, or the folly of the satirist's current victim. No one in Jonson's new world is exempt from critical scrutiny; nor is any one character permitted the moral exaltation of the satiric commentator, above the action and aloof from it. All now is grist to the satirist's mill. Jonson creates a unique scenic density as he marshals this raw material into the significant forms of the action with an unpitying moral perspective.

In the creation of his satire, Jonson had not proved fickle to his former sources of inspiration, the ancients. His imagination readily grasped the hilarious possibilities of the extraordinary Roman custom whereby a person with a small fortune presented his money to a much richer man, in the hope that he would eventually be rewarded by a greater legacy than the sum he had originally laid out. These 'legacy-hunters', casting their bread upon the waters in the expectation that it would come back buttered, inevitably laid themselves open to manipulation and exploitation, since the sums of money involved were often very large. The classical world here offered Jonson on a plate an authentic historical example of his personal division of humanity into gullers and gulled; with the added advantage that there was no certainty as to which of the two in this situation would eventually come out on top.

The legacy-hunter provided, however, only a starting-point. There is no known source for *Volpone* in classical literature. Jonson knew the type and the situation from the satires of his well-conned Horace and Juvenal; Pliny, too, among his favourite ancient authors derided this custom and its practitioners. Other analogues certainly known to Jonson were episodes from Petronius' *Satyricon* and Lucian's *Dialogues of the Dead*.[1] But none of these provided the plot for *Volpone*. At most they illuminated the central concept, and offered a few telling details.

The world of classical satire suffered in addition a further remove by Jonson's decision to update the source material. With a confident master-stroke Jonson severed the connection with classical Rome that had proved so ill-fated in the case of *Sejanus*. He decided instead to capitalize upon Italy's Jacobean reputation for exotic vice and rarefied criminality. This inspired blending of classical and Renaissance had been adumbrated in *Sejanus*, whose creation was fuelled by Jonson's

reading of Machiavelli.[2] In *Volpone* there are echoes of the great
Florentine throughout, from Sir Politic's fatuous attempts to model
himself upon 'Nic. Machiavel', to the constant employment of the
advice in *The Prince* that one confederate should not draw into a plot
another who could prove treacherous.

The incorporation of Machiavelli's theories into the revenge
tragedies of Jonson's contemporaries had lent them a savage satirical
glee and a sardonic coloration that intensified the final effect of
darkness. Jonson now set himself the congenial challenge of reproducing this effect in comedy. And although like Jonson's other raw
materials not comic in themselves, Machiavelli's total preoccupation
with human folly and vice, his concentration upon personal frailties as
levers for action by the stronger and cleverer but certainly not better
individuals, proved to be peculiarly compatible to the form of comical
satire as now interpreted by Jonson.

The shift in location from the ancient world to Renaissance Italy
also allowed Jonson to render one single and limited abuse of the
classical world in a much wider 'humours' style. The result, fed from
two very different sources, is intensely real but not realistic. From the
dynamic, blasphemous opening lines of *Volpone*:

> Good morning to the day; and next, my gold!
> Open the shrine, that I may see my saint . . .
>
> (I.i.1–2)

we are drawn into and vividly compelled by this mesmeric and
plausible action. At the same time, it is like nothing else in life or in
literature, a brilliant hybrid world *sui generis*. *Volpone*'s originality as a
comical satire extends too to its dispensing with a satirical commentator, the character of Peregrine only the faintest echo of the 'scourg-
ers' of former times. There is indeed no necessity to incorporate the
Asper/Crites character as the running voice of good; here the moral
standards are incarnated, not preached, the satirical perspective
consistent throughout the play for every character and event.

Corbaccio, for instance, as a picture of the ravages of 'the faint
defects of age' could have been a sympathetic portrait. But Jonson is
ferociously severe on the character's physical infirmities. His deafness,
his failing eyesight, his weak hams are all held up to ridicule as
consorting so ill with his vigorous pursuit of gold and the tenacious
hold on life that he displays. The satirical point is not made at the
expense of his weakness, but in the discrepancy between that and his
bounding ambition. Galloping greed serves to vitalize a virtually

lifeless trunk. Jonson here sternly dismisses a cherished value of the classical world, a respect for the aged; age indeed in his scale of values always compounded rather than excused moral failure.

As the aged are not sacred, nor exempt from satirical scrutiny, neither are the good. Celia and Bonario call upon the audience's sympathy, first of all as virtuous in themselves, and additionally as victims both of Volpone's malpractices and of the staggering callousness and selfishness of their nearest and dearest. Yet Jonson does not feel that virtue is not a fit subject for satirical comedy. Bonario's prevention of Celia's rape by Volpone is the action of a right-thinking man (the only example in the whole den of vipers of this type). Yet he is made to express himself at this point in a hilarious parody of heroic attitudinizing which quite undercuts the impact of his intervention:

> Forbear, foul ravisher, libidinous swine,
> Free the forced lady or thou diest, impostor.
> But that I am loath to snatch thy punishment
> Out of the hand of justice, thou shouldst yet
> Be made the timely sacrifice of vengenance
> Before this altar, and this dross, thy idol.
> Lady, let's quit this place; it is a den
> Of villainy; fear nought, you have a guard;
> And he ere long shall meet his just reward.
>
> (III.vi.267–75)

This satirical colouring washes over Celia, too, who with Bonario is comic both in the rape and trial scenes (III.vi and IV.v). But Jonson's purpose here is not merely that of comic effect. So pervasive are the assumptions fostered by romantic comedy that he needed constantly to subvert the audience's expectations that Celia and Bonario, like any other young couple, would somehow be paired off at the end of the play. On this account, too, Jonson leaves both of them somewhat out of focus, undeveloped and undercharacterized. For the audience to identify with these two would endanger the satiric detachment that Jonson was working for.

The treatment of Celia highlights Jonson's dual perspective on women, the first that of a harsh anti-feminism, the second a clear perception of women either as commodities like Celia herself, or if not marketable then redundant in the masculine world of commerce, like Lady Politic Would-Be. All this meant that Jonson could not create a strong, virtuous woman; and as a result he could not portray love. His satiric perspective only serves to masculinize his women when he does try to lend them human characteristics. The presentation of the females in Jonson is purely external – there is nothing at all to bring Lady Politic Would-Be to life as a woman.

All the elements of *Volpone* indeed are similarly harmonized into Jonson's satiric-didactic schema. This it is that lends significance to the sub-plot of the Politic Would-Bes, giving it the relevance to the main plot that has often been missed or questioned. The career of Sir Pol is throughout an ingenious and ironic gloss upon the superior but no less fated machinations of Volpone himself, and his final humiliating *dégringolade* is a burlesque anticipation of the magnifico's ruin and exposure. As Sir Pol serves as a comic distortion of Volpone in his role of opportunist, politician, speculator and manipulator, so his wife Lady Would-Be caricatures in her antics the more vicious predatory activities of the legacy-hunters Corvino, Corbaccio and Voltore. The couple together embody yet another message for the contemporary audience; through them Jonson savagely derides the behaviour of his countrymen abroad, and warns of the dangers that attend both credulity and over-cleverness.

The conclusion of *Volpone* allowed Jonson to express his final satirical judgements through the disposition of the characters. Although in the epistle later offered as preface to the play Jonson betrayed some unease that his punitive denouement did not accord with the requirement of 'comic laws' that there should be a happy ending, nevertheless he asserted the higher claims of the just punishment of wrongdoers. He was confident too that the degree of avarice, cruelty and perversion revealed in the characters should never be lightly waived, nor the discords and divisions uncovered in the action harmonized into a joyful peaceful conclusion. But overarching all this is the play's irresistible satiric drive, and its conviction that the purpose of satire is to expose and to rebuke, not to send the audience away in a rosy glow of contentment and self-satisfaction. The final sentences of the play are carefully constructed to embody the summary of each character and his central fault, as each is forced to undergo the precise penance to make manifest his true state. Volpone will become an incurably sick and deformed man, his servant Mosca a slave, Voltore an outlaw, Corbaccio a pauper and Corvino a civic joke.[3]

This final multiple motif of deformity and degeneration aptly catches up one of the play's most important themes. Although outwardly healthy, attractive even in his vigour, vitality, high spirits and humour, Volpone is Jonson's crowning realization of a Renaissance cliché of the fair outside and corrupted inner being. Volpone's blasphemous adoration of gold as his 'saint' in the first scene will not hold the same delicious *frisson* for godless modern audiences as it did for Jonson's; but we cannot fail to recognize the barrenness of a life that elevates the cold unresponsive metal over the warmth of human relationships, and the perversion of a man in the prime of life denying his normal sexual instincts in its favour.

Dammed up, these find other outlets. As Volpone fetishizes and eroticizes his gold, so he does the individuals around him. Mosca is the prime recipient of this treatment, petted like a lover when all goes well – 'My joy, my tickling, my delight', 'let me embrace thee' – and then struck down as Volpone's inhuman 'wolfish nature' asserts itself at the last. But all who come within Volpone's orbit are subjected to the same process; his appetite, even to an attractive young woman, has to be primed by the taster that she is 'bright as your gold! and lovely as your gold!' Although boasting that he is 'sensual as the Turk' Volpone seems to set things up in such a way as to cheat himself out of the ordinary sexual pleasures; and finally he expresses a classic perversion of the sexual instinct when he declares that to have caused the false trial of Celia and outwitted the court, delighted him 'more than if I had enjoyed the wench'. In comparison with the exercise of these cruel and destructive skills, 'the pleasure of all womankind's not like it' (V.ii.10–11).

In the character of Volpone Jonson created a human nexus where the personal, the political, and the economic meet. These powerful themes are articulated through a plot combining a strong narrative line with a multiplicity of ancillary incidents into what we recognize as the quintessential Jonsonian formula. *Volpone* was the first of Jonson's plays in which he succeeded in creating one plot element to act as a magnetic centre, drawing the other characters and incidents irresistibly towards it. Around this one centre, opening up from it and always referring back to it, Jonson plots his subplots with a Machiavellian intensity. Volpone's 'wolfish nature' and his unresisted animal instincts provide the play's forward impulsion; and Jonson adroitly controls the accelerating pace of the action for maximum dramatic effect. The clarity and force of this movement is counter-pointed, not obscured, by the other, lesser actions that Jonson builds in; the constructional grasp of the dramatist is everywhere secure, so that each development swings in convincingly and forwards the overall action. Each new inspiration of Mosca and Volpone to torture and delude their distracted victims extends and expands the central plot line, pushing it onward to its conclusion.

Comment upon the excellence of *Volpone*'s conceptual content and the development of its characters and structures, however, can fail to do justice to the play in the theatre. Generations of audiences testify to the effectiveness of this play as a dramatic experience. It is, in fact, pure theatre in every aspect. It uses stage resources to the full, offering cleverly contrasted crowd scenes, in the mountebank episode and the trial, which are themselves contrasted with the intimate domestic scenes between Volpone and Mosca, or Corvino and Celia. It incorporates an ascending series of climaxes like the rape attempt, that like the final catastrophe of the uncasing of Volpone itself, are conceived and excuted as fully realized dramatic moments, veritable *coups de théâtre* uniting spectators and actors in one stunning moment of revelation. It provides variety of tone, scene, character and pace, all within a firm but not rigid frame; and it offers wonderful parts for actors. In the use of stage space, and in the management of theatrical illusion and effect, Jonson makes a play and creates a world.

A comedy world, of course; and taking Jonson's aims and achievements too seriously can bury under a heavy weight the play's wide-ranging and rich humour. *Volpone* focuses Jonson's gifts both for verbal humour and for comic stage business. As Volpone and Mosca banter together, as Lady Politic Would-Be sweeps in with the repellent greeting 'How does my Volp?', or as Corvino switches from calling his wife 'locust, whore and crocodile' to 'sweet Celia', we hear the comedy writer at work; while as we watch Mosca guiding the 'blind' Volpone's hand to snap up presented jewels, Lady Would-Be fretting about her curls sticking up, or Voltore reading the will which proclaims 'Mosca the heir' in the sight of all the other hopeful beneficiaries, we see the consummate skill of the master of stage comedy and fertile inventor of comic business. As Jonson himself proudly sensed when writing his prologue, he had written 'a hit', a verdict which was freely awarded in his own time, and which has never since been withdrawn.

The range of Jonson's consummate craftsmanship at this point is further evident in the writing of *Epicene*. Not only does this comedy follow hard on the heels of *Volpone*, it also represents an entirely new departure for Jonson in terms of form, themes and style. Nowhere does Jonson attempt to repeat the elements of the preceding success, nor fall back on characters or devices likely to succeed with his *bête noire*, the uninformed audience. Yet at first glance the play appears to be a reversion to earlier methods. Once more Jonson has demonstrably turned to the classics for his plot; Libanius provided him with the story of the surly man who married a talkative wife, while Plautus offered in his *Casina*, taken from Greek sources, the situation of a man tricked into marrying a boy instead of a girl. Among Jonson's non-dramatic materials are Juvenal's sixth satire against women, relieved by Ovid's warmer commentary on male–female relations in his *Ars Amatoria*.

Followers of Jonson's development will also note a resurgence of his former preoccupation with humours. The character of Morose, who can endure no noise and seeks to refashion his society after his own anti-social obsession, is a pure humour in both the superficial and the deeper meanings exploited by Jonson. His exaggerated predilection for silence has ossified into a paranoid inability to tolerate the slightest disturbance of his peace. This humour makes him the enemy of the world, and all the people in it; the nearer, the deadlier, as his nephew Dauphine finds. Jonson graphically renders the situation in an establishing speech of Act I, scene i, where 'humours' theory and vocabulary both explicitly and implicitly place the type for us:

TRUEWIT: When saw you Dauphine Eugenie?

CLERIMONT: Not these three days. . . . He is very melan-
cholic, I hear.

TRUEWIT: Sick of the uncle, is he? I met that stiff piece of
formality, his uncle, yesterday, with a huge turban of
nightcaps on his head, buckled over his ears.

CLERIMONT: Oh, that's his custom when he walks abroad. He
can endure no noise, man.

TRUEWIT: So I have heard. But is the disease so ridiculous in
him as it is made [that] . . . a trumpet should fright him
terribly, or the hautboys?

CLERIMONT: Out of his senses. The waits of the city have a
pension of him not to come near that ward. . . .

BOY: Why sir, he hath chosen a street to lie in so narrow at both
ends that it will receive no coaches nor carts nor any of these
common noises. . . .

TRUEWIT: A good wag. How does he for the bells?

CLERIMONT: . . . by reason of the sickness, the perpetuity of
ringing has made him devise a room with double walls and
treble ceilings, the windows close shut and caulked, and
there he lives by candlelight.

(I.i.131–77)

Morose, then, both has and is a virulently destructive social disease. He embodies Jonson's developed conviction that 'in natural bodies, so likewise in minds, there is no disease or distemperature, but is caused either by some abounding humour, or perverse affection'.[4]

To take these elements in isolation, however, is to falsify the overall effect of the play. Jonson combines all his disparate materials into a new, compelling and dramatic whole. His fusion of classical plot suggestions provides intrigue and conflict; his management of themes and characters provides food for laughter and for thought. There were Renaissance elements too; from Aretino came the device of the delayed disclosure of the sex of the 'bride'.[5] What unites all these threads into one fabric is the daring contemporary perspective that Jonson chose to give his action. This is the first of Jonson's plays to be conceived and set in his own London, at the time when he was writing. The present-day treatment brings a determinedly fresh and topical slant, and acts as a unifying force.

For Jonson sets his London scene very precisely, both in time and place. He alludes, for instance, to a new statue at Aldgate unveiled in 1609 only a few months before the play was acted (I.i.122); his characters refer familiarly to Westminster Hall, the Cockpit, London Bridge, Paris Gardens and Billingsgate (IV.iv.12–14); Jonson even knows that fashionable women go for their hair-pieces to Silver Street (IV.ii.84). The perpetual ringing of the bells for the victims of the plague which so torments Morose was occasioned by the visitation of 1609 which kept the theatres closed for much of that year. Within this well-known world, Jonson's characters are also located with great care as to their educational and cultural background. While the educated are reaching for their Pliny and Paracelsus in a case of suspected dementia, Trusty the serving-maid trots out her parents' recourse, *The Sick Man's Salve* and Greene's *Groatsworth of Wit*. The kind of effortless placing of detail both affords Jonson a dramatic short-cut and deepens the texture of the portrayal for the audience.

As with *Volpone*, Jonson found a fruitful contemporary vehicle for his satire. Morose's agoraphobia becomes in Jonson's hands a means of indicting not only the malady but its source, the noise and bustle of a London mushrooming at an alarming rate, so that overcrowding, overbuilding and overpopulation were becoming a serious threat to the health and welfare of the inhabitants. The gradual evolution of England from a feudal agrarian to a monopoly capitalist economy, most acutely experienced in some of its phases in the metropolis, is given a vivid actuality in the language and behaviour of the fishwives, orange-women, broom-men, hammermen, prentices, waits and bell-men who throng Morose's disordered fancy; these are both products and producers of the new society Jonson regarded with such reserve and disdain. The split between old values and new habits is sardoni-cally highlighted in Truewit's cynical advice on how to win a woman: 'Give cherries at time of year, or apricots; and say they were sent you out of the country, though you bought 'em in Cheapside' (IV.i.108–10).

Yet as the title of the play makes plain, Jonson's satire is not primarily directed at society in general. What engrosses his attention is the 'epicene', the no-man's, no-woman's land between the normal male and the normal female. To a modern ear the associations of the word are weakness and contemptibility; Jonson expresses it as some-thing altogether more horrific and threatening. In his scale of values it denoted a monstrous departure from the norm, a creature having the characteristics of both sexes and the identity of neither. Epicene herself is the figurehead, but by no means the only example, of this dangerous intersexuality. Many of the other characters are similarly epicene, from the effeminate gulls Sir Amorous and Jack Daw, through the over-womanned, undermanned Captain Otter, to the mannish college ladies whose principal, Lady Centaur, is both figuratively and literally an unnatural hybrid of no true gender.

As this suggests, Jonson's concern is not simply with the superfices of manners and behaviour, but with more fundamental concepts. As one sex changes its nature, so the other must too, since sexual definition proceeds by a continuous process of opposition and ex-clusion. Any failure by a member of one sex to assert its true kind creates a vacuum that the other must inexorably invade:

DAUPHINE: Tom Otter? What's he?
LA FOOLE: Captain Otter, sir. . . . His wife . . . commands all
    at home.
CLERIMONT: Then she is Captain Otter?
LA FOOLE: You say very well, sir.

(I.iv.23–31)

By satirizing deviants of both sexes, effeminate men and mannish women, Jonson seeks to define and illuminate appropriate sexual behaviour, the norm between these extremes. As always his thematic thrust is prescriptive and didactic; he is labouring towards the establishing of what he sees as authentic and natural, the decorum of both sexes.

Inevitably the women come off the worse in this arrangement. Given the conditions of his own age, the still-potent presence of Juvenal among the raw materials, and his own rigid sexual stereotypes, it is inevitable that Jonson's was a sexual portrait of brute anti-feminism. Jacobean public opinion took its cue from a monarch who despite his wide education had an irredeemably gross view of heterosexual relations and of women in particular. The changing social conditions of the period nevertheless encouraged many women to seek to improve upon their traditionally inferior lot, and in the 'college of women' Jonson was grappling with a contemporary issue every bit as relevant as the evolution of a mercantile society with London as the metropolis of capitalism. James's personal attitude is encapsulated in the legendary encounter with a brilliant and highly educated woman, when his sole demand was *'But can she spin?'* This hardened into public policy in such acts as James's ordering the Bishop of London to instruct his clergy to preach against 'the insolency of women and their wearing of broad-brimmed hats, pointed doublets, [with] their hair cut short or shorn'. Within a fortnight, as a contemporary newsletter reported, 'our pulpits ring continually of the insolency and impudency of women'.[6] The theme and its phraseology could have come straight out of *Epicene*, and demonstrate Jonson's topical, even prophetic insight; these events did not take place until 1620.

Equally weighty among Jonson's non-dramatic influences in the handling of this theme was the malignant spirit of Juvenal. To some extent this satirist's frenzied misogyny was softened by Jonson's admixture of ideas, motifs and images from Ovid, whose view of love as an art, a sport and a civilized pastime allowed for a higher view of women than Juvenal (or Jonson) could ever attain. Truewit's extended disquisition upon women, praising their feminine skills and urging men to admire and to court them, derives both tone and content from the Ovidian perspective:

> Women ought to repair the losses time and years have made i' their features, with dressings. And an intelligent woman, if she know by herself the least defect, will be most curious to hide it, and it becomes her. If she be short, let her sit much, lest when she stands she be thought to sit. If she have an ill foot, let her wear her gown the longer and her shoe the thinner . . . you

115

must approach them i' their own height, their own line. . . . If
she love wit, give verses. . . . If valour, talk of your
sword. . . . Men should love wisely, and all women.

(IV.i, 31–6, 88–93, 131)

Yet all this, however congenial and flattering to women it may
appear on one level, is merely a rhetorical flurry, as the lecture format
makes clear. The words are spouted, not felt, and certainly not,
within the play, lived. There the Juvenalian hatred and contempt
triumph through the structural device of the 'college of ladies' that
permits Jonson to display the full range of his anti-feminism. And
writing for a boy company as he was, meant that Jonson did not need
to stint himself in the creation of female characters, nor restrict
himself to the conventional pair of girls as in the adult companies. He
could have as many female grotesques as his imagination could
engender.

Through the collegiates Jonson mounts his attack on women in two
mutually conflicting perspectives. Viewed from the first, Lady Centaur, Mrs Otter and the other women are censured as mannish and
unnatural because they seek learning and eschew the conventional
female servitude of helpmeet and adornment to a man's life. Satiric
targets here include their loud assertive behaviour, the assumption of
'most masculine or rather hermaphroditical authority', their pretensions to learning, and above all their determined refusal to bear
children, procured through their own potions and concoctions.
Although suggestedly modelled on real people, Jonson's college
ladies become non-women, spurious imitation men who unsex themselves and become unnatural, sterile monsters, like Madame Centaur,
half man, half horse, and no part woman.

Yet Jonson's female characters are, with a grand illogic, equally
censured when they try to be, or behave, like women. The time-
honoured techniques of female adornment and allurement, the cos-
metic skills or arts of coquetry, Jonson viewed with deep suspicion and
pilloried with tireless venom. His undiscriminating onslaught
stigmatizes all such devices, and the women who employ them, as
ugly and unnatural. In the portrait of Mrs Otter, Jonson achieves a
total reification and disintegration of the female; she is reduced to
'titivilitium' ['a vile thing of no value'], 'a scurvy clogdogdo, an
unlucky thing', while subsequently in Otter's famous speech she
emerges as a horrible monster-machine, broken down into her
component parts:

She has a peruke that's like a pound of hemp made up in shoe-threads. . . . A most vile face! And yet she spends me forty pounds a year in mercury and hogs-bones. All her teeth were made in the Blackfriars, both her eyebrows i' the Strand, and her hair in Silver Street. Every part of the town owns a piece of her. . . . She takes herself asunder still when she goes to bed, into some twenty boxes, and about next day noon is put together again like a great German clock; and so comes forth and rings a tedious 'larum to the whole house, and then is quiet again for an hour, but for her quarters.

(IV.ii.78–92)

In a manner that anticipates Swift, Jonson goes for an accumulatory technique of heaping up distasteful and disagreeable detail into an overwhelmingly rebarbative whole. Mrs Otter tries so hard to maximize her feminine charms that she turns herself into a sexless collapsible non-person.

For Jonson, then, women overreach themselves and fail grotesquely in attempting to be either more masculine or more feminine. Underlying this inherently contradictory reproach is the deep Juvenalian conviction that women are, intrinsically and inescapably, foul and false. Both their imitation of the masculine and their cultivation of the feminine modes offer proof positive of their hollowness and degeneracy. Nor are they only intellectually spurious. They are different in kind from men, alien and threatening; in Otter's suggestive Latin, 'mala bestia', 'the evil beast'. The savage satirizing of the college woman's sexuality has a note of hysteria in the portrayal of rampant, animal lecherousness; women are creatures who 'love to be horsed', bitches perpetually on heat, greedy predators who will pursue and strike down any male for appetite. Jonson's strident insistence on the relentless and coarse physicality of women encompasses both the lowest personal detail and the widest mythical resonance – 'the spitting, the coughing, the laughter, the sneezing, the farting, dancing, noise of the music and the masculine and loud commanding, and urging the whole family, make him think he has married a Fury'. Other mythological non-women invoked in the play include the Gorgon, Medusa, and the Amazons.

Given the primacy of language in Jonson's imagination, however, it is not surprising that speech is the main area in which women offend. In *Epicene* Jonson dramatized a rooted contemporary prejudice, handed down from the Middle Ages, that 'to be slow in words is

117

a woman's only virtue' (*The Two Gentlemen of Verona*, III.i.326). In a characteristically Jonsonian formulation, speech is directly linked with dominance, so that after her first metamorphosis from silent maid to talkative wife, Epicene is made to instruct a servant: 'Speak to him, fellow, speak to him. I'll have none of this coerced, unnatural dumbness in my house, in a family where I govern' (III.v.48–50). Similarly Mrs Otter maintains her rule over her husband by her constant barrage of bullying prose:

> Who gives you your maintenance, I pray you? Who allows you your horsemeat and your man's meat? Your three suits of apparel a year? Your four pair of stockings, one silk, three worsted? Your clean linen, your bands and your cuffs when I can get you to wear 'em? 'Tis marvel you have 'em on now.
>
> (III.i.34–9)

With education, women become even worse than this, as in Truewit's caricature of the domineering of puffed-up wives: 'If learned, there never was such a parrot' (II.ii.76). The female scholar only uses her learning to torment her husband by incessantly rattling Latin and Greek. Jonson's view of the collegiate ladies is amply expressed in the final Jonsonian contrivance for them; they are at last struck dumb and 'stand mute' when Epicene is revealed.

Speech, then, is a masculine prerogative which women wrongfully usurp and then use as an instrument of the control that rightly belongs to men. Not all members of the ruling sex are worthy of their high prerogative, however, in Jonson's view; while the women are satirized for speaking at all, the men are satirized only if they speak incorrectly. Jonson is at pains to establish, through careful punctuation and control of syntax, the garrulous, disordered speech of those who squander what was to Jonson the one gift that raises man above the animal:

> But let that go, antiquity is not respected now – I had a brace of fat does sent to me, gentlemen, and half a dozen of pheasants, a dozen or two of godwits, and some other fowl, which I would have eaten while they are good, and in good company – there will be a great lady or two, my lady Haughty, my lady Centaur, Mistress Dol Mavis – and they come a' purpose to see the silent woman, Mistress Epicene, that Sir John Daw has promised to bring thither.
>
> (I.iv.41–9)

Like the silent woman, the chattering man exemplifies Jonson's concept of the inversion of the normal. As the women masculinize themselves, so La Foole and Daw denote their effeminacy by this breathless, gossipy style. Their wilful unmanning of themselves is echoed in another vein later in the play with the ritual castration of these two by the 'real' men of the party.

With both male and female characters, the speech Jonson gives them is no mere decoration, nor even simply a means of characterization; it is organically related to the movement of the plot. Epicene's role as the silent, whispering, simple girl leads directly to her first metamorphosis, into the loud, dominant, demanding matron and woman of fashion. Having led both Morose and the college ladies a fine dance with this device, Jonson exerts his dramatist's prerogative to change Epicene again; this time with a decisive reversion to the character's true, masculine self. At this revelation it is significant that not only Epicene and the college ladies, but Morose too, are all rendered speechless – they have talked themselves to a standstill and worn themselves away into nothingness. The same fate overtakes the garrulous gulls of the subplot, La Foole and Daw, whose action in this as in the rest of the play is adroitly arranged to parallel and mimic the action of the Morose intrigue.

The play's ascending series of reversals is carefully orchestrated. From the first ingenious conceit of building a play around the binary opposition of sound and silence, the action pursues an apparently zig-zag course which in fact proves to lead directly to Jonson's desired end. Truewit's intervention to dissuade Morose from marriage, for instance, appears to defeat its object when Morose is thereby prompted to speed up his nuptials in order to be certain of disinheriting Dauphine by his action. Yet in actuality Truewit's deed serves Dauphine's covert purpose of precipitating his uncle into the disastrous non-marriage with Epicene. Similarly, when La Foole and Daw gang up on Epicene, their intention is to aggrandize their own reputations as men of the world by the destruction of hers. Again, the expected result is the opposite of what was intended, yet results in Jonson's long-term aim of the public annihilation of all their pretensions, both social and personal. Nothing occurs haphazardly; all strands of the action are caught up in the final denouement to demonstrate Jonson's moral values and judgements.

On the structural level *Epicene* is a highly assured play. It is equally confident, too, in its stagecraft. Beginning with the basic staple of drama, speech, Jonson contrives an ingenious and elaborate series of

119

comments upon it in highly dramatic terms. Mrs Otter's entrances, for instance, are wonderfully rumbustious pieces of theatre, as she erupts like a thunderclap amid the bemused males. The humiliation of La Foole and Daw could only work in the theatre, as it is essentially visual in itself, in addition to gaining from the effect of the audience within the play as the collegiate ladies look down on the scene from above. Again, the revelation that Epicene is a boy, made by the removal of his wig, is nothing in verbal terms – yet the stage effect is a visual shock that comes as a stunning *coup de théâtre*. In the less spectacular moments, too, Jonson displays his sense of the dramatic, and his control of the medium, in the contrast and variety of group with individual scenes, for instance, or of male and female characters, and exits and entrances.

Yet with all its brilliances, *Epicene* has proved unpalatable to post-seventeenth-century audiences. The residual thread of farce, inherent in the material from its classical origins, results in an action which has been found too brutal to permit of unqualified enjoyment. The tormenting of Morose in Act II, scene ii, for instance, the harsh physical punishment of the gulls and their ignominious public exposure are not for sensitive spirits, nor for an age interested in the psychological verities of human behaviour. Jonson approached his characters and his material in the riotous humour of the caricaturist; *Epicene* is cast in the mould of his comical satires, yet with the addition of such bite, penetration and contemporary topical purchase as make its lashes cruelly painful rather than formal and conventional. The comical satire inheritance also accounts for the structural difficulty of Truewit; as a legacy from the earlier dramatic mode (the satiric commentator, repository of true values and undisputed final arbiter). Truewit is out of place in an even more slightly naturalistic mode. Not even his repeatedly professed friendship for Dauphine can therefore succeed in giving him the authority to intervene so consistently in the affairs of the other characters.

A farce such as *Epicene* directly opposes itself to romantic comedy in taking the lowest possible view of human motive. Jonson's characters seek money, prestige, social status, or sex; if possible a combination of all these. Apart from Truewit whose questionable status has been noticed, and Clerimont, who exists solely to provide within the play an audience for the various intrigues, each character lives in a monomaniacal world observed by Jonson strictly from the outside. The English theatre has never, either before Jonson or since, been accustomed to intellectual farce, or 'comical satire' in Jonson's mode, save perhaps in the brief, doomed flowering of Joe Orton. So *Epicene* remains an oddity, a strange production whose demonstrable merits are unlikely ever to be well known in their true arena of the stage.

With *The Alchemist* Jonson hit on his most potent central conceit. More than any other of his previous inventions, the figure of the alchemist enabled Jonson to reconcile his moral and social preoccupations into one dazzling unity; through this he was able to comment upon human nature both in its eternal aspects and in its contemporary social formations. This conceit also satisfied Jonson's various requirements as a practising craftsman-dramatist and comedy-writer – it suggested plots, characters and structure, all within a framework of humour ranging from the simply daft to the extravagantly grotesque. These elements combine to form Jonson's best-loved comedy (*Volpone* being his most admired) by audiences and actors alike.

Alchemy offered Jonson a perfect target for his satire. Ridiculous in itself, it nevertheless had a considerable importance and influence. For the sincere, the idealistic, or the gullible it operated as a quasi-religion, with its demands that the alchemist live a pure and humble life, its hidden secrets, and its promise of better things, when all baseness would be dissolved into refined excellence. Jonson by contrast operated alternately, and often simultaneously, within a strenuous classicism and a profound Christianity – neither of which systems of belief could have any truck with the undigested learning, unfocused rhetoric, and woolly spirituality that were alchemy.

At the other end of the scale, alchemical practice opened up a vista of fraud, opportunism, greed and exploitation to confirm the darkest satirical view of humankind. Alchemy was such a tangled mixture of misplaced experimentation and bizarre humbug that Jonson did not need to exaggerate anything at all to achieve a satiric effect. His considered and detailed portrait of alchemy in this play successfully incorporates the varied, often contradictory perspectives in which the subject and its practitioners could be viewed by contemporaries. Yet we are never left in any doubt as to Jonson's own orientation, nor as to the suitability of alchemy for harsh satirical scrutiny.[7]

Alchemy afforded Jonson not only a ripe subject for satire in its own right; it served, too, as the focus for further satire, most notably upon the Puritans. In a straightforward dramatic equation, Jonson uses the characters of Tribulation Wholesome and Ananias to assert that Puritans were in the same business of spiritual and material fraud as alchemists were, so that for canting, lying and cheating there was nothing to choose between them. Puritanism in Jonson's view was as likely to lead its followers to salvation, as alchemy to turn its believers' lead into gold.

Yet Puritanism held the deeper threat of the two, in its combination of far more complex social, political and religious elements than ever alchemy could aspire to. Jonson signals this in the play by the treatment he accords to the two Puritan characters, Ananias and Tribulation Wholesome, over all the other dupes. They are handled in attentive detail, closely observed and never underrated. Unlike the other gulls with their tame domestic aspirations, these scoundrelly zealots are rendered dangerous by their desire for power and their belief in their own authority. Their narrow 'precision' and breathtaking hypocrisy insulate them from any rational objection to their courses. This for Jonson is the unforgivable offence, and these are the grounds of his attack. It is interesting that he does not confuse the issue, as so many of his contemporaries do, with imputing to the Puritans wild revolutionary plans to overthrow the government, or a lewd and vicious sexuality operating uncontrollably under the cover of rigid virtue. Jonson centres his attack, and scores right on his chosen target:

TRIBULATION: Truly, sir, they are
Ways that the godly Brethren have invented,
For propagation of the glorious cause,
As very notable means, and whereby also
Themselves grow soon and profitably famous.

(III.ii.97–101)

Jonson's satire in *The Alchemist* is not only directed at individual objects or targets. The whole world of London-on-the-make becomes his purview. Both alchemy and Puritanism are set within the context of a fast-growing capitalism which glorified money-making and individualistic self-aggrandizement. The activities of Face, Subtle and Doll are an ironic commentary upon the dedication of their larger society to acquisitiveness and consumerism. They can only rise upon the backs of others similarly desperate to claw their way up. Dapper's request for a 'rifling fly' to enable him to win at cards and horse-races; Drugger's anxiety over the best location for his doors, shelves and pots in his new shop to ensure good business; Mammon's unbounded 'covetise' for sensual experience, power and plenty; even Surly's capitulation to the chance of grabbing the rich widow Pliant when he has preserved his detachment from all the toils of the situation up to that point: all these express, in their cleverly differentiated ways, the hungry urges and desires of the new capitalism.

As with *Epicene*, Jonson ties these general observations very closely into a known and observed reality of contemporary London. The location in *The Alchemist* is given with a documentary-style precision; it is not merely that 'our scene is London'; the audience is set down firmly with the characters 'here, in the 'Friars', Jonson's own neighbourhood. From this house, so intensely realized that its very doors, windows and cubbyholes take on a life of their own and participate in the dramatic action, Jonson leads the spectators out in the imagination into contemporary London, so persuasively that Pie Corner, Temple Church, Sea-Coal Lane, Bedlam and the China Houses become as real to us as if we had seen them. What we see is one room of a house; but we feel the whole of London teeming and throbbing just outside the door:

DOLL: Yonder fishwife
   Will not away. And there's your giantess,
   The bawd of Lambeth.

(I.iv.1–2)

As these imaginary characters batter on the door to try to see 'Master Doctor', it becomes clear, too, how serviceable the 'alchemist' conceit is to Jonson in terms of plot and structure. The pretensions of this pseudo-science and its practitioners to more-than-human knowledge and wisdom draw all the characters towards 'Doctor' Subtle like a magnet. Jonson needs no elaborate plotting to bring his personnel together and engage them in mutual action. This makes for great economy in the exposition, allowing Jonson to plunge directly into the development of the action proper. His invention was never more plausible nor more fertile; on to the simple farce notion, borrowed from Plautus, of an absent old man's house being misused by rogues, Jonson hung a plot of dazzling complexity and breathtaking speed.

Jonson achieves this by first creating the dupes, whose actions form the staple of the plot, as separate individuals with distinct and different frameworks of desire. Then, by increasing the pace of their appearance and contriving some strategic overlapping, he shows how their centres of interest first coincide and then begin to converge. He implicates them in each others' fortunes, all eventually competing for the same prizes, as in the contest over the winning of the widow Pliant. Each time a thread threatens to break loose, as with Surly's disgusted departure from the house, Jonson works it back into the fabric again, enriching the texture by a new addition like that of the Spanish masquerade, for instance. The knaves and fools are all eventually involved, and enthusiastically too, in gulling others and in deceiving themselves. This witty plotting of Jonson has a further advantage yet, that it ensures a high and accelerating pace for the action. As the gulls come tumbling into the house each supplies a fresh impetus; when all are active together, the play pulsates with movement, and gathering excitement:

SUBTLE: Are they gone?
FACE: All's clear.
SUBTLE: The widow is come.
FACE: And your quarrelling disciple?
SUBTLE: Ay.
FACE: I must to my Captainship again, then.
SUBTLE: Stay, bring 'em in first. . . .

                               To the door, man!
                                (IV.ii.1–6)

As this shows, both Subtle and Face, to an even greater extent, are put to the extremes of their resources simply to keep all their dupes suspended in the air. Compare the swiftness and precision of their stage-management with that of Mosca in the earlier scenes from *Volpone*; structurally the episodes in which Dapper, Drugger, the Puritans and Mammon call at the tricksters' house resemble the visits of Voltore, Corvino, Corbaccio and Lady Would-Be to the 'crafty-sick' Volpone. But the pace of the earlier play is much more stately and measured than the increasingly frantic manoeuvres of *The Alchemist*, as befits the relative social status of the different crooks.

By involving all the dupes with one another (and eventually with the three rogues too, as Face and Subtle contend over Pliant, and Mammon offers Doll to make her his 'empress'), and by overlapping and accelerating the action, Jonson avoids the potential trap of his plot breaking down into nothing more than a series of unconnected episodes. We see in this the progression Jonson has made from the earlier 'comical satires' whose weakness was the serial parade of fools and knaves with plenty of talking and too little action, characters who offered themselves for a static literary analysis rather than dramatic interaction. Now Jonson was able to vary and deepen his material to extract from it its greatest possible comic and dramatic content. This technique also leads him to a more powerful and convincing climax than he had earlier been able to contrive. As characters, interest, hopes and follies take off and whirl around in increasingly wild revolutions, loops and parabolas, the situation and its managers proceed to a level of frenzy at which something will inevitably have to give. The forward thrust of the plot from Act III, the controlled and irresistible narrative tension, all surge triumphantly on to the Act V final explosion of the house of deceit, a structural movement symbolically anticipated in Act IV with the blowing up of the 'alchemist's' laboratory and the 'destruction' of the stone.

And as with *Epicene*, Jonson tantalizes his audience with a surprise ending. The expected disaster comes out in an unexpected way. We are not prepared for Face's final and stunning metamorphosis when under the persona of the colourless Jeremy he sinks his vivid masquerades as Face, the Captain and Lungs. Nor do we anticipate the final severance between the two rogues, so that Face is allowed to triumph, retaining the spoils and his maker's renewed affection, while Subtle barely escapes over the wall in his shirt. Retribution, either comic or serious, passes one by and strikes the other down. Face remains in the house, the magnetic centre that has provided the simple, dominant overarching structure of the play. He is the master of this little world, complete and rounded of itself, by which Jonson has avoided the redundant scene-shifting so beloved of other contemporary dramatists.

For *The Alchemist* forms the pinnacle of Jonson's achievement in avoiding the widely different localities of romantic drama. Most of his plays are set in the same city; here, Jonson achieves a concentration unique in Elizabethan drama, by restricting all the action to one room in one house, and the street outside it. And it is noteworthy that it is not until the end of the play, with the collapse of the rogues' little world, that the outside world is let in. Not until Act V, with the return of Lovewit, does Jonson open the action to the world and the people outside the house. This final twist is one of the most stunning features of a consistently impressive plot which was almost totally Jonson's invention. Apart from the Plautine idea, and possible hints from other slight pieces both classical and Renaissance, there is no known source for this plot.

Jonson's original choice of alchemy as his central subject also had a vital, and vitalizing, effect upon his use of language in the play. The genuine basis of scientific learning which underpinned it, together with the vulgar and fraudulent malpractices which encompassed it, made possible a variety of dictions, ranging from the educated to the coarse. In giving speech both to 'gown'd man' and guttersnipe, and to many layers of birth and breeding in between, Jonson extended his linguistic facility to its fullest potential. The scholar in him rose to the opportunity to parody the false scholarship of the 'learned doctor' and his assistant:

> SUBTLE: I mean to tinct C in sand-heat tomorrow,
>   And give him imbibition.
> MAMMON: Of white oil?
> SUBTLE: No sir, of red. F is come over the helm, too,
>   I thank my Maker, in St Mary's bath,
>   And shows his *lac virginis*. Blessed be Heaven.
>   I sent you of his faeces there, calcined.
>   Out of that calx I ha' won the salt of mercury.
> MAMMON: By pouring on the rectified water?
> SUBTLE: Yes, and reverberating in Athanor.
>
> (II.iii.58–67)

Mammon, too, is an educated speaker, albeit of a more orthodox bent than this; and the presentation of his disordered, gargantuan appetites allows Jonson to heap up references to Pythagoras, Hercules and Solomon alongside contemporary eroticism and the poet 'that writ so subtly of the fart', with a random profusion and disregard of distinction that in itself encapsulates this gross sybarite:

> MAMMON: Now, Epicure,
>   Heighten thyself to talk to her all in gold;
>   Rain her as many showers as Jove did drops
>   Unto his Danae; show the god a miser
>   Compared with Mammon. What? The stone will do't.
>   She shall feel gold, taste gold, hear gold, sleep gold:
>   Nay, we will *concumbere* [fornicate] gold.
>
> (IV.i.24–30)

Mammon is the most exaggerated, but not the only, example of one who makes a religion out of gold. To drive home this point, Jonson carefully shows how the pseudo-science of alchemy is in fact often a blasphemous parody of Christianity. Among the terms in which it is described by its practitioners and followers in the play are 'state of grace', 'spirit', 'sublimed' and 'exalted'. This perversion of a genuine impulse of faith and idealism to the worship of 'filthy pelf' picks up on the *Volpone* theme – 'Open the shrine, that I may see my saint!' – and amplifies it in a more categoric but equally sombre and satiric way.

Mammon, especially in his encounters with Face, Subtle and Doll, is made the centre of the play's mock-heroic rhetoric and bombast that are among its greatest delights in performance. But Jonson's happiest inventions remain those at the lower end of the linguistic scale; Jonson is unchallengeably our greatest example of what Rudyard Kipling called 'the poet of the cuss-word and the swear'. He possessed himself of a rich and luscious vocabulary of abuse, and frequently seems at his most commanding and zestful when creating a filthy row or bitter quarrel. This need not necessarily be confined to two people; see the flood of vituperation that breaks as the gulls come together to realize what has befallen them:

MAMMON: Where is this collier?
SURLY: And my captain Face?
MAMMON: These day-owls.
SURLY: That are birding in men's purses.
MAMMON: Madam Suppository.
KASTRIL: Doxy, my sister.
ANANIAS: Locusts
  Of the foul pit.
TRIBULATION: Profane as Bel, and the Dragon.
ANANIAS: Worse than the grasshoppers, or the lice of Egypt.
                                          (V.v.11–15)

As this suggests, the sensuous element is always present in Jonson's vilification. The play opens with one of the more horripilating of Jonson's images of execration:

FACE: Sirrah, I'll strip you –
SUBTLE: What to do? Lick figs
  Out at my –

                                          (I.i.3–4)

This splendidly evocative unfinished insult sets the standard for the rest of the play. When Surly exclaims in disgust, 'O this ferret / Is rank as any pole-cat' (II.iii.80–1); when Face reminds Subtle of the days when 'like the Father of Hunger, you did walk / Piteously costive, with your pinched-horn nose' (I.i.27–8); or when Subtle ingratiatingly assures the disguised Surly,

You shall be soaked and stroked, and tubbed and rubbed:
And scrubbed and fubbed, dear Don, before you go.
You shall, in faith, my scurvy baboon Don
Be curried, clawed, and flawed, and tawed indeed
                                          (IV.iv.97–101)

the auditors experience the kind of insult that is not only heard, but seen, felt, even tasted.

Jonson's control of tirade and disputation, although ever-fertile, is not haphazard. Each character has his or her own pattern of peculiar jargon, or mode of rhetoric. There is, too, an underlying image matrix by which the crooks are repeatedly compared with dogs in a variety of abusive terms ('Mongrel', 'cur', 'mastiff', 'bitch'). A secondary image chain associates them with vermin, insects, 'lice' and 'locusts', creatures who live on a lower than human plane and prey upon mankind. This is throughout contrasted with the frame of reference in which the rogues locate themselves, as 'captains' and commanders in a great and proud scheme that subtly anticipates Mammon's ludicrous pretensions. Although immediately recognizable to Surly as 'rank ferrets' keeping a bawdy-house, to themselves they are serious business people engaged in a 'venture tripartite' which is felt to be so binding that even at a crisis of the action Face and Subtle have to take time out to negotiate their positions:

FACE: What dost thou say to draw her to't. Ha?
And tell her, 'tis her fortune. All our venture
Now lies upon it. . . .
The credit of our house is too engaged.
SUBTLE: You made me an offer for my share erewhile.
What wilt thou gi' me, i'faith?
FACE: O, by that light . . .
I'll not buy now . . .

(IV.iii.64–73)

As successful 'venturers', the three rightly pride themselves upon their many and varied achievements; in their own eyes, they are indeed the only stars in their firmament. They signal this to each other in the good times by the use of an elaborate and pretentious courtesy between themselves – they style each other 'your worship', 'captain', 'sovereign', in increasing degrees of exaltation. This contrasts grimly with what we know of the uneasy reality of the relations between them; a vicious self-seeking, hostility and greed, thinly patched over by temporary mutual interest.

The three central characters illustrate a factor of *The Alchemist* that applies equally to all the other speakers, the skill with which Jonson homogenizes a variety of languages, dictions and jargons into a total style which assumes more than a verbal importance in the play. On a simple level, the play's speech both establishes and sustains its characteristic and highly individualized tone; vivid, coarse, sexual, tactile, throbbing with vitality and immediacy. On a deeper level the language serves too to establish the moral framework. No character speaks without the implicit sense of the author's presence guiding the appropriate value-judgement, as much through the audience's emotions and senses as through the intellect; who can repress a shudder at the carefully contrived descent, the brilliant use of bathos, in Face's declaration that Doll must make herself ready to receive a male customer?

> Where is she?
> She must prepare perfumes, delicate linen,
> The bath in chief, a banquet, and her wit,
> For she must milk his epididymis.
> (III.iii.18–20)

Jonson's success in creating a viable dramatic framework for the expression of his moral preoccupations means that *The Alchemist* must be regarded as his ultimate achievement in the form of comical satire. Within a structural framework whose excellence led Coleridge to hail it as one of the three most perfect plots in literature, Jonson achieves not simply a satiric analysis of alchemy, but a fine level of moral distinction between the dupes. Dapper and Drugger are simple fools whose wants are strictly limited by their restricted horizons. Yet within this category, Jonson carefully differentiates between Drugger, who is prepared to put in at least some work to obtain his fortune, and Dapper, who hopes to get his entirely through play. Their long-term hopes are contrasted, too; where Drugger is ravished by Subtle's vision of his rising within the Grocers Company and becoming a civic dignitary, Dapper wants to give up his employment as a lawyer's clerk, become a playboy, and live off gaming. Kastril and his sister Pliant are by contrast again pure country cousins, innocents abroad, desperate to find some entrée into the fashionable life of London, and vulnerable to any shark who will offer to show them the way.

Mammon and the Puritans form another contrasted pair, but on another plane entirely. Here, simple 'humours' have grown into monsters of greed, compelled by their very natures to root out and gobble up what they crave. Apparently strongly contrasted by Epicure's limitless hedonism and the Puritans' rigid austerity, they are nevertheless linked at a deeper functional level of a strenuously working greed; and both parties have the imaginative capacity denied to the simpler creatures, to see themselves glorified, in Tribulation's phrase, as 'temporal lords'.

Then again, in another of the play's impressively contrived structural pairings, Mammon is coupled with Surly, whose overgrown humour similarly sets off that of Mammon. Surly's role as sceptic in the early stages of the play leads audiences naturally to identify with him, and to see him as the one balanced character in a nest of fools and rogues. This is to overlook Jonson's careful placing of him with and against Mammon; this illustrates the moral that if it is ridiculous to be ready to believe anything, as Mammon is, it is equally blind to credit nothing. From the moment of their first entrance together, the audience must see that Surly is riding for a fall just as surely as Mammon is. An empty cynic, he is just as determined to construct the world in terms of his own version of it as the gross knight is; and he is equally ready to rise opportunistically to the moment and seize the main chance for himself as any of the other dupes. Within this framework, his declaration to Pliant – 'I am a bachelor / Worth naught' – takes on a more than literal significance.

As *The Alchemist* is Jonson's most achieved satire, so it is his most adroit and varied comedy. The richness of the original subject allows Jonson to demonstrate his comic virtuosity, and he runs through the different types of humour with unfailing command and resource. From the violent physical farce of the opening sequence, unquestionably one of the most stunning first scenes in drama, Jonson ranges through hilarious play-acting scenes like Doll's raving blue-stocking routine or her masquerade as 'the Queen of Fairy'. In this and in other sequences Jonson gives free rein to his taste for the scatological, handled with characteristic vigour, wit and style. As Dapper is retrieved, rumpled and reeking, from the privy where he has been stowed away, the high spot of his encounter with his 'aunt of Fairy' comes when he is invited to 'kiss her departing part' (V.iv.57). This eminently theatrical knockabout visual style of comedy is throughout executed and illuminated with a consistent ironical vision, so that the slightest things are made funny. Subtle's assurance to Surly that 'lead and other metals' 'would be gold if they had time'; Doll's promotion from Doll Common through Doll Proper and Doll Singular to Doll Particular; Drugger's innocent question to Face, 'Did you never see me play the fool?'; all these and countless other lines would all raise a separate and distinct laugh in performance but that others, equally well-turned, come so hard on their heels.

Jonson's control here extends through every aspect of the play to include the audience as well. Jonson plays the audience of *The Alchemist* like an angler with a fish, now overwhelming them with the power of the dramatic illusion, now twitching them out of it. He wishes simultaneously to convince us with the vigour of the performance, and to remind us that it is all play-acting. This dual perspective is established from the first, when in the Argument Jonson tells us of the 'servant', the 'cheater and his punk' who, having established their arena of operations, 'all begin to act'. At the crisis of the explosion of the illusory 'stone', 'it, and they, and all in fume are gone'; a dismissal and distancing that recall the Shakespearean 'the best in this kind are but shadows':

> these our actors,
> As I foretold you, were all spirits, and
> Are melted into air, into thin air;
> And like the baseless fabric of this vision . . .
> Leave not a rack behind.
> *(The Tempest*, IV.i.148–56)

Within the play the metaphor of play-acting insistently recurs; all three of the rogues play part upon part within their own original part and are highly conscious of this. Consider the multiple levels of meaning and understanding which underlie the apparently simple discussion between the three:

DOLL: Or by this hand, I shall grow factious too,
   And take my part and leave you.
FACE: 'Tis his fault.
   He ever murmurs and objects his pains,
   And says, the weight of all lies upon him.
SUBTLE: Why, so it does.
FACE: How does it? Do not we
   Sustain our parts?
SUBTLE: Yes, but they are not equal.
DOLL: Why, if your part exceed today, I hope
   Ours may, tomorrow, match it.

> (I.i.140–7)

At this and many similar moments we feel Jonson's relish of the wit with which he exploits the drama's relation with the spectator, the thin line between reality and illusion. Throughout the play, with great delicacy and skill, Jonson often seems to be working both outside and inside the framework of dramatic illusion simultaneously.

At the end of the play Jonson's management of this tricky no man's land is so confident that he can make Face take the audience into his confidence about the dramatic conventions governing their entertainment, appealing to their judgement as educated and participant viewers, 'understanders', in Jonson's term:

> Gentlemen;
> My part a little fell in this last scene,
> Yet 'twas decorum . . .
>
> (V.v.157–9)

In *The Alchemist*, Jonson's relationship with the audience was at its happiest. As before, he maintained throughout the didactic and pedagogic role, instructing the spectators not only in moral values and habits, but also in the fine art of comedy. Yet the relaxed geniality with which this is accomplished robs it of all its previous tension and irritability. For once Jonson was able to feel supremely, undefensively confident that his play was good, and would be admired. As the Prologue predicts, 'two short hours' are wished away to general satisfaction.

Ultimately, though, the success of *The Alchemist* is traceable back to the power of the original central conceit, and Jonson's masterly deployment of it. It became the perfect expressive vehicle for Jonson's convictions, and of his mature abilities. Alchemy's true function, to which the pursuit of gold from base metal was but a side-track, was the extraction of the quintessence of matter. In *The Alchemist* all the characters are involved in a personal act of alchemy; they desire desperately to transmute themselves into something richer and better than they are. This in itself, rich as it is in humour and insight, repays the original notion of the play. But beyond this Jonson succeeds in making his whole drama a metaphor of transmutation; in using it as an instrument of dramatic analysis as exact as any chemical process, by which the essential nature of men and things is laid bare and brought forth. In the successful resolution of *The Alchemist* Jonson finally realized the aims of 'comical satire', and in so doing vindicated his longstanding faith in this strange and self-discovered form.

7

TO COME FORTH WORTH THE IVY, OR THE BAYS

Jonson's climactic use of the 'comical satire' formula in *The Alchemist* was an unclouded triumph. It enabled him to work out both a dramatic experience and a relationship with the audience that proved to be agreeable to all. Never again was Jonson able to be as relaxed as he was in the composition of this piece. And with its completion, his restless search for artistic status and supremacy began again in disregard of his comic achievements to date.

For Jonson still needed the validation that even the greatest success in the public theatre could never bestow. Comedies for 'the common stage' could not bestow 'the bays', nor the coveted title of 'Ben Jonson, poet'. He knew himself now for a consummate craftsman. But was it art? And how was he to convince the indifferent multitude, let alone confound the hissing claque of his particular enemies? Then again, the experience of the court masques had accustomed him to the free right of address to the highest in the land. This in turn had raised his ambitions to educate and elevate his auditors on the long-cherished Sidneyan principles of 'instruction by delight'. In a deliberate and determined change of direction, therefore, Jonson made the second bid of his career 'to sing high and aloof', in order 'to make readers understanders'. At the moment of his highest realization in the form of comedy, Jonson abandoned it to return to an earlier battlefield, that of classical tragedy.

Jonson's creation of *Catiline* in 1611 is highly problematical in a number of ways. What prompted it? Eight years had passed since the humiliating stage failure of *Sejanus*. But that play had made an impressive recovery from the original débâcle, gaining ground particularly among the 'understanders' whom Jonson most urgently wanted to convert to his way of thinking: one contemporary admitted, 'I amongst others hissed *Sejanus* off the stage, yet after sat it out, not only patiently but with content and admiration' (HS IX, 191). This belated vindication of the earlier tragedy can only have encouraged Jonson to try again 'the tragic race'. *Catiline* very clearly builds upon *Sejanus*, and in so doing inevitably reproduces its weaknesses as well as its strengths.

Of immediate interest is Jonson's reversion to the purely classical for his subject-matter, when his three previous successes had flourished as a judicious blend of ancient with modern. As in the writing of *Sejanus*, Jonson's reliance upon his principal source, Sallust's *Bellum Catilinae*, was not slavish. Jonson avoided reproducing Sallust's prejudice against the nobility, for instance; and as a son of the Renaissance he felt more warmly about Cicero than Sallust did. In addition, Jonson's pronounced intellectual independence led him to turn to other versions of the story; he incorporates suggestions both from Plutarch and Dio Cassius that Caesar was more implicated in the conspiracy than his cool public demeanour at the time would suggest. By this Jonson gave historical status to rumours which Sallust dismisses as false; as a dramatic historian he knew the duty to represent opinion as well as acknowledged fact. Where his sources agreed, Jonson represented the truth conscientiously and in detail; where they disagreed he exercised his prerogative as a judge; where they were silent, the dramatist's responsibility to fill in.

More significant developments occurred as Jonson struggled to fuse the historian's and the poet's task of representing 'truth of argument'. Although in his own copy of Sallust Jonson carefully marked, and by this token considered and studied, passages relating Catiline's virtues, no trace of them appeared in the finished play. Jonson in fact undercut Catiline's reforming zeal, showing it to be merely the hollow manipulative populism of a man devoid of any other political resource. Equally, Jonson promoted Cicero to a more prominent part than he plays in Sallust's version of events. To Jonson, as poet and as historian, Catiline was an irredeemably evil man; had his virtues been genuine he could never have behaved as he did; while Cicero's importance to Rome and to the whole of the civilized world was self-evidently such that his part in the narration of events must correspond to it.[1]

Jonson's reversal to a purely classical mode, with subject-matter firmly grounded in ancient authority and unimpeachable sources anxiously conflated, is matched by his reversion to tragedy after his comic successes. Despite these recent triumphs, on his own admission Jonson nurtured a deep suspicion of comedy as a form: tragedy was, both in his and received opinion, the higher form. The decision to turn to tragedy at this point demonstrates that Jonson had not transcended the disgust with his profession so movingly outlined to Salisbury in 1605 when, imprisoned for his part in the scandalous *Eastward Ho!* affair, he wrote to the earl regretting that his 'fortune' necessitated 'so despised a course'. Arguably the recent successes in themselves produced this reaction. For his own self-esteem Jonson needed to prove that he could achieve in a vein of high seriousness; popular acclaim, however desired, was as profoundly distrusted and despised. On this perverse scale of values, the stage failure of *Catiline*, its inability to tickle the vulgar palate, was in itself proof positive that it was, as Jonson claimed, 'a legitimate poem'.

Yet a poem of what? Jonson's intentions have remained resolutely opaque, despite many different attempts at critical clarification. The challenge of *Catiline* for modern readers (and the last spectators of the play were laid to rest nearly three hundred years ago) is to set aside Shakespearean expectations of the tragedy of psychological insight, the exploration of emotional states, and the haunting evocation of loss and suffering. Yet there is abundant contemporary evidence testifying to the deep chord struck by Shakespeare's treatment of 'the grieved Moor', for instance. If therefore we have difficulty with Jonson's deliberate displacement of interest from a 'true soul's tragedy' to 'Catiline His Conspiracy', there are grounds for thinking that his audiences could have done so too.

For a conspiracy does not readily serve as the centrepiece of a drama. Catiline's cohorts in complicity neither emerge as a unified band of plotters, nor crystallize out as recognizable individuals. Lentulus, Cethegus, Autronius, Vargunteius and the rest are under-characterized in a way that can only be deliberate, given Jonson's skill in characterization. They remain dull and hollow figures, neither grounded in any known reality, nor brought to life within the world of the play. Exchanges like this demonstrate Jonson's conscious decision to reduce them to ciphers:

CATILINE: So may my blood be drawn and so drunk up
  As is this slave's.
LONGINUS: And so be mine.
LENTULUS: And mine.
AUTRONIUS: And mine.
VARGUNTEIUS: And mine.
CETHEGUS: Swell me my bowl yet fuller.

Here do I drink this as I would do Cato's,
  Or the new fellow Cicero's, with that vow
  Which Catiline hath given.
CURIUS: So do I.
LECCA: And I.
BESTIA: And I.
FULVIUS: And I.
GABINUS: And all of us.

                                                      (I.497–503)

Clearly this scene would be heightened in performance by the grisly
stage business of drinking blood. Yet equally clearly Jonson has
chosen to produce this repetitive speech with its semi-comic echo
effect to suggest that all the conspirators speak with the voice of
one mindless thug. When they do speak as individuals, they
are shallow and uncompelling, hollow braggarts mouthing unfelt
hyperbole.

If not 'His Conspiracy', then what of Catiline himself as a centre of
the play? Jonson gives him a more flourishing send-off than any other
villain of the contemporary drama, when Sylla, himself a legend of
monstrous cruelty, is sent as a herald from the nether world to
trumpet Catiline's 'incests, murders, rapes':

                  thy forcing first a Vestal nun;
  Thy parricide, late, on thine own only son,
  After his mother, to make way
  For thy last wicked nuptials; worse than they
  That blaze, the last act of thy incestuous life
  Which got thee at once a daughter and a wife.

                                                      (I.30–6)

But from the beginning, the irreconcilable tensions inherent in
Jonson's portrayal of Catiline are plain. While this catalogue of
vicious crime unfolds in a speech of over seventy lines, Rome's public
enemy number one is seated quietly 'in his study', according to
Jonson's stage directions. Tyrannized both by the classical prohibition against violence on stage and by his own distaste for unconvincing dramatic representation, Jonson was forced always to describe or
relate Catiline's evil deeds, rather than show them. The great
conspirator comes across therefore as a paper tiger, who despite the
insults of others and the imprecations of his own tongue does not

succeed in injuring a single individual in the course of the play.
Catiline is made to plot, threaten, rave and bluster with a vengeance,
but he is in actuality far less dangerous to the characters around him
than Hamlet, or even Romeo.

And nowhere are the limitations of Jonson's method more painfully
experienced than in the Act IV, scene ii crisis of the action. While the
great orator Cicero impeaches Catiline in a majestic series of speeches
that taken together run to the unprecedented length of almost 300
lines, Catiline is denied any effective response. At first refuting the
charges, Catiline then falls back on his social rank in an attempt to
outflank the 'ambitious orator', and then stalks out to banishment
with the windy bluster of 'Fall I will with all, ere fall alone' (line 451).
Catiline's despatch is brought about in fifty lines; what we have then is
not the spectacle of a tragic fall, but that of a man who having stepped
on a land-mine without noticing it, seems totally unaware that he is
being blown up.

Cicero, the architect of Catiline's ruin, would seem in outline to
offer himself as a viable alternative hero. The paradigm of the
Renaissance man, virtuous and scholarly but capable of decisive action
at need, he undertakes nothing rashly or without reflection, yet his
courage is never 'sicklied o'er with the pale cast of thought'. Even
more significantly within Jonson's scale of values, he shows himself to
be a master of language in many different modes:

> O Rome, in what a sickness art thou fallen,
> How dangerous and deadly, when thy head
> Is drowned in sleep, and all thy body fevery . . .
> (III.ii.204–6)

> Poor misled men. Your states are yet worth pity,
> If you would hear, and change your savage minds.
> Leave to be mad, forsake your purposes
> Of treason, rapine, murder, fire and horror.
> The Commonwealth hath eyes that wake as sharply
> Over her life, as you do for her ruin.
> (III.v.19–24)

> Dost thou not blush, pernicious Catiline?
> Or hath the paleness of thy guilt drunk up
> Thy blood, and drawn thy veins as dry of that
> As is thy heart of truth, thy breast of virtue?
> (IV.ii.112–15)

Yet as these extracts suggest, the coldly impersonal nature of Cicero's speech precludes his emergence as the charismatic focus of the drama. When Fulvia, the mistress of one of the conspirators, comes to warn Cicero of the impending doom of Rome, Jonson negates any potential for dramatic interaction by making Cicero address her as if she were a public meeting, in a series of rhetorical rhyming questions:

> Is there a heaven, and gods, and can it be
> They should so slowly hear, so slowly see?
> Hath Jove no thunder, or is Jove become
> Stupid as thou art, O near-wretched Rome?
>
> (III.i.1–4)

And so on for forty-seven lines. Finally, Jonson's habit of rendering much of Cicero's speech as direct translation of the Latin original clinches the formal, unnatural effect, as in this greeting to the Senate:

> What may be happy and auspicious still
> To Rome and hers. Honoured and conscript Fathers . . .
>
> (IV.ii.5–6)

Nor is the portrait of Cicero untinged with irony. Jonson never wholly endorses him either as a 'virtuous prince' or as a successful leader, 'the only father of his country', in Cato's phrase (V.iv.211). In the short term, Jonson demonstrates some significant similarities between Cicero and the traitor whom he seeks to extirpate; both are politically ambitious, both plot with and depend upon their supporters, both use dubious means and instruments to attain their own ends. In the longer term, Cicero's was only a temporary triumph; as Jonson and all his educated 'understanders' well knew, the hero of this hour was to be the victim of another, caught in the fatal toils of a later, more successful *putsch* than Catiline's.

Cicero will not serve, then, as the centre that *Catiline* seems to lack. Still less will any of the female characters do; all the women are trivial, slight, or weak, alternately vain, selfish, greedy and demanding, narrowed to the point of caricature by Jonson's anti-feminism. Of this contemptible bunch, Jonson's bitterest satire is reserved for Sempronia as a learned lady. In another echo of *Epicene*, and as a further expression of Jonson's misogyny, all the evil in men too is presented in female terms. The male conspirators are lascivious and hysterical, effeminate abortions of nature. While corrupt males usurp female weakness, Sempronia apes masculine learning and Fulvia takes command of events. The men abdicate rational control, and the women grasp for dominance, when 'the time is out of joint' as it is here.

The central difficulty of *Catiline*, then, results from Jonson's original decision to chronicle the fate of an institution (Rome) via an abstraction (the conspiracy) rather than that of a tragic hero. The republic of Rome, frequently personified as a suffering woman, is the true centre of the drama; to her all the characters refer their actions and concerns, and to her fate their own is totally subordinate. For Jonson, the tragic, heroic crisis of conscience typically associated with Shakespearean tragedy is quite beside the point; all his characters have made their crucial decisions before the play opens. For him the tragedy lies in the growth of a man of blood and destruction within the heart of great Rome, a man moreover who as a member of the patrician class, 'a noble', should have been most closely identified with the continuance of her greatness. This tragedy is intensified and deepened by the fact that Cicero's was only a temporary triumph; the true sorrow lies in the spectacle of the greatest civilization the world had ever known tearing itself apart and, despite the efforts of men of conscience and goodwill, failing to find the remedy for its terminal catastrophe. Behind the frenzy of Catiline's speeches, behind even the Senate's attempts through reasoned debate to find the appropriate means of handling the crisis, we hear the rising howls of the Vandal hordes at the gates of Rome, and the long crashing sound of her fall.

Catiline thus assumes its true shape as the moral history of a decaying state, with Rome herself as the tragic protagonist. In keeping with this scheme, which differs profoundly from that of *Sejanus* despite surface similarities, the drama is consistently more sententious than its predecessor, with a higher proportion of rhetoric and oratory to dramatic action. In the attempt to translate moral philosophy into effective political action, Jonson's characters quote, debate, speechify, lean on proverbs and maxims, and consolidate their positions through speech. The effect of this is to massify both issues and individuals, turning them into monoliths that collide but never dramatically conflict. Jonson had both the intellectual insight and the erudition to create a formidable political drama of the classical world, effectively creating a new and unique form in the drama of the period, and still unfamiliar to the English despite later examples occurring in European drama. But he could not make it into a play.

Then too, Jonson saw himself as a historiographer in dramatic form. He wanted to make his play acceptable as history and as poetry, both of which commanded respect by virtue of their own high form and their power as teaching instruments. *Catiline* undoubtedly satisfied its creator's demanding criteria, and may be regarded as a success upon its own terms. But those terms were necessarily and deliberately exclusive. Its full appreciation requires an interest in ideas, a committed classicism, and a faith in the moral power of history. Jonson's possession of all these attributes made him intolerant of those without them. But audiences cannot be expected to master an unfamiliar chunk of ancient history as a prerequisite to appreciating a play. Jonson's history is good, within the limits of his sources; no seventeenth-century clocks chime in his ancient Rome, no streets are anachronistically thronged with members of the Watch or men with hats plucked about their faces. But accuracy does not make for accessibility. Nor, paradoxically enough, does it make for realism. Jonson's careful mosaic of authentic classical detail does not ultimately coalesce to form a convincing world. And as he does not generate one, so he cannot terminate it; he lacks the Shakespearean facility to close down the world of the play at the end of the drama, with issues resolved, dramatic impetus spent, and new initiatives beckoning. Jonson's method, and his fidelity to a wider concept of history than Shakespeare possessed, precludes his 'rounding off' in this way. But the sensation produced is not so much that of the historical flow, the eternal continuities that he sought, but of incompletion.

And however successful *Catiline* is on its own terms, those terms could never be widely successful. Nor are they in themselves *dramatically* successful; quite simply, the elements do not add up to make true theatre. Jonson's chosen events, though popular in his own time and interesting enough in any, lack intrinsic tension; their movement is all one way. Similarly public figures and political types like Cicero, Caesar and Cato have to be vitalized by the dramatist, for they carry no intrinsic dramatic charge. Jonson's preference for confrontation over interaction between the major characters militates against any development, while his setting of scenes of crisis in the Senate (a habit carried over from *Sejanus*) inevitably means that critical exchanges assume the format of political debate rather than dramatic conflict.

In addition, Jonson appears to reject or throw away individual opportunities for dramatic realization. The crusty Cato, Cicero's faithful ally, demonstrates here and there a talent for vilification which peps up any scene in which he appears, but he is consistently under-used, and his relationships with Cicero and Catiline remain under-exploited. Similarly Catiline's love for Aurelia, extravagantly expressed in the first scene of the play, could have been deployed to diversify the character of the 'great criminal', and to lend a little sparkle in a bleak expanse. But once introduced, Aurelia is effectively dropped, and with her go any opportunities to open up the play in a new direction. In place of these genuine dramatic openings, Jonson gives us Sylla's ghost, or choric interventions which interrupt the flow of the action and disengage the audience from it.

Finally, Jonson's chosen mode of composition is in itself essentially and inherently undramatic, even unplayable. In *Catiline*, action and dialogue are throughout not *gestic*; they do not convey what stage movements and dramatic actions should accompany the lines. When in the opening scene of *The Alchemist*, Subtle threatens Face, 'I'll gum your silks . . . I shall mar / All that the tailor has made, if you approach', a vivid picture of the stage action presents itself, Subtle holding out a strong chemical in a menacing fashion, and Face only prevented from making a violent assault by the fear of having whatever Subtle holds, flung all over him. The action would be just as compelling and even funnier, if Subtle's liquid, his 'good strong water', were interpreted, as in some modern productions, to mean the contents of his chamber pot. Jonson's comedies abound in moments like this, where the director merely has to body out the business and movement lying present within the lines themselves.

Reminiscent flashes of this technique occur in *Catiline* to indicate that Jonson could have worked in this way had he chosen to. When at the climax of the confrontation between Cicero and Catiline this exchange occurs:

CATILINE: Well, I will leave you, fathers; I will go
  But, my fine dainty speaker –
CICERO: What now, Fury,
  Wilt thou assault me here?
SENATORS: Help, aid the Consul.

(IV.ii.431–3)

we do not need the stage direction '*He turns suddenly on Cicero*' to tell us what is going on. That action then flows rapidly and naturally into Catiline's next swift change, when on the line 'See, Fathers, laugh you not? Who threatened him?' he appeals to the assembly with mock-innocence and a savage irony. Yet such moments in *Catiline* are extremely rare, and the director of any production would be hard pressed to devise how to stage the twenty-, thirty-, forty-line blocks of rolling oratory and rhodomontade. Jonson further makes unreal

141

and unnecessary demands upon his actors, too; Thespis himself would have found it difficult to keep discovering new and varied reactions, while standing around for the 300 lines of Cicero's climactic oration in Act IV.

For all these reasons, despite the many advances in Jonson's craftsmanship in the interim, *Catiline* does not come as near to success as *Sejanus* did, either as tragedy or as drama. But there were other, more serious consequences in store for Jonson. His return to the same territory as before, with an even less positive result, led inevitably to the renewal of his conflict with his audience. His Horatian distaste for *profanum vulgus*, 'the ignorant mob', was enshrined within the play itself; as Cicero wakes and watches for the good of Rome, conferring with senators and other ruling interests, the unspoken and spoken basis of their actions is the conviction that the body politic, the untutored multitude, was incapable of grasping issues and judging rationally of characters and actions. As the representatives of the people, the Chorus is made to confess this capacity for misjudgement and the related tendency to fly to dangerously wrong conclusions:

> One while, we thought him innocent;
> And then we accused
> The Consul for his malice spent,
> And power abused.
> Since that we hear he is in arms;
> We think not so:
> Yet charge the Consul with our harms
> That let him go.
> So on our censure of the state
> We still do wander;
> And make the careful magistrate
> The mark of slander.
>   (IV.867–78)

If the people could not judge of political matters, still more were they unable to discriminate in matters historical and poetical. In the address 'to the . . . ordinary' reader written by Jonson for the 1611 publication of *Catiline*, he waxed ponderously sarcastic about his audience's inability to form any worthwhile opinion: 'though you commend the first two acts with the people, because they are the worst, and dislike the oration of Cicero, in regard you read some pieces of it at school and understand them not yet, I shall find the way to forgive you.' As this shows, Jonson could neither comprehend nor forgive the approach of the uninitiated to the fruits of his muse.

One arm of his self-defence was this heavily condescending and aggressive response to those whom he took to be his detractors. The other was the appeal to the 'understanders', to 'the Reader Extraordinary', 'the better man' to whom alone Jonson was prepared to 'submit [him]self and [his] work'. In choosing William Herbert, Earl of Pembroke, as the play's dedicatee, Jonson was not merely paying a debt of gratitude to one whose patronage had been and was to be very important to him. He was also trying to single out and to demonstrate the epitome of the 'understander'; the cultivated, educated nobleman whose 'great and singular faculty of judgment', and ability to 'vindicate truth from error' contrasted so sharply with the 'crude and airy reports' of the 'thick and dark' ignorance of 'these jig-given times' (dedication to *Catiline*, lines 1–9).

As this shows, Jonson's experience of the stage failure of his tragedy had not minimized the exigence of his demand for an active critical involvement of the audience in the experience of the play. More, he commanded rather than invited the educated, discriminating, chosen members of his audience to join with him in evolving the appropriate scale of values. It is a painful irony that while Jonson possessed such an enlightened view of the active participation of the audience with the dramatist in the creation of a communality of experience, thought and emotion, his insecurity and defensiveness caused him to limit the community to an ever-decreasing number. As he himself wrote in the preface to *Catiline*: 'The commendation of good things may fall within a many, their approbation but in a few; for the most commend out of affection, self-tickling, an easiness, or imitation; but men judge only out of knowledge. That is the trying faculty.' Indeed it is; and it tried Jonson, and found him out.

In the writing of *Catiline* Jonson had set himself to employ the highest standards of classical, historical and literary technique. But theatregoers and dramatic critics alike are resistant to plays written to satisfy extra-dramatic and extra-theatrical criteria. Characteristically Jonson could not lie down under an intellectual or a theatrical rebuff; he volleyed and thundered. However, the security of classical and conventional authority on which he had implicitly depended to shore up his extreme position was not enough. And when the smoke of hostilities died away, Jonson had not succeeded in coercing more than a handful of 'understanders' to join him in his estimate of the play's merits. Jonson himself did not lose his faith; but he found it easier to preserve in retreat than in action. As had happened before with Jonson's defeat in the 'War of the Theatres', the rejection of his play precipitated the wounded titan of the contemporary drama into another three-year retirement from the public stage.

Although once again in full retreat from 'the loathed stage', Jonson could afford to take full satisfaction in another area of his professional activities. The pre-eminent success of his greatest plays and the traditional classification of him as a dramatist first and foremost have tended to obscure both the importance and the continuing achievement of Jonson's masques. After his brilliant debut with *The Masque of Blackness*, between the years 1606 and 1611 that gave *Volpone*, *Epicene*, *The Alchemist* and *Catiline* to the world, Jonson wrote one masque or entertainment every year, two in three years, and three in the *annus mirabilis* of 1608, a total of eleven in all. Superficially at least, Jonson was first a professional masque-maker during this period, and only secondarily a dramatist.

But Jonson's masques were far more than routine, 'money-get' productions to him. Just as he was attempting to use the conventional form of the stage play to make his own statement about life, theatre, morality and the art of writing plays, so too his response to the masque was one of confident and self-determined artistry. His resolution to raise this form, too, by the power of his craft resulted in a series of improvements and developments of the form that indicate Jonson's continued quest to discover the potential of the masque and to use it to the full.

The masque was no easy form within which to work, let alone to innovate, as Jonson by now knew well. In James's reign it took on its distinctive but limited format of a combat of concepts taking place within a mythologized Golden Age pastoral setting, where the critical intervention of some virtuous quality results in the triumph of right. In its predetermined form and outcome, in occasion, in audience, the masque was in every way contrasted with the public theatre which had been Jonson's artistic base. Length too was a factor; the majority of Jonson's masque texts are between 200 and 400 lines in length, about the size of one substantial scene in a play. It should not be assumed, though, that this made a masque easier to write because shorter, or that an evening's masque entertainment was briefer than an afternoon in the theatre. Jonson's masque texts are more properly regarded as libretti, representing as they do merely the skeleton of the finished performance.

Yet to Jonson, his skeleton provided both the supporting framework and the conceptual backbone for what would otherwise be an empty show. Jonson took his masque-making every bit as seriously as his plays or poetry, evolving an intimidating body of critical theory by which he regulated and substantiated his masque-writing practices. As early as 1603, when he began work on what was to be *The King's Entertainment* in the following year, Jonson was giving active consideration to the artistic problem of uniting separate elements of meaning into one meaningful whole:

> the nature and property of these devices being to present always some one entire body or figure, consisting of distinct members, and each of those expressing itself in its own active sphere; yet all with that general harmony so connexed and disposed as no one little part can be missing to the illustration of the whole.
>
> (HS VII, 90–1)

Jonson's grasp of the essential difference between these shows and the drama emerges clearly here in his use of metaphors drawn from music and the visual arts to encapsulate his concept of the masque.

The management and blending of the masque elements did not in itself constitute a theoretical problem of a high order; the resolution of any difficulties lay well within the craftsmanship and skill of the masque-maker. More serious and eventually beyond even Jonson's considerable power to control, is the status of the text within an essentially non-literary form; and the related difficulty of preserving an accurate record of a masque when the text can be the only part capable of preservation. In the prologue to *Hymenaei* Jonson tackled this by asserting the supremacy of the text as embodying the 'soul' of a masque; this is what appeals to 'understanding' over mere 'sense', and what as a result guarantees the survival of the masque, since it is 'impressing and lasting'. The impression of the senses is but 'momentary'; without 'the most high and hearty inventions to furnish the inward parts', 'the glory of these solemnities had perished like a blaze'. The writer's invention alone, 'grounded on antiquity and solid learnings', can lead the spectator or reader forward to 'lay hold on more removed mysteries'.

This exaltation of the poet above the designer was and remained Jonson's position on his masque-making – as he tersely stated elsewhere, 'the pen is more noble than the pencil' (HS VIII, 610). In these early stages, however, Jonson was not experiencing these differences as discords. His conception of the roles of writer and designer and so far as is known his practical experience too, was at this time one of co-operation rather than competition. He did not then perceive the pre-eminence of the writer as under any threat, and was therefore generous in his initial tributes to the work of his collaborator.

And nothing could detract from Jonson's elevated view of the masque as a form; these were 'noble solemnities', that 'glorify the court'. In the preface to *Hymenaei* Jonson satirized those who considered masques to be only 'transitory devices' when in fact they were acts of love demonstrating 'a most real affection in the personaters' for the persons to whom they were addressed. As the 'personaters' were members of the aristocracy and royalty, then 'the nobility of the invention should be answerable to the dignity' of the presenters. For although aware of the difference of the masque from previous forms, Jonson still clung to the conviction that it should satisfy the established criteria of literary worth, consciously working according to 'that rule of the best artist [Horace] to suffer no object of delight to pass without his mixture of profit and example' (preface to *The Masque of Queens*, HS X, 282).

Given the weight that Jonson attached to the masque and the frequent opportunities he made over these years to flesh out his theories and to learn from practice, it is not surprising that the masques of these years show a tremendous formal improvement and progression in craftsmanship. His first masque, *Of Blackness*, had demonstrated the power of a spectacular central conceit; in *Hymenaei*, his next venture, he attempted to extend the central concept through strenuous and elaborate 'invention' into a unified celebration of harmony and concord (the Platonic theory given a light wash of Christian colouring in the standard Renaissance manner). The idea of *unio*, 'union', interpreted according to its widest possible range of meanings from the personal through the political to the philosophical, is more than the single notion of the earlier masque, strong though that was in Jonson's ingenious and illuminatory handling. It had become, in fact, a conceptual framework, a unifying concept that satisfied Jonson's feeling that the masque should present 'one entire body or figure' to which all its parts organically related.[2]

In contriving and developing an ordered progression of thought in the masque, Jonson also reinforced the plot-line. Given the conventional elements of the masque, not much could be expected or

146

achieved in the way of narrative; confronted with Queen Anne's desire to appear as a blackamoor, the dramatist in Jonson could have been forgiven for finding very little story value in the device. But in the exposition and unravelling of the central conceits, in the leading of the spectators towards the 'more removed mysteries' that he aimed at, Jonson contrived to give his masques if not plots, then at least the intellectual sinews so noticeably absent in the productions of others. He frequently made use of the time-honoured but ever-serviceable motif of the quest; the daughters of Niger are seeking the source of beauty in the masques *Of Blackness* and *Of Beauty*; while Venus' search for her lost son Cupid lends a quasi-dramatic vigour to *The Hue and Cry after Cupid*, later known as *The Haddington Masque*:

> Beauties, have you seen this toy,
> Called love, a little boy,
> Almost naked, wanton, blind,
> Cruel now, and then as kind?
> If he be among you, say;
> He is Venus' runaway.
>
> (lines 86–91)

Another crucial development, both more radical and more visible, was Jonson's development of the anti-masque. Jonson constantly sought ways to work against the masque tendency to be static, to settle into a series of pictures. Within the confines of the form he explored the possibility of introducing some conflict and contrast, and in so doing vitalized what in other hands generally proved to be no more than tableaux or pageant-style entertainments. *Hymenaei* was Jonson's first attempt to bring in the element of discord that was to ripen into the fully fledged anti-masque. Four Humours (Melancholy, Phlegm, Blood and Choler) and four affections (Joy, Hope, Dread and Sorrow) try to disturb the ceremonies with their ungoverned behaviour, threatening to destroy the body, but are rebuked and restrained by Hymen, the spirit of the wedding feast, and Reason. In the proceedings on the following night, the Debate of Truth and Opinion, with the ritualized 'battle of the barriers', continued the conflict motif.

Encouraged by the success of this experiment, Jonson took it further. *The Hue and Cry after Cupid*, on the poet's own declaration, contained Jonson's first full attempt at an anti-masque. At this early stage of his masque-making career, Jonson had tried the limits of the form and found them too confining; there had to be room for some opposition to the main proceedings, and some humour. The anti-masque was the means Jonson devised to fill this gap.

In *Hymenaei*, the element of discord is provided as a part of, yet still within, the masque. As Jonson uncovered the value of an element of contrast, so the anti-masque began to split off from the masque proper and assume a distinct and separate identity, with the related functions both of introducing the main masque and preparing for it by a strong contrast. In the *Hue and Cry after Cupid*, Jonson took this development a step further by introducing characters who had no part to play in the masque, but existed solely to serve the purpose of providing a contrast and relieving the solemn scene with humour. The Haddington anti-masquers were a troupe of twelve boys, 'most anticly attired'; on their cue they 'fell into a subtle capricious dance, to as odd a music, each of them bearing two torches, and nodding with their antique faces, with other variety of ridiculous gesture'. Set against the stately formality of the adult speeches and dances, the little boys were a great hit, and 'gave much occasion of mirth and delight to the spectators' (lines 171–5).

The most remarkable feature of this sequence is its brevity; the boys, who appear as attendants of Cupid, do not speak, or act; they simply dance, look comical, and pull faces. Yet clearly they struck the right note, both in theory and practice. When Jonson came to write his next masque, *Of Queens*, he completed the evolution of the anti-masque by removing it from the main body of the show, and giving it the status of an introductory piece in its own right:

And because Her Majesty [Queen Anne], best knowing that a principal part of life in these spectacles lay in their variety, had commanded me to think on some dance, or shew, that might precede hers, and have the place of a *foil*, or *false masque*; I was careful to decline not only from others but from mine own steps in that kind, since the last year I had an antimasque of boys; and therefore now devised that twelve women, in the habits of hags or witches, sustaining the persons of Ignorance, Suspicion, Credulity etc. (the opposites to good fame) should fill that part; not as a masque, but as a spectacle of strangeness producing multiplicity of gesture, and not unaptly sorting with the current, and whole fall of the device.

(lines 10–22)

Jonson's hags (played of course by adult performers capable of sustaining a greater dramatic burden than the boys) dance, chant,

sing, conjure, and summon up their dame in an extended sequence of
more than 250 lines – an episode longer than the first scene of *The
Alchemist*, for instance. For once discovered, the anti-masque proved
to be Jonson's delight. In the conceptual scheme of things it
embodied the disharmony over which harmony must constantly
struggle to prevail, and hence deepened the intellectual and allegorical content of each masque; but in simpler terms it offered Jonson the
chance to offset the grand and highflown action of the masque proper
with something vitally different. By the time he came to write *Oberon
the Fairy Prince* Jonson could create a full anti-masque of satyrs, whose
coarseness aptly sets off Oberon's delicacy and grace. They are fun to
watch, they are funny to listen to, and they provide an expert lead-in
to the main masque:

SATYR 4: What is there now to do?
SATYR 5: Are there any nymphs to woo?
SATYR 4: If there be, let me have two.
SILENUS: Chaster language. These are nights
   Solemn to the shining rites
   Of the Fairy prince and knights. . . .
SATYR 2: Will they come abroad anon?
SATYR 3: Shall we see young Oberon? . . .
SILENUS: Satyrs, he doth fill with grace
   Every season, every place; Beauty dwells but in his face,
   He's the height of all our race . . .

(lines 44–65)

As this suggests, although Jonson used the anti-masque as an
occasion of comedy, he was careful that the humour did not overstep
the bounds of decorum, either social or artistic. The racy, bawdy
laughter of *The Alchemist* belongs to another world entirely. Nor was
the anti-masque always a vehicle for humour. In the final masque of
1611, Jonson wrote a serious debate between the Sphinx and Cupid,
allegorically representing Ignorance in its most monstrous form
tyrannizing over Love, which it attempts to destroy before being
thwarted by the priests of the Muses representing the power of
wisdom. It would be too much to suggest that this episode has any
true dramatic conflict; yet its strength is such that the succeeding part
seems weak by comparison. Even allowing for the impact of the
music, dance and spectacle that necessarily are unrepresented in the
printed text, the scene is highly interesting in its clear implications
that the anti-masque was increasingly coming to engross Jonson's

creative energies. This it was that provided an outlet for the more distinctive, as opposed to conventional, aspects of his genius, his delight in grotesque absurdities, witches and monsters, for example. The anti-masque came eventually to outgrow the masque in size as well as in significance; a study of the relative lengths of masque and anti-masque in these pieces shows the latter coming to outstrip the masque in the proportion of two-thirds to one-third.

Within a short time, then, Jonson had both consolidated the masque as he found it and introduced vital and valuable innovations. His principles of composition remained constant – congruity, continuity and contrast, all governed by the demands of decorum – and these led him to experimentation and discovery through a series of brilliant variations and appositions. Jonson ranged freely and confidently through this rigid and ungiving form, modifying both its conventions and his theories in the light of every new experience of creation.

For Jonson clearly relished all these new opportunities. As with the earlier entertainments, he delighted in the purely visual, for every character and scene specifying detail, colour and style: 'a personated bride, supported, her hair flowing and loose, sprinkled with gray; on her head a garland of roses, like a turret; her garments white, and on her back a wether's fleece, hanging down; her zone or girdle about her waist of white wool, fastened with the Herculean knot' (*Hymenaei*, lines 56–61). As Jonson was at pains to establish in the writing of *The Masque of Queens*, his was an active if not a controlling interest in the design – he prescribed properties and described the pictures that he had in his mind's eye, just as they demanded to be set down.

Jonson's later tensions with his designer have tended to overshadow what was initially an unmixed delight in 'what was most taking in the spectacle' (HS X, 232). The masque offered, as the public stage did not, the romance of sheer splendour; and in the brilliance, the colour, the spangles, Jonson uncovered a sense of wonder that had never succeeded in finding expression through the drama. Indeed the visual spectacle, the song, dance and music united to form a harmonious whole in Jonson's imagination. In direct contrast, he also relished the impact of disharmony and discord, and frequently introduced 'wild noise' and 'hollow and infernal music' into his later masques. He enjoyed creating visually expressive symbolism through movement and dance, like the final circle in *Hymenaei* when all the performers are 'linked hand in hand; so heart in heart'. He recognized the power of movement not only to illustrate but to embody the theme: 'Here they danced forth a most neat and curious measure, full of subtlety and device, which was so excellently performed, as it seemed to take away that spirit which the invention gave to it: and left it doubtful whether the forms flowed more perfectly from the author's brain, or their feet' (HS VII, 220–1).

Yet these enchanting shows never for Jonson existed simply for their own sake and in their own right; they were formed to express the beauty of their 'soul', the concept that united and dignified the whole endeavour. The creation of the 'soul' was for Jonson the true exercise of his part; he found an irresistible opportunity for intellectual gymnastics in the devising of allegory and symbol that then had to be worked out through a central unifying conceit and a plethora of local detail. In the act of peopling his masque universes with appropriate figures, Jonson was able to call upon a richly diversified parade of classical, mythological and allegorical beings. Hymen, Reason, Venus, Vulcan, the Three Graces, the Cyclops and many more rub shoulders with Merlin and the Lady of the Lake. Jonson's masque-making gave him free rein to bring to life the make-believe characters who had thronged his imagination since boyhood. In the masque Jonson could enlarge his fertile fantasy beyond the strait-jacket of the realistic; he could even suspend the laws of nature, time and history.

For nothing other than this total creative freedom and power could, in Jonson's eyes, do justice to the importance of the occasion. However flimsy any masque text may now appear to a modern reader, it is clear that Jonson and his contemporaries took these ceremonials very seriously indeed. Jonson in fact seized on them as a chance to handle in a new way some of his abiding thematic preoccupations. Chief among these was his sense of the active presence of the evils of darkness, fear and suspicion; like his monstrous Sphinx in *Love Freed from Ignorance and Folly*, Ignorance is the prime vice from which all others emanate. Hence it is the duty of the good to be vigilant – to maintain the sacred flame of the threatened good, and particularly as the good is incarnated in what Shakespeare called 'lawful rule and right supremacy'.

For to Jonson (and not to Jonson only) the critical factor in all this was the king. He alone could hold the balance between warring factors, could reconcile oppositions and harmonize dissent, both by his actions and by his example. He was the principal earthly link in the golden chain binding all sublunary beings eventually to God; he was the sole bastion against those mutinous and seditious subjects who chose to rampage in their ignorance and disturb the right and true order of things.

This was the significance of James in Jonson's conceptual framework; and this, rather than simple flattery, was the reason that Jonson so consistently elevated and eulogized one who, taken simply as a man, could not hope to live up to the picture Jonson portrayed. But James could not be taken merely as an ordinary man. He was both the king, and the emblem of kingship; and as the last English monarch to rule before the doctrine of the Divine Right of Kings became insupportable, he was also his country's chief lawgiver, minister and priest. In the masques, Jonson repeatedly stressed the pre-eminence of the king's position:

> Britain's the world, the world without.
> The King's the eye, as we do call
> The sun the eye of this great all.
> (*Love Freed from Ignorance and Folly*,
> lines 285–7)

Again and again Jonson was to find the way to praise and compliment James, in any number of elegant variations; the treatment of Oberon, for instance, in the masque of that name, elevates first the prince himself, then by extension refers all praise and glory to the king:

> This royal judge of our contention
> Will prop, I know, what I have undergone;
> To whose right sacred highness I resign
> Low at his feet this starry crown of mine,
> To show his rule and judgment is divine.
> These doves to him I consecrate withal
> To note his innocence, without spot or gall;
> These serpents for his wisdom; and these rays
> To show his piercing splendour; these bright keys
> Designing power to ope the ported skies,
> And speak their glories to his subjects' eyes.
> Lastly this heart, with which all hearts be true:
> And Truth in him make treason ever rue.
> (lines 932–44)

On one level, this is patently designed to tickle the vanity of the king who took himself for the British Solomon. But in stressing James's wide powers and the constant need for truth, wisdom and integrity in

152

the exercise of them, Jonson conveys an important message while in the final couplet reminding the king of the penalty to be paid for neglecting it.

The masque then provided Jonson with a form of direct address to the king and court, in effect to all the high officials of the land (the mythological and allegorical figures are of crucial importance here, since 'Truth' or 'Reason' could speak plainly and prescriptively to the king, where a mere mortal could not so presume). Yet there were pitfalls, and Jonson could not in the nature of things entirely avoid them. Each masque, for instance, had a different starting-point, and the writing assignment often had to satisfy some strange exigencies. Consider, for instance, Queen Anne's demand that Jonson come up with a sequel to *The Masque of Blackness* three years after he had written it; only now the nymphs were to be white, not black, there were to be four more of them, and the whole thing was to be plausibly revamped and the inconsistencies explained away. Jonson's urbane prose glosses over the difficulties, but they must have been considerable:

> It was her Highness' pleasure again to glorify the court, and command that I should think on some fit presentment, which should answer the former, still keeping them the same persons, the daughters of Niger, but their beauties varied, according to promise, and their times of absence excused, with four more added to their number.
>
> To which limits, when I had apted my invention . . .
>
> (*The Masque of Beauty*, lines 2–9)

Responding successfully to the half-baked notions and passing whims of his capricious patrons was only one of the hurdles to be overcome by the masque-maker; another was contriving to please a sophisticated but demanding audience. Like modern soap opera, masques were required always to be the same, but different, familiar yet fresh. In Jonson's constant search for new and ingenious figures and allegories, the pressure on him to satisfy these opposed requirements is palpable. Undoubtedly at times Jonson tried too hard to be clever, and toppled over into obscurity. To read the masques, with their battery of explanatory notes giving a detailed account of every significance and implication – 'by this Sphinx was understood Ignorance' – is to wonder how much an audience, denied the assistance of the text, could possibly have grasped on the basis of their one solitary experience of the piece in performance. As Jonson burrows ever deeper into his allegories and figures, heaping up fresh meanings through the excavation of every personal, political, social and sexual application, the masques threaten to become purely cerebral, an agglomeration of attributes rather than a harmonized experience.

Jonson's masques did not always succeed in achieving the clarity of meaning that he both desired and claimed for them. He never lost his belief that profound symbolism could speak allusively to a subtle intelligence; but his own notations to his masques show his awareness that not all spectators could satisfy this criterion. In the preface to *Hymenaei*, Jonson was withering about those who found his masques too erudite; 'where it steps beyond their little, or (let me not wrong 'em) no brain at all'. Later in the same masque, he glosses his characters of the Humours and the Affections with a contempt only thinly veiled by heavy condescension:

> And for the allegory, though it be here very clear, and such as might well escape a candle, yet because there are some must complain of darkness, that have but thick eyes, I am content to hold them this light.

> (HS X, 213)

Characteristically Jonson refused to accept these reactions as any valid criticism of his work – as he declared defiantly, 'It is not my fault if I fill them out nectar, and they run to metheglin' (HS X, 210) (an insult that combined all that a canary-drinking Englishman could convey of ignorance and barbarism). Later, in a magnanimous exercise of Christian charity, Jonson introduced *Hymenaei*'s final song with the pronouncement, '[I] do heartily forgive those whom it chanceth not to please' (lines 440–1). Since it is often assumed that Jonson enjoyed better relations with the more educated court than he did with the audiences of the public theatre, it is fascinating to see him here reproducing exactly the same attitudes and stances that had clouded the reception of so much of his dramatic work; and it further demonstrates the truth of his statement to Drummond that he was not intimidated by the nobility, and would not flatter to save his life.

These outbursts of Jonson's irritability do not, however, diminish the reality of his achievement in the masque form. He breathed new life into a moribund hybrid through his belief in the power of the poet's invention to knit together spectacle, song, dance and language into a poetic 'soul' disseminated through and uniting as one all the senses of sight, hearing and apprehension. He toiled to raise the level of the masque through his careful framing and composition of his pieces from a positive mosaic of sources, often confused and corrupted by their passage through the centuries. To the skills of this scholarship he added the experience of a practising dramatist, and incorporated within his masques as much in the way of contrast and conflict as this weak-sided form would support. Nor was it always so serious as Jonson's own commentary would have us believe; the frolics of naughty boys, laughing Graces, fairies and satyrs have a light-hearted playfulness quite at variance with the common idea of masques as occasions of stiff and stately formality.

Impressive, too, is Jonson's use of an enormous variety of verse forms; to the ear attuned simply to the prose and verse contrast of the plays, the masques are a revelation. Jonson is adept, for instance, at the short verse line conventionally associated with supernatural creatures; consider the sharp accelerating rhythms of this chant with which he builds up the tension of the witches' coven in *The Masque of Queens*:

> Dame, dame, the watch is set:
> Quickly come, we are all met.
> From the lakes and from the fens,
> From the rocks and from the dens,
> From the woods and from the caves,
> From the churchyard, from the graves,
> From the dungeon, from the tree
> That they die on, here are we.
>
> (lines 53–60)

Following this, Jonson modulates effortlessly through lines of differing length, then breaks into a charm whose jagged driving rhythms are achieved by the unusual combination of iambic with anapaestic feet:

> The Owl is abroad, the Bat and the Toad,
> And so is the Cat-a-Mountain;
> The Ant and the Mole both sit in a hole,
> And Frog peeps out of the fountain.
> The dogs they do bay and the timbrells play,
> The spindle now is a-turning;
> The moon it is red, and the stars are fled,
> But all the sky is a-burning.
>
> (lines 75–82)

As Jonson is at his most rhythmically varied and versatile in these masques, so was he boldly experimental with rhyme. He attempted a

155

range of different rhyme schemes, from the simplest couplet to the elaboration of stanzaic construction, all with equal facility and success. These newer forms, however could not dislodge his favourite rhymed couplets of iambic pentameters from their primacy in his estimation; he continued to reserve this form, which as he told Drummond he loved above any other, for his most important characters at their most important moments, of summary and conclusion, for instance. But in the lead-up to these climactic utterances, he allowed his maturing technical skill full play in the contrivance of the maximum amount of variation and contrast. Perhaps the happiest moments, however, are those in which Jonson was able to give free rein to a delicate lyrical grace hardly to be expected of the satirical dramatist or stern allegorist:

> To rest, to rest; the herald of the day,
> Bright Phosphorus commands you hence; obey.
> The moon is pale and spent; and winged night
> Makes headlong haste, to fly the morning's sight;
> Who now is rising from her blushing wars
> And with her rosy hand puts back the stars.
> Of which myself, the last, her harbinger
> But stay to warn you, that you not defer
> Your parting longer. Then do I give way,
> As night hath done, and so must you, to day.
> (*Oberon the Fairy Prince*, lines 434–43)

Such moments of elegiac tenderness are not common in the masques; but the general level of the poetry is such that taken with the strength of the structuring concepts and Jonson's established constructional ability, the different elements combined to raise the art of masque composition to a higher level than it would have seemed capable of.

For 'raising his art' remained Jonson's abiding preoccupation. The ongoing struggle of these years had been 'to make readers, understanders', and to create a 'legitimate poem'. It was solely to this end that Jonson had abandoned plays 'of the comic thread' in favour of the 'higher' form of tragedy. For this purpose, too, Jonson strove strenuously to stretch, even crack, the stiff sinews of the masque form, to elevate it both in form and content. And to this drive Jonson's colleagues and contemporaries owed his great innovation of the anti-masque by which the form was rendered so very much more interesting and flexible than it could otherwise have been.

Jonson's continued experimentalism further betrays his determination not to relax his self-imposed programme of the perfection of his craft. So, far from resting on his laurels, he still saw himself as one who had yet 'to come forth worth the ivy, or the bays' of the true poet. His decision at this juncture to change direction and renew his former initiative in tragic writing had its price; all that was gained from that exercise resolved itself into another theatrical flop. Yet the success of this phase of Jonson's career is not to be measured in terms of the box-office response to *Catiline*, nor even in the undoubted progress of the masque in Jonson's hands. What emerged from these years was the groundwork for Jonson's genuine and unqualified triumph, his 'grand climacteric': the achievement of the Folio and Jonson's emergence as 'the Poet'.

8

THE POET

With the 1616 Folio Jonson brought his achievement to its peak, and carefully enshrined it in the form that he correctly estimated would outlast any other kind of monument. The lovely book that his printer eventually produced contained nine plays, nineteen masques and two collections of Jonson's poetry. Taken together, these form a staggering display of Jonson's range and power. Their combined effect is, however, very much greater than the sum of the parts, substantial though each of these is in its own right. The Folio, great in every sense of the word, warrants throughout the validity of Jonson's claim to the title *poeta regius* 'the royal poet',[1] or more simply, 'the poet', which, as Drummond noted, 'in his merry humour he was wont to name himself' (HS I, 150).

For the Folio is far more than simply a collection by Jonson of his literary productions up to that date. It is in fact a careful construction of Jonson's output into a very literary structure, whose intention was to elevate both the writings and the writer. Jonson brought to the task of assembling his work a clear idea of how he wanted to stage himself both as a worthy inheritor of the literary past and as a claimant to the attention of the future. He wanted to be seen to be a poet, according to the highest and most ancient of classical standards, looking back to Horace, Virgil, Ovid, Plautus and Pliny; and he wanted the 'understanders' of later ages to read him with the same delight and profit that he had derived from the mighty dead. Accordingly he selected and arranged his work by these standards, rather than by those of popular success. He had determined that the works were both to create and to live up to the career of a poet and man of letters, rather than submit to the stigma of ex-bricklayer turned playhouse hack.

In accordance with this aim, Jonson's presentation of his work

158

throughout the Folio was rigidly controlled. He deliberately excluded anything he considered not consonant with the high level both of his best work and of the serious pretensions of the volume. Firmly discarded, for instance, were all the early or apprentice works; Jonson comes before his public with *Every Man in his Humour* as a fully fledged dramatist, not perhaps at the level of mastery he is to attain, but evidently no novice. Among these earliest excluded pieces, the only wholly Jonsonian production to survive was *The Case is Altered*. Jonson was equally hard on his early tragedies – he left out not only those written before 1598 and glowingly praised by Francis Meres, but also such plays as *Richard Crookback*, for which he was paid by Henslowe in 1602.

The Henslowe connection, indeed, was one that Jonson was most anxious to suppress, since this it was that branded him as one of the contemporary theatre's journeymen hack 'playwrights', in his own disparaging phrase, ready to turn a hand to anything, and able to codge up a play to order from any materials at hand. Jonson had no wish to preserve plays on which he had worked to any other writer's plot, with others of Henslowe's stable. He excluded, therefore, everything of which he was not the sole and total author, with an immeasurable gain to the Folio in artistic integrity, whatever the loss to the interests of literary history.

The plays that survived Jonson's rigorous selection procedure demonstrate his determination to present his play-writing as a well-shaped career ascending through different stages of development. In the order in which he printed them, first come the 'humour' plays and the comical satires. This phase is crowned with a Roman tragedy. Next follow the mature comedies, again both comical and satirical, and again crowned and contrasted with a Roman tragedy. The full list clearly shows the desired phasal structure:

Comedy: *Every Man in his Humour*
          Every Man out of his Humour
          Cynthia's Revels
          Poetaster
Tragedy: *Sejanus*
Comedy: *Volpone*
          Epicene
          The Alchemist
Tragedy: *Catiline*

It is easy to see how a loose, bifurcated romance like *The Case Is Altered*, the additions to *The Spanish Tragedy*, hack work, or co-authorship would disrupt the pattern of this achievement. Nor would they have any place in what Jonson wanted to have considered as a literary canon.

Daring and imaginative though this ambition was in its time, it was only part of Jonson's wider design. He wished his plays to live in the best form that he was capable of bringing them to, and consequently printed *Every Man in his Humour* in a revised text substantially different from the original version. Scholars have debated the precise date for this revision,[2] but all are agreed that it was undertaken by Jonson at the height of his powers, and in his mature comedy manner.

The most profound and structural of the changes, for instance, removes the action and personnel from Italy, and re-sets it in London, a locale that Jonson only began to exploit dramatically after 1609. Naturally the London setting, imposed upon the play at a later date, could not be organic and integral to the drama in the way that it is in *The Alchemist* or *Bartholomew Fair*. But the vivid immediacy of the local colouring, the gain both in scenic density and depth of characterization, fully declare the correctness of Jonson's judgement. Dwelling on the difference between a Hogsden man and one who owns 'Middlesex land', or calling up 'the citizens that come a-ducking to Islington ponds', Jonson makes sport of the favourite English pastime of social placing while simultaneously illuminating for us his characters and their frames of reference.

But Jonson did not merely change the setting of *Every Man in his Humour*. He worked through the entire text line by line, sharpening and polishing his effects, and deleting or rewriting passages that he found unsatisfactory. Cut or pruned back are the earlier version's frequent and rather high-flown references to 'sacred poesie'; although he had not abandoned his faith in poetry, Jonson showed by this action his recognition that such episodes have little dramatic value, and cannot advance a play. The effect of Jonson's alterations is to tighten the plot, to clarify and speed up the rambling denouement, to enrich the characters and to build up the fictional world of the drama. All these improvements move the play and its characters much nearer towards the expression of Jonson's idiosyncratic rhetoric of realism; its characters may not sound any more like real people, but they sound more and more like real Jonson.

Of all the nine plays in the Folio, *Every Man in his Humour* received by far the most drastic revision; yet even here Jonson was engaged in improvement rather than in reconstruction. He did not make any changes to the main story-line, or vary the order of the scenes, for instance; all his touches attest to his fundamental faith in the play; he knew that it was both sound as a drama and effective as a comedy. The other plays received less and less alteration as the time drew near when Jonson had to hand them over to the printer for publication; and the latest plays received no rewriting at all. Yet the minute attention that Jonson gave to every capital letter and comma both in his redrafting and in the proof stage, bears continuing witness to the seriousness with which he carried out his desire to preserve, in the best, highest and clearest form, only those representations of his dramatic powers that he thought capable of standing the scrutiny of later ages.

And in the event, who could fault his critical judgement? This collection of dramas is a corpus of great might, in which Jonson can be seen repeatedly extending his range and yet sustaining his highest flight. From the cosy domesticity of *Every Man in his Humour*, Jonson wings off into the shrill satirical 'War of the Theatres' plays; thereafter he manages the moral authority of *Sejanus* as if the petty squibs of personal spite had never been. His restless artistic temperament combined with his wide reading and experience of life to produce a series of plays where, though each builds on the other, none is anything but wholly fresh and original. Jonson may have mythologized his dramatic career and its separate stages. But he did not falsify it. However Jonson's plays were trimmed and dressed for the hoped-for readership, and however many of their brothers and sisters died in silence so that they might live and grow, each of them unaided merits our attention and regard, while taken together they unfold Jonson's extensive skills as a dramatist and his unwearying determination to test those skills as thoroughly as possible.

Subsequent generations have confirmed and enhanced Jonson's own rating of himself as a dramatist whose major productions were 'poems' and as a result entitled to serious study. To his own generation, however, his contribution as a masque-maker rated equal if not greater prominence. Denied the opportunity ever to experience one of these rich trifles, post-Restoration Jonsonians have tended to underestimate or to dismiss his work in this field. Jonson's own procedure is all the corrective needed to such an attitude; he included nineteen of these 'ephemeral' pieces in his Folio as a plain statement of his belief in their capacity both to endure in their own right and to enhance his literary legacy to after-times.

Like the plays, these too are arranged in such a way as to suggest

Jonson's idea of their relative importance. First come the early entertainments, the public welcomes offered to the king and queen and the private celebrations of their presence in the houses of the great:

The King's Entertainment on Passing to his Coronation
A Panegyre on the King's Entrance to Parliament
The Entertainment at Althorp
The Entertainment at Highgate
The Entertainment for the Two Kings at Theobalds
The Entertainment for the King and Queen at Theobalds

Continuing the royal theme, and with obvious pride in the circumstances, Jonson entitled the next section 'Masques at Court'. Here again he imposed a patterning that rejects chronology of events as the organizing principle. At the head of the list stand the two masques that Jonson made for Queen Anne, the masques *Of Blackness* and *Of Beauty*. These had a particular significance since they represented the special honour done to Jonson by the participation of the queen herself. Further, *Of Blackness* had been Jonson's breakthrough into the world of court masquing, a circumstance no writer would be likely to forget; and both were linked not only in theme and circumstances of production, but also in being both controversial and successful.

Following on these come two that were also clearly linked in Jonson's mind, the pair of celebrated wedding masques written for the nuptials of courtiers whom royal favour had rendered almost royal themselves. *Hymenaei* and the *Haddington Masque* had both retained favour in Jonson's eyes, despite the scandal that had gathered round the first. . . . Learning after the event of the sordid adulterous relationship that lay behind the marriage of the Countess of Essex with the king's favourite the Earl of Somerset, and in particular of the countess's cold-blooded murder of the earl's secretary who had opposed the match, the disgusted Jonson struck out the names of the bridal couple from the Folio's printed text. But he thought too well of *Hymenaei* to delete it altogether.

In addition, he would not have wished to disturb the system he had constructed of printing these masques in pairs. As with the queen's masques, so with her son's; the two pieces that Jonson wrote specifically for Prince Henry are also bracketed together, the *Speeches at Prince Henry's Barriers* and the *Masque of Oberon the Fairy Prince*. The remaining masques are all linked as celebrations of the king and his court, most frequently in some variation of the classical Golden Age terminology and symbolism. And just as in the ordering of his plays, Jonson clearly desired his readers to accept his masque output as a totality, to be seen on an ascending curve of competence and control. This rearrangement of the individual masques, denying the order of their composition, however satisfying in its symmetry, serves to obscure rather than to highlight the true story of Jonson's developing mastery of this branch of his art.

Formally, for instance, he continued to play boldly with the apposition of masque and anti-masque. During this phase, the anti-masque swelled to its greatest proportions, and then declined in its importance to the whole. At the peak of Jonson's interest in the anti-masque, *Love Restored*, written and performed in 1612, boasts an anti-masque that occupies two-thirds of its 300 lines. Admittedly the last hundred lines had more importance than this might imply, since they expressed the development of the allegory and the climax of the action, while important later elements like music and dance are only slightly represented in the libretto-like masque text. These, with the addition of spectacle and 'shew', would alter the apparent proportions of the masque in performance. But Jonson clearly found more mileage in his vigorous anti-masque characters than in the formal, ceremonial conclusions to the festivities. In *Love Restored*, the anti-masquer Robin Goodfellow seems to speak for the author as he rudely attacks the formal masque proceedings:

> Are these your court-sports? Would I had kept me to my gambols of the country still, selling of fish, short service, shoeing the wild mare, or roasting of robin red-breast. . . . I am the honest plain country spirit, and harmless, Robin Goodfellow, he that sweeps the hearth and the house clean, riddles for the country maids and does all their other drudgery while they are at hot cockles. . . .
>
> (lines 51–9)

James's courtiers would not have had to be literary critics to distinguish the difference between this light and larky introduction and the spiritless rhymed couplets that followed it:

> So will they keep their measures true,
> And make still their proportions new,
> Till all become one harmony,
> Of honour, and of courtesy,
> True valour and urbanity

Of confidence, alacrity
Of promptness and of industry,
Ability, reality [royalty].

(lines 261–8)

This uninspired verse, a shopping-list of virtues composed of inter-changeable abstractions, shows Jonson's writing at its most flat-footed, and clearly indicates where his creative heart lay.

In the next of Jonson's pieces, *The Irish Masque at Court* (1613), the take-over by the anti-masque is almost complete. Of the masque's 190 lines, 150 are given to the Irish anti-masquers. These characters, naive, feckless and charming in the time-out-of-mind caricature of stage Irishmen, are creatures from the world of the drama, cousins if not prototypes of Captain Whit, the Irish bawd in *Bartholomew Fair* (1614). They were clearly a delight to their creator, who would not otherwise have drawn out their interlude to such lengths, nor taken such pains to try to set down phonetically every nuance and inflection of Irish speech:

DENNIS: Peash Dermock, here ish te king.
DERMOCK: Phair ish te king?
DONNELL: Phich ish te king?
DENNIS: Tat ish te king.
DERMOCK: Ish tat te king? got blesh him.
DENNIS: Peash, ant take heet, vat tou shaysht, man.

(lines 13–18)

Yet such pseudo-realism of dialogue can hardly disguise the fact that crudely satirized bog-trogging peasants are leagues apart from the world of the masque. Their earthy reality and vitality explode the fragile and top-heavy masque fiction, toppling it from its insub-stantial foundation already overloaded with myth and allegory.

Jonson never again allowed his dramatic impulses and abilities to run away with him like this. By the time he came to *The Golden Age Restored*, Jonson had made an interesting reversion to his earlier practice; of 240 lines, the anti-masque occupies a mere thirty-five, and the emphasis is once more not on speech, but on sound and sight, music, dance and spectacle:

(A tumult and clashing of arms, heard within) . . .
  Iron Age presents itself, calling forth the evils . . .

. . . Rise, rise then up, thou Grandam vice
Of all my issue, Avarice,

164

Bring with thee Fraud and Slander,
Corruption with the golden hands
Or any subtle ill that stands
    To be a more commander.
Thy boys, Ambition, Pride and Scorn,
Force, Rapine, and thy babe last born,
Smooth Treachery, call hither . . .

The anti-masque, and their dance, two drums, trumpets, and a confusion of martial music: at the end of which Pallas showing her shield.

(lines 25–68)

In the next masque, *Mercury Vindicated from the Alchemists at Court*, the anti-masque is both shorter and tied into the allegorical scheme of the whole in such a way as to draw its teeth as an independent entertainment.

As this suggests, the level of Jonson's masque achievement was highly uneven. *Love Restored* never lives up to its good and lively opening. It lacks, too, a central visual image, a fatal weakness in an essentially spectacular form. Similarly the *Irish Masque*, although founded upon a vivacious and serviceable conceit, and obviously successful at the time despite misgivings expressed by those of tenderer conscience, was still essentially literary rather than visual in conception, notwithstanding Jonson's provision of harps and 'Irish gowns'.

In strong contrast *A Challenge at Tilt* employs a delightful and effective central conceit; for this entertainment on the day after an important court marriage, Jonson introduces two cupids doing battle, one on behalf of the bridegroom, one for the bride. This provided an appropriate and witty lead-in to the ritualized combat of two teams of courtiers which the 'challenge' format was designed to introduce; and the contest was aptly and plausibly resolved by the final appearance of Hymen to unite as one the interests of both man and woman. For *Mercury Vindicated from the Alchemists at Court* (1616) Jonson again came up with an impressive visual idea to get his masque off to a good start, without benefit of the kind of anti-masque which threatens to take over from its parent:

After the loud music, the scene discovered; being a laboratory, or Alchemists' workhouse; Vulcan looking to the registers, while a Cyclops, tending the fire, to the Cornets began to sing:

165

CYCLOPS.

Soft subtle fire, thou soul of art,
   Now do thy part
On weaker Nature, that through age is lamed.
   Take but thy time, now she is old,
   And the sun her friend grown cold,
She will no more in strife with thee be named . . .

The song ended, Mercury appeared, thrusting out his head, and after-
wards his body, at the tunnel of the middle furnace; which Vulcan espied,
crying:

VULCAN.

Stay, see, our Mercury is coming forth; Art and all the elements
assist!

(lines 1–21)

As this suggests, despite his very obvious feeling for the masque,
Jonson's best moments within it all tend to the dramatic. Yet there
was no by-passing the central imperative of the masque, that in
essence, if the separate elements of this hybrid were to be harmonized
into one, it had to be a poetic unity, not dramatic. There is a
considerable spill-over in this period of Jonson's masque-making
between his dramatic writing and his writing for the masque. Not
only is there a sudden burst of stage Irishmen, alchemists and so forth;
but Jonson borrows from the stage other theatrical techniques like the
induction, the technique of direct address to the audience, and the use
of dialogue and dramatic monologue as opposed to allegorical speech
of a recitative nature. Equally redolent of the hurly-burly of the
theatre rather than the rarefied atmosphere of the court is the
humour, often very broad, that Jonson was now introducing into
the masque. Robin Goodfellow in a comic monologue describes his
attempts to gain entrance to the court, to join the festivities:

Never poor goblin was put so to his shifts, to get in . . . then
took I another figure, of an old tire-woman, but tired of that too
for none of the masquers would take note of me. . . . Then I
pretended to be a musician, marry, I could not show mine
instrument, and that bred a discord.

(lines 62–97)

The ascending flurry of puns, the coarse humour and innuendo, all
mark their kinship with the public stage work of Jonson's mature

phase, rather than with the self-conscious and stately formal and allegorical masques with which Jonson began, when his only medium for masque-making was the solemnly rhyming heroic couplet. Yet however rewarding to the reader these flashes of drama, their use and relevance within the masque are strictly limited, since the entire form is built around the non-dramatic rituals of music and dance, and must be resolved in a non-dramatic, non-verbal, essentially spectacular way.

Jonson scored in his masque-making, however, through his constant experimentation, which combined with his now-assured technical skill to produce stylistic effects of great variety and interest. *Love Restored*, for instance, modulates effortlessly from prose into song and thence into easy, progressive rhymed couplets, while *Mercury Vindicated from the Alchemists at Court* reverses this format, moving from song into prose at the opening. *The Golden Age Restored* gives a particularly impressive view of Jonson's virtuosity, consisting as it does of a variety of metrical forms, including some unusual stanzaic forms themselves both rhythmically and metrically varied:

> But, as of old, all now be gold.
> Move, move then to these sounds.
> And, do not only walk your solemn rounds
> But give those light and airy bounds
> That fit the genie of these gladder grounds.

> *PALLAS.*
> Already? Do not all things smile?

> *ASTRAEA.*
> But when they have enjoyed awhile
> The age's quickening power.

> *AGE.*
> That every thought a seed doth bring,
> And every look a plant doth spring
> And every breath a flower.
> (lines 148–58)

And as always, the masque continued to afford Jonson the chance to handle a strange thought, or to express a lyrical impulse, as no other form could do:

Now, ladies, to glad your aspects once again with the sight of love, and make a Spring smile in your faces, which must have

167

looked like winter without me; behold me, not like a servant now, but a champion, and in my true figure, as I used to reign and revel in your fancies, tickling your soft ears with my feathers, and laying little straws about your hearts, to kindle bonfires [that] shall flame out at your eyes.

(A Challenge at Tilt, lines 97–104)

> The earth unploughed shall yield her crop,
> Pure honey from the oak shall drop,
>   The fountain shall run milk:
> The thistle shall the lily bear
> And every bramble roses wear,
>   And every worm make silk.
> *(The Golden Age Restored*, lines 163–8)

Stylistically, then, these masques consistently show Jonson writing near or at the height of his dramatic and poetic ability; and though he does not altogether avoid the pedestrian, he never descends into dullness. Richly varied and vividly experimental, the masques are distinguished by the confidence of Jonson's established artistry, a confidence that nowhere emerges more clearly than in the poet's relations with the audience; consider the anti-masque to *Love Restored*, for instance, when Jonson imports the Induction from the theatre in order to be able to make a cheeky direct address to the audience, and to the king, too, as its principal member: 'Good faith an't please your Majesty, your masquers are all at a stand . . . a pretty fine speech was taken up o' the poet, too, which if he never be paid for, now, 'tis no matter' (lines 6–12). The *Challenge at Tilt* goes even further in the direction of that audacious, even salacious humour that King James relished:

FIRST CUPID: . . . was it not I that yesternight, waited on the bride into the nuptial chamber, and against the bride groom came, made her the throne of love? . . .
SECOND CUPID: And did not I bring on the blushing bridegroom to taste those joys? and made him think all stay a torment?

(lines 41–4 and 53–4)

Jonson was writing here with one eye on the monarch who, even by the standards of his own time, was felt to concern himself too grossly with such matters. Jonson's consciousness of the king expressed itself again in *The Irish Masque*, where the whole of the anti-masque played off the presence of the king and his 'sweet face' among the audience. For Jonson never lost sight of the central function of the ritual, which was to praise and glorify the king and his court. It is to Jonson's credit that he managed largely to avoid the most egregious and vain flattery; but equally he never missed an opportunity to honour or commend the king. Amongst a variety of techniques employed by Jonson for this necessary purpose, foremost was direct praise of 'the virtue of his Majesty, who projecteth so powerful beams of light and heat through this hemisphere' that he was able to thaw ice. Equally important was Jonson's ability to introduce and play upon the king's known interests and habits, as in the extract above.

Given Jonson's determination to subject his own work to stern criticism by the highest and oldest standards available to him, it is not to be supposed that he was equally delighted with all his masques. But from their inclusion in the Folio it is clear that Jonson deemed them worthy of being offered to posterity rather than consigned to obscurity. In their variety, strangeness and undeniable flashes of power they support Jonson's view of them; while in the wider literary perspective they play an invaluable part in our understanding of Jonson's writing, his mastery of other modes, and his awareness of himself as a developing artist.

Jonson's contemporaries admired his masques; posterity found his highest achievement in the plays. There is no doubt, however, of Jonson's own order of priorities; by deliberately placing his *Epigrams* at the head of the Folio, and by dedicating them to the Earl of Pembroke as 'the ripest of my studies', Jonson demonstrated his own conviction that his poems were more important than anything he had written for performance. Jonson was not unaware of the worth and significance of his plays and masques. But his experience of both these forms was fraught with constraints and tensions. Writing for the stage in particular Jonson viewed with great ambivalence, oscillating between evangelistic reformatory urges and bitter disillusion. Only in his poetry was Jonson writing in a manner and form with which he felt entirely comfortable. And any claim to be among the great poets had to rest, in the final analysis, on poetry.

For Jonson, poetry set the standard which he hoped all his work would attain, and by which he hoped to be judged. He always described himself as 'a poet', if not '*the* poet', and his dramas not as plays, but 'poems'. He made a clear distinction between his own 'poems' for the stage and the lesser work of the hack or 'playwright'. This word, a coinage newly minted by Jonson, encapsulates both his disdain and his sense of distance from those who were dramatists first and foremost. It was as a poet that Jonson wanted to be evaluated and remembered.

The 1616 Folio contains two collections of Jonson's poems, the *Epigrams* and *Forest*. Although published together, these are essentially separate enterprises. The *Epigrams* had originally been gathered together with a view to independent publication; they were licensed for issue in 1612 as a self-contained volume. When circumstances delayed their appearance, and the idea developed of issuing the Folio, they were incorporated in the larger work. The collection of epigrams, 133 short poems in all, each devoted to the examination of one central comment or conceit, is characterized by its integrity and sense of unity; there is an overall structure, albeit of a loose kind, and the pieces are put together in a way that gives the reader the sense of a full experience, with beginning, middle and end.[3] The *Forest*, by contrast, has no such predetermined basis of organization; the fifteen poems are assembled simply as examples of Jonson's poetic 'studies', his exercises in craftsmanship. Even so, 'the poet' did not want his reader to like them any the less for all that; he expected this collection to be received as constituting a body of work comparable with the *Epigrams*, and not merely as a random compilation. This is made plain in Jonson's explanation of his unusual title as referring to 'works of diverse nature and matter', all growing together like 'a wood or *forest*'. To Jonson then, his poems together composed a small forest, and were not to be seen as individual poetic trees. As with the *Epigrams*, a unity is invoked; not the structural unity of the earlier collection but an association through similarities of tone and content that serves to link the individual pieces into one larger experience.

Within these self-imposed frameworks, Jonson 'the poet' ranges freely among examples of the epigram, lyric, dedication, memorial, epistle and panegyric. In each of these Jonson explored and reworked the poetic forms and conventions of the past. For from the outset it is apparent that the poems are the central repository of Jonson's classicism and, by extension, of his deepest poetic values.

No reader, however, who has once heard the authentic tones of Jonson's 'singing voice' could long harbour the notion that he had made himself merely the mouthpiece of another 'poet antique or deceased'. In his varied essays in these poetic forms, Jonson was able to adapt and extend the methods of his classical forebears, rather than simply taking over their ideas and phrases. Where Martial invented insulting names for his satiric targets, so did Jonson; where Martial castigated character types identified by trade or profession, so did Jonson; but Jonson's names are entirely original and his satiric portraits totally reworked in a native vein. His 'Cheverel the Lawyer', 'Old-End-Gatherer', 'Old Colt', 'Sir Cod', 'Lieutenant Shift' and 'Groom Idiot' are no citizens of ancient Rome but inhabitants of St Paul's, Ludgate, or Pie Corner. Jonson himself drew attention to the similarity, and yet the significant differences between Martial's time and literary task, and his own:

'To the Ghost of Martial'

Martial, thou gavest far nobler epigrams
To thy Domitian, than I can my James.
But in my royal subject I pass thee,
Thou flattered thine, mine cannot flattered be.

(Epigram 36)

'My James' – Jonson's poems often sound this possessive, personal note. The *Epigrams* in particular enshrine his own concerns, whether with fools, knaves, cheaters and punks, or with his patrons who include the highest in the land. With his poems, as with his friends, Jonson could castigate the sin of usury in the person of the punningly named 'Bank':

'On Bank the Usurer'

Bank feels no lameness of his knotty gout;
His money travels for him, in and out.
And though the soundest legs go every day
He toils to be at hell as soon as they.

(Epigram 31)

Among other sins and gross social offences that Jonson notices in the epigrams are lechery, pride, avarice, covetousness, lying and greed. Yet his world of poetry is equally illuminated by records of encounters with those whom Jonson offers as the beautiful and gifted, like the Countess of Rutland and Lady Mary Wroth, where he flatters splendidly, but does not cringe. Jonson used his poetry as other writers use a diary, to note, observe, take down and commit to memory the highlights (and the lowlights) of his unusually rich and varied life, from the taverns of the Fleet to the Court of St James.

171

Criticism has made much of the personal nature of Jonson's poetry: his constant presence in his own work, his rueful and truthful self-appreciation, his endearing talent for self-deprecation and his touching fury when insulted or put down. Yet this formulation, accurate as far as it goes, is only one half of the sum. Jonson's poems are not monologues, making a dreary obsessional parade of ego-events. On the contrary, they are dialogues, in which he engages his friends or opponents within the poem itself, addressing, praising, haranguing, or castigating them, but never permitting them not to participate in the occasion. Consider how many of Jonson's poems begin with direct address, and how adroitly he contrived a multiplicity of variations on this technique so that no two of his poems have the same opening:

> Donne, the delight of Phoebus and each Muse . . .

> Lucy, you brightness of our sphere . . .

> Do what you come for, Captain, with your news . . .

> Were they that named you prophets?

Such is the vitalizing power of Jonson's imagination that he can, for the purposes of a poetic debate, personalize a house, even an abstraction:

> Thou art not, Penshurst, built to envious show . . .

> Why, disease, dost thou molest
> Ladies, and of them the best?

From these arresting beginnings Jonson goes on to create a true dialogue between himself and the object of his poem. He gives advice, asks questions, and ventures his observations candidly upon their affairs, ranging from politics, to poetry, to the pox. So vivid is Jonson's management of direct address that he summons up his friends and enemies in person, constructing the interlocutor within the poem:

> When I would know thee, Goodyere, my thought looks
> Upon thy well-made choice of friends and books;
> Then do I love thee, and behold thy ends
> In making thy friends books, and thy books friends.
>
> (Epigram 86)

The presentation is even more immediate, and the impact more telling, when the other party to the duologue is handled humorously or satirically. Here is Jonson's Captain Hungry, the braggart soldier who trades his small snippets of military news for a free meal, reacting to Jonson's description of his tricks:

> Nay, now you puff, tusk, and draw up your chin,
>   Twirl the poor chain you run a-feasting in.
> Come, be not angry; you are Hungry; eat.
>   Do what you came for, Captain; there's your meat.
>
> (Epigram 107)

Throughout the epigrams, Jonson created character as in a play. He borrowed from the drama these dramatic techniques of speech, and evolved a naturalistic vernacular which yet retains the sharp authority of poetry. The poems give the whole world of Jonson's society, with every member in his or her place, from the king downwards. So convincing is this world that Jonson can blend his fictional accounts of real people with realistic accounts of fictional characters, to achieve a convincing homogeneity.

This relaxed naturalism, with the lively incorporation of the demotic, is the diametric opposite of what posterity has been conditioned to expect from 'learned Jonson', high priest of the classical vein. The impression is rather one of simply overhearing Jonson having a colourful encounter with a colourful character. But this impression is deceptive. Behind all the created characters who throng Jonson's *Epigrams* and *Forest* stands another party to the exchange, the reader. Jonson's never-wavering sense of this relationship informs every one of his poetic pieces. He speaks to many men and women, in a variety of voices, sometimes coarse, sometimes respectful, grave, or gay; yet always in the knowledge that others are sharing the exchange. Jonson's is public, not private verse; and it is his constant consciousness of the reader outside the little world of the poem that prevents Jonson's poetry from being personal in the way that has often been assumed.

For the reader of Jonson's poems has a far more active part to play than that traditionally assigned. Jonson's reader is expected to be his pupil, learning from everything that the poet says; since these are 'the ripest of [Jonson's] studies', he demands that the reader must study too, to read, mark, learn, and understand. Thus the reader must become the ideal audience, in the poetic theatre where Jonson stages his real and imaginary characters, borrowing the metaphor of the 'theatre of poetry' from Martial: his claque, booing and hissing whatever Jonson finds fault with, at his bidding; and, ultimately, his friend, one that he can rely upon to share his standards and accept his assessments.

Jonson does not expect this idealized reader to appear by magic. On the contrary, he tries very hard to create him or her, just as he had attempted to fashion the ideal audience from the random group of playgoers in the theatre. From the very first epigram, 'To the Reader', with its warning growl

> Pray thee, take care, that takest my book in hand,
> To read it well; that is, to understand

Jonson shows his constant concern to provoke, direct, and above all to determine the reader's response. The first section of the *Epigrams* is in fact dedicated to the exclusion of the unworthy; Jonson wants to keep out those whose stupidity or spite would hinder true understanding. Jonson's strenuous intellectualism could not tolerate the idea of his poems being taken up by a mere consumer; Epigram 56 attacks 'the sluggish gaping auditor' who devours all and 'marks not whose 'twas first'. Unwelcome too are the assorted lightweights or nitwits whom Jonson arraigns in the epigrams as 'playwright', 'censorious court-ling', or 'old-end-gatherer' [plagiarist]. Jonson sought, and tried to ensure, a readership worthy to join with him in the celebration of the high rite of poetry.

Because of this, Jonson's relation with the reader, although close and constant, is not personal; the ideal reader, despite Jonson's obsession with him or her, is an unreal fiction, created to impersonal, external poetic standards. So too is Jonson's own poetic persona as it comes through in the *Epigrams* and *Forest*. Jonson's poetry is constantly praised for being 'personal'; and judged only by the standards of the inane poetic posturings of some of his contempor-aries, it is. But even a relatively superficial survey shows that Jonson 'the poet' is as careful a creation as 'the reader'.

Consider, to begin with, how many of the events of his personal life were rigidly debarred from the poetry. The epigrammatic biography of 'the poet' was achieved by winnowing out the dissenter, the homicide, the husband, the libertine, the prankster; all of these are roles played by Jonson in life, but not in this branch of his art.[4] Where in the poetry is Jonson's account of his numerous brushes with the authorities, the murderous brawl in which the actor Gabriel Spencer died by Jonson's hand, his addiction to 'venery' and especially to married women, his drunken roistering with his courtier friend Sir John Roe and his practical jokes like the masquerade as a fortune-teller? The dignified bard in his 'singing robes' embodying the classical ideals of restraint and moderation, the austere moralist upholding Golden Age standards of virtue in condemnation of modern meanness and vice, not only covers but directly conflicts with other known realities of Jonson's inner and outer existence. The Apollonian vision of the poet was only achieved by a rigorous self-censorship of the Dionysian, and by a consistent self-imaging along the wished-for lines.

This careful and skilful construction of the poetic self had certain clear consequences for the body of Jonson's poetry as a whole. First is the unusually strong and recurrent concern with morality; no other contemporary poet hits this note as often as Jonson does, nor with such an intensity of desperation; contrast his non-dramatic work with Shakespeare's as an instance. Virtue, infamy, heaven and hell, false and true, worth and worthlessness; these are the almost obsessional preoccupations of Jonson's poems, worked and reworked with endless freshness and fascination. He considers countless examples of active virtue, and of the operation of morality in a social context, in writers, soldiers, statesmen; he examines the concept of virtue embodied in the monarchy and aristocracy; he describes the goodness in the mutual love of friends.

These of course are set against a compelling cast of the weak and the wicked through whom Jonson attacked social vice in decayed lechers, corrupt traders, sharp lawyers, and literary rogues of one sort or another like the 'poet-ape' (Epigram 56). It is a gallery of the good or the grotesque; and though none of Jonson's moral judgements can be disputed, their tendency and prevalence tell us as much about him as about the objects of his scrutiny.

The other obvious result of Jonson's pre-determination to elevate his poetic persona comes in his handling of the theme of love. For a man who was in turn a son, husband and father, in addition to an amorist and womanizer for as long as his natural powers held out, if his rueful aside on 'making a little winter love in a dark corner' is anything to go by, Jonson was remarkably tight-lipped on the score of his emotional and sexual life. Apart from the two tender but distanced accounts of his two children's deaths (Epigrams 22 and 45), Jonson repudiated from his world of poetry the mother who would have chosen death rather than dishonour for him, the honest shrew of a wife, and the women who shared his bed but were not allowed to share his place in history even by association. In their stead come 'his lady, then Mistress Cary' (Epigram 126); Lucy, Countess of Bedford (Epigram 76); Elizabeth, Countess of Rutland (*Forest* 12); Katherine, Lady d'Aubigny (*Forest* 13); even 'a gentlewoman, virtuous and noble' (*Forest* 4) in preference to flesh-and-blood women who did not have the good fortune to be of aristocratic birth, and Jonson's patrons.

This is not to say that Jonson does not deal with love. As the masques consistently suggest, Jonson had a lyric voice that was among the most consistently under-used of his gifts. Where he gave free rein to this, Jonson could produce and evoke sensations of simple sweetness and delight:

> Kiss me, sweet; the wary lover
> Can your favours keep and cover,
> When the common courting jay
> All your bounties will betray.
> Kiss again; no creature comes;
> Kiss, and score up wealthy sums
> On my lips, thus hardly sundered
> While you breathe; first give a hundred . . .
> Till you equal with the store,
> All the grass that Romney yields,
> Or the sands in Chelsea fields,
> Or the drops in silver Thames,
> Or the stars that gild his streams
> In the silent summer nights,
> When youths ply their stolen delights . . .
>
> (*Forest* 6)

Yet these experiences are rather described than felt; and the reader may well feel that the speaker is rather assembling the constituent parts of the lyric moment with an eye to its effect upon another, than minting it new and fresh through the power and immediacy of his own passion.

This love-song, as a poem that has in any case strayed into the collection from the very different world of the drama, may perhaps be adjudged a special case. But Jonson is always at a disadvantage on this ground, so much so that his deficiency in this department has passed into the Jonson mythology. Jonson himself began his *Forest* with a characteristic (and characteristically evasive) comment on the subject:

'Why I Write Not of Love'

Some act of Love's, bound to rehearse,
I thought to bind him in my verse:
Which when he felt, 'Away!' quoth he,
'Can poets hope to fetter me?
It is enough they once did get
Mars and my mother in their net:
I wear not these my wings in vain.'
With which he fled me; and again
Into my rhymes could ne'er be got
By any art. Then wonder not
That since, my numbers are so cold,
When Love is fled, and I grow old.

(Forest 1)

This statement neatly side-steps the original question, 'Why write I not of love', by answering it not in terms of love, but of poetry. This is in fact Jonson's main theme in all his verse, its staple and substantive; the making of poetry, and of the poet who makes it. Jonson's pieces are more centrally concerned with working in and through the medium of poetry than they are with their nominal subjects. While dealing on one level with Edward Alleyn, with Parliament, with 'Mill, my lady's woman', or with Death, Jonson uses his poems to generalize from his starting-point in order to draw in others of the same tradition or in the same vein. Simply to name Pembroke, for instance, is 'an epigram on all mankind' (Epigram 102); the tribute to Lord Monteagle (Epigram 60) is a monument in verse, as opposed to brass or marble; while the 'Epitaph on Elizabeth, L.H.' assumes the reader's knowledge of a variety of epitaphs and the techniques for writing them, taking this as a challenge to produce something different yet still related to the subject:

Wouldst thou hear what man can say
In a little? Reader, stay.
Underneath this stone doth lie
As much beauty as could die . . .

(Epigram 124)

At moments such as this, Jonson's poems achieve a level of presentation at which they comment upon themselves. Throughout his many different poetic 'studies', Jonson continued to discuss the poet's task and obligation, the moral duty of poetry to raise noble deeds to posterity by celebrating them, the need to find the right subject. In wider terms his diverse cast of characters enables him to consider the poet's relations with the social world, with the world of literature both past and present, and with his own patrons; consider the subtle, tactful, yet confident management of this relationship in 'To Penshurst' (*Forest* 2), for instance. It was, in short, a full-time occupation, being 'the poet'; small wonder that Jonson the man was squeezed out of consideration in favour of Jonson the maker.

For Jonson, each poem was a critical moment and as such not simply the locus of critical discussion, but the instrument of it. Jonson used his poems as tools of analysis, on the classical precedent again, yet with a wholly original inflection and approach. Pursuing the classical principle of the ethical and didactic function of poetry, he used an epigram, for example, both to teach and to demonstrate the art of writing epigrams:

'To My Mere English Censurer'

> To thee my way in epigrams seems new
> When both it is the old way and the new . . .
> Prithee believe still, and not judge so fast;
> Thy faith is all the knowledge that thou hast.
> (Epigram 18)

In this example, in the attack upon the 'chamber-critic' (Epigrams 52 and 72), or in the several attacks upon 'playwright' (Epigrams 49, 68 and 100), Jonson established and defended the true standard of poetry by the definition of the false. From the opposite standpoint, the identification and praising of true writers and scholars like Camden and Donne (Epigrams 14, 23, 94 and 96) perform the same function. In a series of lucid and forceful statements, Jonson makes his poems his intellectual tools, censuring 'poet-ape' (Epigram 56), for instance, because his works are 'e'en the frippery of wit'. To Jonson, wit was no laughing matter, but a serious business.

These are, in fact, poems of visible control brought to a predetermined conclusion, an end decided in advance by study and thought. Jonson's care and concern are revealed through his poetic style and technique. The language is sparse, the manner unadorned. But this verse is not un-imaged, as has been claimed; it has a firm metaphor base drawn from social and public activities like the stage, games, drinking and amusement. These are counter-weighted by a wide range of classical figures, the whole pantheon of the gods, goddesses and their numerous offspring, as well as all the mythological animals, creatures and events. Yet Jonson's preferred techniques of direct address and plain speech combine to create an effect of great economy and restraint. As Jonson told us, he wrote out all his poems in prose first, 'for so his master Camden had learned him'. This approach has been thought responsible for the prosaic element in Jonson's poetry. But its purpose was to improve the poetry by strengthening its central thought and by purging it of flowery redundancies of expression. These two collections of poetry afford many examples of Jonson's capacity to turn thought into poetry of the greatest lucidity and grace through purposive structure and firmness of phrasing:

> The thing they here call love is blind desire,
> Armed with bow, shafts and fire;
> Inconstant like the sea, of whence 'tis born,
> Rough, swelling like a storm;
> With whom who sails, rides on a surge of fear,
> And boils as if he were
> In a continual tempest. Now true love
> No such effects doth prove;
> That is in essence far more gentle, fine,
> Pure, perfect, nay divine;
> It is a golden chain let down from Heaven
> Whose links are bright and even;
> That falls like sleep on lovers, and combines
> The soft and sweetest minds
> In equal knots . . .
>
> (*Forest* 11)

As this shows, Jonson's verse is not sensuous; he uses sights and smells in the nature of stage-dressing, and rather tends to inform the readers that something shines bright or smells sweet than invite them to experience it for themselves. Yet such is the nature of Jonson's mature verse, its drive and strength concealed by an easy, confident flow, that his lines are never impoverished nor emotionally under-nourishing; the reader shares fully in the warmth pulsing between poet and recipient in the verse epistle 'Inviting a Friend to Supper':

> Tonight, grave sir, both my poor house and I
> Do equally desire your company;
> Not that we think us worthy such a guest,
> But that your worth will dignify our feast

With those that come; whose grace may make that seem
Something, which else could hope for no esteem.
  It is the fair acceptance, sir, creates
The entertainment perfect, not the cates . . .

(Epigram 101)

Assurance of concept here is perfectly matched by assurance of technique. Jonson's faultless ear produces unfailingly regular rhythms, each line carefully adjusted for any necessary contractions or elisions so that the stress will correctly fall where it is expected. Against the smooth and forward-moving rhythm, the taut phrasing packs each line with meaning, yet never so densely that the lines become clotted and compacted. The weight of each quiet pronouncement is reinforced by end-rhymes of unerring accuracy and authority; despite an occasional adventure into feminine rhyming, or the resort to pairings that are not quite exact either in sound or quantity, Jonson's extraordinary ability to clinch his couplet with strong chiming monosyllables is one of the unsung glories of his verse.

Such pieces as this represent Jonson's highest achievement in verse, the accomplishment of the cool, civilized, Horatian tone to which he aspired. This mode does not preclude the admission of stronger poetic fare; it can encompass a darkly ironic view as the other side of the affirmative assessment of human life, since it is the product of the mature wisdom and personal balance that measure life by the old standards of heroic courtesy, but is unsurprised by any failure to measure up to them. This is Jonson's chosen mode in its most finished expression. It never spills over into empty posturing since Jonson turns this scrutiny upon himself as upon others, striving to maintain its consistency even at the cost of his own natural warmth and impulsiveness.

Yet although Jonson can rise easily and truthfully to the authentic accents of 'the poet', this is only one aspect of his poetic personality. The tone of the *Forest* is more consistently grave and controlled than that of the *Epigrams*; within the earlier collection (which significantly contains pieces stretching over a longer period of time) the contrarieties are only just contained, and inevitably break out here and there. The expression of Jonson's other side, his ungovernable irritability, his vulgarity and coarseness, his destructive arrogance, his relish of what he condemns, all peep out in his poems. Sometimes they are licensed to appear, as self-condemning examples of what a right-thinking poet must demonstrate his hatred of – into this category come the voluptuous, lecherous beasts, the bawds and their diseased customers, the cuckoldy husbands and their adulterous wives, and all the vicious, stinking blots on London society that Jonson manifestly relishes even as he castigates.

The moral stance, in short, supplied Jonson with a legitimate outlet for his fascination with depravity of behaviour, style and taste, and the concentration upon the gross undoubtedly answered something in himself. This Jonson is capable of the crudest and most brutal anti-feminism: consider his terse retort 'To a Friend' who asked him to remove the word 'whore' from the poems:

> To put out the word 'whore' thou dost me woo
> Throughout my book. Troth, put out 'woman', too.
>
> (Epigram 83)

Yet offensive as this is, it is only part of a wider and darker disgust with the whole of the physical world, a world in which young wives are the prey of old lechers, the healthy of the diseased, and the body is both the tomb of the spirit and also a microcosm of all the garbage and waste matter of the universe. When Jonson's imagination moves along these grim and nihilistic lines he can see any man reduced to 'Sir Cod', every woman to 'her quaint [cunt] practice' (Epigrams 41 and 50); a contraction of all human function to that of their sexual parts.

Where Jonson really bursts the bounds of the self-imposed restraint on 'the poet', however, is in his unashamed delight in the excremental. 'On the Famous Voyage', the last in the book of *Epigrams*, is a poem of relentless, joyous and sustained foulness, and sadly therefore not as well known as it deserves to be. Using a mock-heroic introduction –

> No more let Greece her bolder fables tell
> Of Hercules or Theseus going to hell

– Jonson relates the 'famous voyage' of two bold knights through a 'merd-urinous' world. As the two knights in the *Aeneid* rowed across the Styx, so Jonson's two heroes undertake an excremental parody, in which 'arses were heard to croak instead of frogs' and 'each privy's seat / Is filled with buttock'. These are only two of Jonson's grotesque flights of fancy (repulsively anal or zestfully coprophiliac, according to taste). What is both inescapable and compelling is that Jonson chose this subject, and pursued it for 196 lines (which makes it by far the longest poem in the two collections, twice as long as the next longest, the important 'To Penshurst', *Forest* 2, for example); that he decided to include it in what he elsewhere insisted on describing as 'my chaste book'; and that he gave it pride of place at the end of the collection of *Epigrams*, clearly intending it to serve as an *envoy* to send the by now well-trained reader away happy.

'On the Famous Voyage', in short, represents an aspect of Jonson's poetic genius that he saw no reason to deny. It is not couched in the accents of Horace, nor yet of Virgil, despite the introduction of the latter into the prologue. The question of its location within Jonson's poetic range raises yet again the contradictions and paradoxes in this deeply divided artist. What this piece ultimately tells us, though, is that Jonson recognized these opposing impulses in himself, and was honest enough to acknowledge them. By so doing he gave to posterity something far more impressive than simply 'the poet', and far more indicative of his poetic power.

Jonson's literary posterity has not quite reproduced his own view of his poems. None has questioned the status that he afforded them, but the passage of time has reversed his order of priorities, so that his plays are now enjoyed as 'the ripest' of his 'studies', rather than the poems, and their popularity has tended to put Jonson's non-dramatic verse in the shade, with the exception of one or two well-anthologized pieces like 'Drink to me only with thine eyes'. The enjoyment of Jonson's poetry to the full has largely been left to the studious or specialized reader.

Admittedly not all Jonson's poems are equally good. There are a number of times when he cannot escape the charge of merely versifying the occasion. But they are always appetitive, always searching. Through them Jonson teaches that a small poem does not mean a small experience, and shares with the world the inclusiveness of his own vision and awareness. To read the *Epigrams* or the *Forest* is to undergo a rare and dynamic process; that of discovering, poem by poem, Jonson's own record of his personal and artistic development.

9

ALL THY FIGURES ARE ALLOWED

The effect of the great Folio of 1616 is to crystallize Jonson's *oeuvre* in one moment of time, offering it to the world complete and perfect. Yet Jonson was also engaged in other literary work during the years of this demanding project; for his working life did not come to a stop, and he continued to be in demand both for masque-making and in the public theatre.

Jonson's masques, as we have seen, were the most up-to-date of all the works in the Folio. Their position at the very end of the book allowed for the inclusion of work much later than the poetry or drama, so that the 1616 publication brought before the public every masque that Jonson had written up to that point. Nevertheless, in the relatively short span between the publication of the Folio and Jonson's departure for Scotland in 1618, he produced five more masques, which, however, did not make their way into the great record of its achievement. At the end of 1616 Jonson wrote two masques for that Christmas season; *Christmas His Masque* was given at the end of the old year, and *The Vision of Delight* a short while later at the beginning of the new. Less than two months later in 1617 Jonson created one of his few non-royal masques, when *Lovers Made Men* was given by Lord Hay. The next Christmas festivities, at the start of 1618, saw *Pleasure Reconciled to Virtue*, which was subsequently revived with *For the Honour of Wales* as a prologue.

The impression of this body of work taken as a whole is of the overwhelming disparity of the individual pieces. Working within such a demanding form, Jonson continued to try to reproduce his strengths by looking back to past successes, and yet had to satisfy the perennial requirement to come up with something new and unlooked for. The difficulty of accomplishing this within the constraints and limitations of the fragile hybrid form of the masque is evidenced from the slight but unmistakable signs of staleness and strain which crop up in the masques towards the end of this period. Another problem was the need to devise a strongly visual central conceit; no masque would work without it, yet to produce it put Jonson where he least wished to be, in the hands of the designer.

At first, though, these problems were not so apparent. *Christmas His Masque* is a strange and delightful piece by which Jonson demonstrated his virtuosity in the short entertainment, and his ability to surprise and tickle an audience. In place of the stately allegories of earlier masques, Jonson created what resembles nothing so much as a mummers' play; to the highest in the land he gave a demonstration of the kind of show enjoyed by their lowest subjects. In this burlesque of a Christmas performance at a city hall, Jonson brings on Christmas himself, who speaks not only in a good broad vernacular, but in the homely language of old saws and proverbs, tag lines from ballads, and all the rag-bag sounds and speech rhythms of ordinary people – 'Ha! Would you have kept me out? Christmas, old Christmas, Christmas of London and Captain Christmas? . . . 'Tis merry in hall, when beards wag all . . .' (lines 6–10).

As a further contrast with the expectations of highly polished and self-conscious entertainment, Jonson introduces a deliberate element of the cheerful amateurishness and on-the-spot improvisation that recall 'The Lamentable Comedy of Pyramus and Thisbe' from Shakespeare's *A Midsummer Night's Dream*. As the show gets under way, Christmas is startled to realize that they have actually begun, without his noticing the most important figure: 'Bones o' bread, the King! Son Rowland, Son Clem, be ready there in a trice; quick, boys!' This old device, which apparently never failed to tickle the king, is carried on throughout. Additionally, half the props are forgotten, as are important items of costume, and the mother of one of the actors blunders in halfway through to see her boy perform, insisting on prompting him with such determined maternal solicitude that she puts him quite out of his part.

In this endearing piece Jonson pushed the masque as far as it could go from its formal origins. With his next production, *The Vision of Delight*, he reverted to the older style as if *Christmas* had never been. Nothing could be stronger than this contrast of low humour with high fantasy. In the elaborate allegory of *The Vision of Delight*, with its heavy reliance upon mythology and abstraction, Jonson imagined the audience as experiencing a communal dream, and exhibits the masquers to them as the figures in their dream landscape. The conceit of the 'vision', in which illusion and reality mingle, allowed Jonson to create a fusion of sleep, dreams, waking, poetry and imagination, as this invocation to his central character makes plain:

> Break, Phant'sie, from thy cave of cloud,
>   And spread thy purple wings;
> Now all thy figures are allowed,
>   And various shapes of things;
> Create of airy forms a stream . . .
>   And though it be a waking dream

THE CHOIR:
> Yet let it like an odour rise
>   To all the senses here,
> And fall like sleep upon their eyes,
>   Or music in their ear.

(lines 44–54)

The greater flexibility of Jonson's language over modern English allowed him to incorporate both 'fancy' and 'fantasy' in this figure, who, with 'Wonder' and 'Delight', formed a grave and graceful trio to lead what was evidently one of the most splendid of Jonson's masques. In formal terms, although not longer, it is fuller and more complex than most; the action, such as it is, is repeatedly broken up by song and dance and the masque incorporates two 'antic' dances as anti-masques. The reversion of the anti-masque to the non-verbal, danced original that Jonson had moved away from, in itself indicates the nature of the development. In place of Jonson's textual developments once again the visual element is predominant. The opening description of the set indicates that the masque is to take place attended by the currently admired novelties of the designer's art; '*The Scene. A street in perspective of fair building discovered*' (line 1). As the masque proceeds, various directions lead us to imagine what this must have been like as a spectacle: '*Here the Night rises, and took her chariot bespangled with stars*' (lines 32–3); '*the scene here changed to cloud*' (line 55); '*here the bower opens, and the masquers are discovered as the glories of spring*' (lines 170–1). Add to this constant succession of visual stimuli and a higher proportion of music than usual in this sophisticated performance, with many of the lines 'spake in song' (*stylo recitativo*), and the displacement of the text from the central position that Jonson had tried so strenuously to maintain becomes very obvious. The writing of this masque is notably fresh, inventive and unusual. But with such

185

competition from the other masque elements, this must have gone unremarked by many of the spectators.

Given these developments, *Lovers Made Men* seems to be reaching back to previous work, evoking as it does the distinctive form of Jonson's earliest entertainments. As the stage-setting informs the reader:

> The front before the scene was an Arch Triumphal. On the top of which humanity . . . sat with her lap full of flowers, scattering them with her right hand; and holding a golden chain in her left hand; to show both the freedom and the bonds of courtesy, with this inscription *Super Omnia Vultus* ['Appearance Above All'].

Yet Jonson could not turn back the clock. In an acknowledgement of the masque's inexorable drift away from its origins, 'the whole masque', as Jonson wrote, 'was *sung*, after the Italian manner, *stylo recitatavo*, by Master Nicholas Lanier, who ordered and made both the scene and the music' (lines 26–8). The complete take-over by the music led Herford and Simpson to describe this production as 'the first English opera' (X, 566). Further, Jonson himself minimized the dramatic content by making the masquers and the anti-masquers identical to one another, not contrasted as they had been. This device, ingenious but not original, may have been intended as a delicate compliment to Lord Hay, since Campion had used it as long before as 1607 in the masque he wrote for Lord Hay's wedding. But there is a distinct loss in the abandoning of what had previously been one of Jonson's most lively and serviceable masque techniques.

The running-down of the anti-masque was continued in *Pleasure Reconciled to Virtue*. The main impact of this masque, known from contemporary accounts to be considerable, was the visual effect of the opening:

> *The Scene the Mountain Atlas.*

> His top ending in the figure of an old man, his head and beard all hoary and frost; as if his shoulders were covered with snow, the rest wood and rock; a grove of ivy at his feet; out of which, to a wild music of cymbals, flutes and tabors, is brought forth Comus, the god of cheer or the belly, riding in triumph, his head crowned with roses and other flowers, his hair curled . . .

> (HS VII, 479)

As with the opening effect, so with the anti-masques; both are spectacular visual contrivances in the form of dances, one of monsters and the other of 'pigmees' – the ever-serviceable little boys again – and are totally non-verbal.

Yet Jonson had clearly taken pains with his part. The text of *Pleasure Reconciled to Virtue* is carefully wrought, with closely calculated transitions between the Rabelaisian flashes of the humour of 'the belly' and the elevated allegorical moments occurring in the second half of the masque, when Mercury descends to crown Hercules as an 'active friend of virtue'. This blending of the jolly manner of the *Christmas* masque with the more abstract style of the mythological figures is achieved through the use of song; the masque is not entirely sung, but there is a high proportion of lyric material, which facilitates and covers the changes of tone and direction within the piece.

Nevertheless, *Pleasure Reconciled to Virtue* did not succeed; the text was not finally strong enough to pull together all the disparate elements that it sought to harmonize into a poetic unity. To retrieve the failure Jonson added another piece, *For the Honour of Wales*, hastily got together before the revival of the masque at Shrovetide. The decision to write an entertainment on 'goats and Welsh speeches' committed Jonson to the kind of dialogue, and the type of humour, previously essayed in *The Irish Masque at Court* whose foundation was the sole and simple notion that all the non-English (and non-Scottish) inhabitants of the British Isles are unfailingly good for a laugh. Yet despite (or perhaps because of) Jonson's detailed attention to their speech, incorporating Welsh phrases not only into their dialogue but even into their songs, Griffith, Jenkin and Evan remain resolutely unfunny:

> I do say, an't please his Madestee, I do not like him with aull his heart; he is pludged in by the ears, without all piddies and mercies, or proprieties, or decorums. I will do injuries to no man before his Madestee . . .
>
> (lines 53–6)

Much may have been done in performance to redeem this sorry stuff. It is impossible to estimate how much difference good singing might have made; had any genuine Welsh tenors been imported for the occasion, much might have been retrieved. Nevertheless, the piece did not please.

Jonson's masque-making towards the end of this period conveys a very real sense of strain. Writing for a collaborative medium meant that the importance of his contribution ebbed and flowed, and the masques began to lose the earlier confidence of the textual security

187

they had held at the heart of the enterprise. These pieces in fact are less clearly Jonson's; his primacy has been encroached upon by the other 'makers'. None of these masques could be adjudged a failure on verbal or artistic grounds. But none has either the sparkle, the poise, or the excitement of experimentation that distinguish the masques of the first phase. What we have, however, if not Jonson writing to the full extent of his range, is a strong sense of the working author engaged to the full in his difficult task, and a continuing reminder of his ever-impressive variety of concept and technique.

These masques of Jonson's, whether good, bad, or indifferent, have all suffered the same fate; being only 'the glory of an hour' they passed away with their hour beyond the recovery of later ages. But this crowded phase of Jonson's career also contained some of his work in the public form of the theatre, which came too late for inclusion in the Folio and yet can stand comparison with the best of Jonsonian drama. The writing of *Bartholomew Fair* in 1614, and *The Devil is an Ass* in 1616, crowned and completed the achievement of Jonson's creative maturity.

For his return to the stage following a gap of more than three years after the production of *Catiline*, Jonson once more returned to comedy. *Bartholomew Fair* demonstrates how thoroughly Jonson had assimilated the lessons of his earlier experiences of working in comical satire; yet it also manages both a breadth of vision and a series of fresh artistic impulses which show that the previous vein neither is being simply repeated, nor has been played out. The drama is both comical and satirical, after the earlier models of Jonson's comedies; but the humour is both broader and more humane than Jonson has accustomed his auditors to, and the play's final injunction, 'Remember you are but Adam, flesh and blood', is delivered in the spirit of understanding and tolerance, rather than of stinging rebuke. In addition, Jonson incorporated dramatic moments and events of a sort that he had not handled before, in his continued efforts to find new methods of dealing with his recurrent dramatic preoccupations.

Most evident, of course, is the continuation of Jonson's study of 'humours'; both the psychology and the methodology of 'humours' had survived, like a subterranean stream, to feed Jonson's newer comedy creations. From the first character in the play, the naive and self-satisfied lawyer Littlewit, the note is struck of fatuous pretension, self-ignorance, overweening pride and stupid greed. Certain of the characters, like Wasp, are handled very successfully in the 'humours' manner. The audience never learns why this busy little man is so constantly irritable to the point of insanity; we are simply given a buzzing, stinging creature whose nature it is to light upon those around him with convulsive rankling insults like his favourite, 'Turd in your teeth!'

With other characters too Jonson pushes the dominant humour to its outer limits of grotesquery, giving, in each case, a virtuoso demonstration of his 'humours' technique and philosophy. The Puritans of *The Alchemist*, although credited with narrow bigotry, greed, crookedness and credulity, come off fairly lightly in comparison with the Puritan elder of *Bartholomew Fair*, Zeal-of-the-Land Busy. This joyous creation of Jonson's comic art combines a lean wit with a fat head. He is made to preach purity and restraint while gourmandizing himself upon anything he can lay hold of; he claims spiritual authority as a 'Rabbi' and prophet of the 'revealed religion', when his knowledge and grace extend no further than that of any other ex-baker (his former trade before he turned to 'seeing visions'). This arch-hypocrite is introduced to the spectators before he appears on stage in a most memorable vignette, when he is reported 'fast by the teeth in the cold turkey-pie in the cupboard, with a great white loaf on his left hand, and a glass of malmsey on his right' (I.vi.34–6). Behind this vigorous comic image, the parodic echo of the Christian communion of bread and wine administers a latent satiric rebuke of the false priest, as well as of the sinner through greed.

In the fair itself, the gross and stupid Busy is paralleled by the pig-woman Ursula. Where he offers to feed souls, she feeds bodies; and Jonson is clear about which of the two is the more honest trade. The gargantuan Ursula is a stunningly original and compelling dramatic creation; through the evocation of the Great Bear ('Ursa Major' is one of her nicknames) and through her close identification with her pigs, she is projected as the embodiment of a huge and greasy animal, more an elemental force than a simple character, a force of ungoverned and ungovernable vitality, eternal and enduring:

> What! My lean Ursula! My she-bear! Art thou alive yet with the
> litter of pigs to groan out another *Bartholomew Fair?*
>
> (II.iii.1–3)

Yet despite her size, her strength and domination in the world of the fair, Ursula is wholly and assertively female. This is expressed through the imagery of the play: she is the 'Mother of the Fair', 'mother of the pigs', the 'womb and bed of enormity', and 'the sow of Smithfield'. She has been in her time (some twenty-two years) punk, pinnace and 'bawd', working her way through the ranks until, like Shakespeare's Mistress Overdone, she has 'worn her eyes almost out in the service' (*Measure for Measure*, I.ii.102). In her own eyes, though, the middle-aged, massive Ursula is still no more than 'a plain plump soft wench of the suburbs, juicy and wholesome' (II.v.83–4).

These larger-than-life figures dominate the play but do not over-balance it; Jonson's achievement here is to have created a world of humours, where everyone is similarly afflicted to a greater or lesser degree. A new slant in *Bartholomew Fair*, however, is discernible through the jargon of the characters as a new word, 'vapours', takes the place of 'humours'. 'Humours' refer to a physiological and hence psychological imbalance, only secondarily indicating affectation and a ridiculous striving to be what one is not. A 'vapour' is equivalent to a warp or perversity of flesh and blood, an original sin in temperament. 'Humours' make people withdraw into singularity; 'vapours' make people obtrude themselves, meddle and quarrel. The puppet show which brings to a climax all the tensions and conflicts of the play is thus the *locus classicus* of vapouring, an orgy of humours out-humouring each other and themselves.[1]

The fair then is both the site and the expression of all these clashing desires and determinations, to the point of becoming one great comic 'humour' in itself. As such it forms an instructive comparison with *The Alchemist*; the fair echoes the alchemist's house as the shop where cheats and rogues sell hopes, dreams and fantasies. Although the plays have much in common in their handling both of humours and gulls (the constant stock-in-trade of Jonson's dramaturgy) yet the settings could hardly be more strongly contrasted. Where in the earlier plays Jonson set himself the considerable technical challenge of confining his entire created world of teeming London life to one room, here he has adopted the even more tricky task of putting a known real world, that of the famous fair, into the confines of a stage. He meets this by employing an ancient but still serviceable metaphor, that of the world as a stage. His 'Bartholomew birds' speak and act in the knowledge that theirs is a public performance; they make their annual appearance, go through their roles as cut-purse, horse-courser, pig-woman, or punk – then take the money and run.

Within this framework the structure of the play is carefully contrived to follow the metaphor through. Jonson gives us not one but two prefaces to the main action, so that the audience eventually encounters the fair through a series of receding perspectives. The play opens in the theatre with one of Jonson's favourite devices, the

Induction, when an actor playing the Stage-Keeper comes on to address the audience as if on behalf of the back-stage staff:

> Gentlemen, have a little patience, they are e'en upon coming, instantly. He that should begin the play, Master Littlewit the Proctor, has a stitch new fallen in his black silk stocking; 'twill be drawn up ere you can tell twenty.

(lines 1–5)

This artful assumption of naturalism modulates to stage realism through the use of a legal metaphor; two more characters, a scrivener and another member of the 'stage staff', the book-holder or prompter, are brought on to deliver and to conclude an agreement between the playwright and the audience as to the rights, duties and expectations of both parts. That done, the play can begin, and by an ingenious glide Jonson takes us from the 'real' scrivener of the Induction to the character of the lawyer Littlewit in the 'real' play.

Even here though, the play has started only to whet the audience's appetite. Until all the main characters and their interests have been established in the first scene, the action proper, that of the fair, does not begin. With this ingenious and suggestive handling of the play-within-the-play motif, Jonson attempts to sharpen the audience's critical awareness of the overlapping of 'reality' and 'illusion' by deliberately blurring the boundaries between them. He seeks simultaneously to prod the spectators into making these crucial distinctions, and yet also to engage their co-operation in his fiction through this witty demonstration of its possibilities and limitations. And underlying this deft and humorous management of the shifting perspectives is the unchallengeable contention: 'All the world's a stage . . .'.

For only on the sprawling stage of the fair can the action of the drama be played out. Critics have observed the relative plotlessness of *Bartholomew Fair* after the clockwork mechanisms of *The Alchemist*. Jonson's technique here is broadly that of simply bringing his characters to the fair and allowing the rest of the play to write itself. This method can hardly fail, since the fair contains in microcosm all the opportunities and temptations of the larger ('real') world outside; men and women, traders and customers, knaves and gulls, poor and rich, jostle in this gaudy, vital milieu whose one moral imperative is 'getting and spending', in all senses of the phrase. The traders' cry, 'What is't you lack? . . . What do you buy?', epitomizes that unshaken faith in the greed and acquisitiveness of others which was

191

always one of Jonson's prime satiric targets; and the folly of this attitude is hilariously summed up in the character of Cokes, who, longing to spend his money, in effect gives it away, when the fair's resident cutpurse takes it as a professional challenge to relieve him of his various purses.

Bartholomew Fair equally supplied Jonson with a brilliant conceit for the expression and complication of his characters' destinies, through its in-built sense of occasion. 'Bartholmas', the ancient festival of high summer at the end of August, was a day of licence, hallowed time out of mind. Londoners in fact so far extended the traditional laxity of legal, civil and moral rules and norms at this time that eventually the fair had to be suppressed by the authorities. This real-life factor was Jonson's inspiration and artistic justification for a drama of licence, in which every commandment and prohibition is held up to scrutiny and put to the test in the rough-and-tumble of experience, usually breaking down under the pressure.

For the fair, taking place at harvest time, combined the elements of a high Saturnalia with a Bacchanalia. It allowed Jonson to seize upon the existing associations of natural fullness and seasonal completion. He places the accent firmly upon the gratification of the senses and their physical release in eating, drinking, copulating. Even the inevitable corollary, the necessity of evacuation, is unblushingly handled at the height of the action, to considerable comic effect:

> WHIT: . . . shweet Ursh, help this good brave voman to a jordan [chamber pot] . . . bring the velvet woman to de . . .
> URSULA: I bring her? Hang her! heart, must I find a common pot for every punk in your purlieus? . . . Let her sell her hood, and buy a sponge, with a pox to her. My vessel is employed, sir. I have but one, and 'tis the bottom of an old bottle. An honest proctor and his wife are at it, within; if she'll stay her time, so.
>
> (IV.iv.189–200)

It is worth remarking that this theme, the crudest of comic levellers, for which Jonson had previously demonstrated his fondness in 'On the Famous Voyage' (Epigram 133), is carried on throughout the play by such touches as the naming of one of the characters 'Jordan', and by Wasp's special and personal 'noisesome vapour', 'turd in your teeth'.

Jonson's fair, in short, abounds in physicality, in every form and on every level. As much as Shakespeare's romantic comedies, though in a totally different mode, it is a play about mating and matching, a

ribald celebration of elemental urges and instinctive anarchic appetites as the sources of new life, growth and fruition. The problem of
the marriage of Grace Wellborn is the starting-point of the action,
and within it Quarlous, Winwife, Dame Purecraft and Grace all
contract marriages, while Cokes is cheated out of one. This marriage
of the Puritan widow and the pure young heroine on one level of the
action is echoed structurally in the much lower vein of burlesque, by
the mating, indeed 'horsing' of the two married women, the wives of
Proctor Littlewit and Justice Overdo. Despite their previous respect-
ability these two, once in liquor, are startlingly ready to yield to the
blandishments of the horse-courser 'Captain' Jordan Knockem; who
as his name punningly indicates, in his role as bawd or 'whores'-
courser', will, in the shortage of clients, 'knock 'em' himself: 'Sayst
thou, filly? Thou shalt have a leap presently; I'll horse thee myself,
else' (IV.iv.230–1).

In pursuit of a theme that richly supplied him with the action he
needed to simulate the fullness of the fair, Jonson lost no opportunity
to reinforce it through the language. Just as *Epicene* repeatedly stresses
sterility and barrenness, so *Bartholomew Fair* abounds in procreative
imagery and suggestions of sexual fulfilment. The fair itself operates
symbolically as one gigantic orgy, a revel of orgiastic pursuits; it deals
with harvest-time abundance, set against pinching want. The characters are engaged, the pace accelerates, builds to an increasingly
frenzied climax, and after release sinks quietly down to normality
again. Contributory to this orgiastic sense and structure are the
recurrent images drawn from eating and drinking. It is a world of
carnality, a reminder that human beings 'are but Adam, flesh and
blood', and the flesh will out. Jonson's treatment of the theme of
carnality in his play, the tolerant attitude to the uninhibited debauch
that he creates, is unusual in his work; he is not generally so relaxed
about his own Rabelaisian impulses.

This does not imply, of course, that Jonson applauds the rejection
or demolition of constituted authority. His target in *Bartholomew Fair*
is false or usurped authority, authority that rests upon no true moral
base. Within the three concentric circles of the play, 'Rabbi' Busy
stands for religious authority, Justice Overdo for legal, and Wasp for
the civil authority of the pedagogue. Each of these characters,
'humours'-style, is made to display an obsessive, even ferocious
determination to act out his official role; the divine, the justice and
the tutor are put through motions that become increasingly deranged
as their unsound authority is repeatedly challenged and ultimately

eroded by the irregular processes and anti-authoritarian spirit of the
fair and its denizens. The satirical name of Overdo given by Jonson to
his petty justice applies in fact to them all – the corrosive thrust of
Jonson's examination of authority is located in this ignorant over-
doing, religious, legal and moral. Here is Justice Overdo in full
flight, in his final, not to say terminal, paroxysm of law-giving:

> Look upon me, O London! and see me, O Smithfield! the example
> of justice, and Mirror of Magistrates; the true top of formality,
> and scourge of enormity. Hearken unto my labours and but
> observe my discoveries; and compare Hercules with me, if thou
> dar'st, of old.
>
> (V.vi.33–8)

For this hubristic bombast, with its parody of a popular contemporary figure, the Virtuous Magistrate who discovers all evil, Overdo
is rewarded with public exposure as his careful observations are shown
to be false and his pronouncements ludicrous, and his whole conduct
proves to have been as much a product of the fair as that of the most
confirmed villain within it. Overdo's experience of an ignominious
public failure where he had expected a predetermined public
triumph, is brought about not only through his own injudicious
conduct, but that of his wife. Jonson's compact stage direction caps it
all: '*Mistress Overdo is sick, and her husband is silenced*' (V.vi.67 ff). This
final proceeding confirms Jonson's treatment throughout, completing a consistent and sustained comment upon the importance of
authority through a detailed analysis of its malfunction; see, he crows,
the folly of fools trying to correct folly!

In *Bartholomew Fair* Jonson found the perfect medium for these
serious considerations, that of stage comedy. The success of the play
and its message depends upon its total realization in theatrical terms.
For not only is this play funny; it is dramatically funny and consequently highly serious as Jonson finds the way to dramatize his
concerns, to present them in visual terms yet without the sacrifice of
artistic autonomy that he had to make in the masque. On the simple
level of stagecraftsmanship, Jonson's control in this play is faultless.
In comparison with the difficulties evinced in *The Case Is Altered* when
the young dramatist had to handle more than two speakers in the same
scene, there is now the matured ability to manage the 'full stage' that
Jonson so loved. *Bartholomew Fair* has twenty-three speaking parts,
plus at least fourteen supernumeraries with appearances and incidental lines, not to mention the off-the-line mugging that bit-part actors

have to do; yet Jonson disposes of this massive cast of over forty players without the slightest sense of strain.

This is achieved through the same technique as that employed by Shakespeare in all his war scenes, the breaking down of the mass into readily identifiable groups, each of which can then be handled in effect as one character. When the play begins, for instance, the spectators are directed to take hold of the Littlewit household, neatly composed of the younger couple (Littlewit and his wife Win), and the older generation, consisting of the mother, Dame Purecraft, and the spiritual 'father', Rabbi Busy. This pseudo-family group remains intact almost to the end of the play, by which time Jonson trusts his audience's grasp on the individuals sufficiently to allow the group to fragment, the members going their separate ways – ways that express their deeper individual preoccupations or personalities. Littlewit goes off to see his puppet play performed, Purecraft pursues her hunt for a husband, Busy gives himself up to wallowing in the fair; and Win-the-Fight Littlewit, left to her own devices, is splendidly eager to fall for Knockem's assurance that she should live 'like a lady', and that the life of 'an honest woman' is 'very scurvy' (IV.v).

This technique of handling linked characters in a group is repeated with the comparable visiting party of Bartholomew Cokes, his tutor, his bride-to-be and her chaperone. Once again Jonson has created two younger members of the troop, male and female, and two of the senior generation. These two, Wasp and Mistress Overdo, resemble those of the Littlewit party; they are no more responsible and steady than their opposite numbers, but betray any claim to the authority of seniority by their foolish behaviour. Another structural parallel is that each party leader, Littlewit and Cokes, is its most foolish member, and each contains, in Busy and Wasp, an alternative leader who is a moral bully of false authority. On a similar structural parallel, the two young heroes Quarlous and Winwife (in so far as Jonson allows them that status) are also handled as a pair until the audience's familiarity with their aims and characters facilitates rapid and easy discrimination between them.

By this consummate technique, Jonson not only promoted the smooth and comprehensible flow of the action, but brought about an effective contrast between these groups and their individual members when the time came for them to splinter off from their parent body. This movement, in fact, determines the rhythms of the plot, as first groups, then individuals, break off and collide in an ever-accelerating tempo until the rupture of pre-existing ties results in new alignments across the board. This is all accomplished without Jonson's ever losing sight of his underlying dramatic purpose, a purpose which is continually felt within the play, surfacing in the stocks scene (IV.i), for instance. Here, in a memorable theatrical episode, Jonson plausibly contrives to have his three representatives of authority lodged in the stocks, simultaneously and side by side. The point of their failure and folly is made in dumb show, illustrating Jonson's vital capacity to imagine in visual, theatrical terms. This satiric-didactic tableau affords a juxtaposition rich in both humour and irony, and redolent of moral and allegorical associations wider than those of the immediate dramatic situation.

For eventually *Bartholomew Fair* reveals itself as a parable upon the theme handled by Shakespeare in *Measure for Measure*: 'Judge not, that ye be not judged'; for 'with what measure ye mete, it shall be measured to you again' (Matthew vii.2). Jonson's is a parable in the comic vein; the farcical elements and warmth of tone prevent it from becoming heavy or oppressive. Again, the question of human frailty is consistently posed in human rather than abstract terms, building to the powerful final injunction:

> Remember you are but Adam, flesh and blood! you have your frailty.
>
> (V.vi.96–7)

Two factors combine to promote the audience's experience of Jonson's message in highly personal and accessible terms. First of these is his by now familiar location of the action in his own London, with settings and characters re-created with a vividness which makes them feel one dimension larger than the reality in which they are faithfully grounded. Both the supposedly virtuous and the self-declared villains live their created lives with an intensity that relentlessly compels the audience's attention; from the mad Trouble-all to the unscrupulous wife-hunters Quarlous and Winwife, from the possessed Purecraft to the resigned Grace, all are fully realized in their character and situation through the comprehensive nature of Jonson's vision and treatment. Their impact on us is heightened by the play's most significant stylistic characteristic, the use of prose. This was to be Jonson's last great essay in this medium; all his subsequent plays make verse the main form. But for the fair, with its vivid, often violent vernacular, its naturalistic mode and its realistic depiction of the low life of the underbelly of London, then prose is the obvious and right choice. In *Bartholomew Fair*, Jonson's taut, rhythmic prose, its flexibility and variety, rose to the supreme exploitation of its resources as a plastic medium:

> WASP: Heart, what have you to do? Cannot a man quarrel in quietness? but he must be put out of it by you? What are you?
>
> BRISTLE: Why, we be His Majesty's Watch, sir.
>
> WASP: Watch? 'Sblood, you are a sweet watch indeed. A body would think [if] you watched well at nights you should be contented to sleep at this time of the day. Get you to your fleas and your flock-beds, you rogues, your kennels, and lie down close.
>
> BRISTLE: Down? Yes, we will down, I warrant you! Down with him in his Majesty's name, down, down with him, and carry him away to the pigeon-holes!
>
> (IV.iv.168–79)

Perhaps because of his confidence in writing consistently at this level, Jonson is able here to be more relaxed than usual with the audience. In *Bartholomew Fair* Jonson came as near as he ever did to negotiating a working relationship with what he elsewhere regarded as the many-headed public enemy of his theatrical endeavours. He seized the nettle of this problem in the Induction, where he went so far, albeit in a humorous vein, as to put before the audience 'articles of agreement, indented, between the spectators or hearers at the Hope on the Bankside in the county of Surrey on the one party; and the author of *Bartholomew Fair* in the said place and county in the other'. In return for promising to deliver 'a new sufficient play . . . merry, and as full of noise as sport, made to delight all and offend none', Jonson set out in full his expectations of the audience.

These are nothing if not stringent. Jonson desires 'that every man here exercise his own judgment', and ironically allows it 'lawful for any man to judge his six pen'orth, his twelve pen'orth, so to his eighteen pence'; but no one must 'censure by contagion', catching a bad opinion of the play like a disease from his neighbour. He must take the play as it comes, and not repine for either the old-fashioned theatrical conventions like those of *The Spanish Tragedy*, or the actualities of the real fair which Jonson does not introduce, like 'a little Davy [bully-boy] to take a toll of the bawds'. Finally Jonson warns against any spectator trying to act as a 'politic pick-lock of the scene', winkling out concealed satiric applications of his innocently intended characterization. In the Induction Jonson both directly states his own critical standards and demonstrates them through his own practice. His affectionate scorn for low popular amusement is shown through the puppet play; his dislike of knockabout fun, comic patter and rhymed extemporization is manifested through the stage-keeper's fervent praise of Tarlton, who exemplified vulgar taste and 'the concupiscence of jigs and dances'. Jonson's own stagecraft is clear, bold and discriminating, and he warns his audience what to expect in advance.

To paraphrase Jonson's original makes it sound much more laboured and self-conscious than it is, especially in performance. Jonson did not take himself so seriously, and the peroration ends with a self-deprecating pat on the back for the author, whose sense of decorum has extended to representing in the play the stink of the bears as it was in real life. Evidently Jonson judged correctly the business of the Induction in getting the audience to the play in the right frame of mind; the play was entirely spared the violent audience reaction that had latterly attended his other productions. On this occasion, as with *Every Man in his Humour*, Jonson 'hit it' with the playgoers. Never again was he to combine in one play the gutsy vigour and winning charm of *Bartholomew Fair*.

The Devil is an Ass is a piece in an altogether darker mode than *Bartholomew Fair*. In the composition of this play, the last of the great comedies, Jonson tackled two contemporary abuses of a far graver nature than any of the venal offences of the fair. With an extraordinary and unpredictable imaginative leap, Jonson seized on and fused together a social problem of his day whose roots lay far back in the distant past and one that was expressing the birth pangs of disorders to come. In his contemporaries' continuing belief in witchcraft, and in their attempts to come to terms with the emergence of a modern capitalist economy, Jonson pinpointed reactions to social change that provided ample satiric meat for the last of his great 'studies of the comic thread'.

Of the two social abuses, Jonson found a first fruitful source of 'study' in demonology and witchcraft. Here he put his finger on a key intellectual issue of his day, one that had vexed the minds of all, from the villager suspicious of an elderly female neighbour, to the highest in the land, the king himself. James had given considerable thought and attention to the subject, of which he believed he had had personal experience, and had published the results of his studies in his *Demonology* (1597). But as the advancement of science and the spread of humanistic questioning combined to undermine older habits of thought, belief in the veracity of medieval demonology and witchcraft became harder to sustain. As he had with *The Alchemist*, Jonson picked up the precise moment at which this critical change was occurring, when educated and intelligent people stopped crediting something which had been unquestioningly accepted as true earlier in their lives. In *The Devil is an Ass*, Jonson sought to further the spread of enlightenment by satirizing the continuance of the old belief, and its consequent potential for exploitation by the unscrupulous.

For naturally an idea of such antiquity (ultimately tracing back to Old Testament roots in the Book of Leviticus) displayed a predictably tenacious hold. Jonson's declaration that only the credulous and the vainly curious could sustain such a belief provides the plot basis of the play; at its start Fitzdottrell (satirically dubbed by Jonson after a bird of proverbial foolishness) expresses the crack-brained desire: 'Would I might see the Devil!' (I.ii.10). His imagination stimulated by old pictures of Satan, Fitzdottrell syllogistically argues for the existence of supernatural manifestations on the grounds that 'if they be not, / Why are there laws against them?' (lines 20–1). Through this character, fatuously impressed by the stage-setting of the self-styled magicians and experts in the field, Jonson makes sport of these pretensions:

> They have their crystals, I do know, and rings,
> And virgin parchment, and their dead men's skulls,
> Their raven wings, their lights and pentacles,
> With characters; I have seen all these. But –
> Would I might see the Devil! I would give
> A hundred of these pictures so to see him
> Once out of the picture.
>
> (I.ii.6–12)

In the unmistakable whiff of quackery and imposture, coupled with the speaker's expressed longing for something that could not be satisfied by any honest or downright proceeding, Jonson creates a framework of knavery and gullibility irresistibly reminiscent of *The Alchemist*.

From this beginning Jonson develops his plot as a two-pronged attack on the dramatic target. The first is mounted through a series of gullible and credulous individuals, whose difficulties are brought to a head in the last scene of the play. Here Fitzdottrell is forced through his own machinations into pretending that he has been possessed by the devil. This imposture, involving a simulated fit with frothing at the mouth and other tricks and contrivances, was based by Jonson

199

upon a real-life occurrence;[2] and within the play, as in real life, the deceit imposes upon all those around, even upon the wisdom of the representative of judgement in the play, the justice Sir Paul Eitherside. In this important last scene, Jonson demonstrates that clinging to ignorance and superstition is not merely a personal nor even an intellectual vice or weakness; it is one with the widest possible implication for society at large, and has social repercussions of the greatest gravity for innocent people victimized by others' malpractices.

On a second level, Jonson uses the theme of the supernatural in the play to raise wider issues of personal behaviour and social relations. Through the quaint and effective notion of making his central character an apprentice devil, one who is still learning the trade, Jonson delivers a caustic attack upon the devilishness in humankind. Young Pug, burning with desire 'to do the commonwealth of Hell some service', is granted his wish to leave the infernal regions and come to earth, although his 'chief', 'great Lucifer', sardonically doubts that he will do any good (that is, evil), there: 'You are too dull a devil to be trusted / Forth in those parts' (I.i.26–7). In Lucifer's grim assessment, humanity has nothing at all to learn about evil from the legions of Hell, 'now . . . as vice stands this present year' (line 80).

Jonson devotes the rest of the play to unfolding his proposition that 'the devil is an ass' in comparison with man. Pug's career on earth consists of a series of adventures in which the human beings invariably out-devil the Devil himself in greed, cruelty, selfishness and ingenuity. Not only are they tirelessly engaged in trying to rob, deceive, fleece and exploit others for their own gain, like the crooked Meercraft, Everill and their agents Engine and Trains; they are determined, too, to make their own hell on earth, bringing upon themselves that which they most fear. Fitzdottrell, for instance, within a dozen lines of his first entrance, confides to the audience his dread of being cuckolded by his wife. Yet his folly, covetousness and disregard of all decent values, lead him to treat his wife as a commodity that he can 'venture' for personal advantage, like Corvino in *Volpone*. By his own actions therefore he exposes her to 'the main mortal thing' that he dreads, her temptation to infidelity. In a structural parallel which would not have been lost on contemporary audiences, Jonson links two horned creatures, the devil and the cuckold, since both, while tormenting others, are themselves tormented with punishments that they have brought upon themselves.

This darker, more pessimistic view of human nature is reinforced and further developed through the second major satiric preoccupation of the play, the abuses of the contemporary economy. As with demonology and witchcraft, Jonson isolated a burning topic of the day that encapsulated the transition from the old order to the new. The movement from the medieval agrarian economy to early capitalism, when trading, venturing and money-making replaced the former ways of living and dealing, seemed to many of those who endured it to be a convulsion in nature. Few of those engaged in economic affairs had more than the slightest grasp on events or their underlying causes; outsiders steered clear of an area that was both incomprehensible and contentious. Dramatists rarely attempted to comment on problems other than the personal; so that 'The Miseries of Enforced Marriage' would be examined, as L. C. Knights observed, but never 'The Miseries of Monopoly'. Jonson was therefore unique in his readiness to take on the subject of the economy, and to give it a full and unblinking scrutiny.

For Jonson saw clearly the corruption and the danger in many of the fiscal practices developing at the time not only unquestioned, but supported by the highest in the land; the members of the aristocracy and the king himself were among their keenest, not to say greediest, supporters. Jonson's primary target was the evil of 'projection', where schemes were floated for all manner of projects, and money raised from those who hoped to get rich quick by them. Jonson was the earliest commentator to identify the potential evil of what at bottom was frequently nothing but an elaborate form of confidence trick.[3] He was also not only on the right track, but ahead of the game: the satiric relevance of the central 'project' in *The Devil is an Ass*, the recovery of 'drowned land', emerges in the existence of several schemes to drain and recapture fenland, for instance, which were patented both around this time and later.

To Jonson, the 'projector', represented in *The Devil is an Ass* by the subtle Meercraft, was the instigator of massive and unmitigated social evil through his unbridled appetite for money. This in turn affected and preyed upon others, infecting them with the same disease, until society was divided into two, those who were projecting, and those being projected upon. Jonson was too intelligent not to perceive some of the advantages to humanity in the new enterprises in science, technology, business and trade. But equally he foresaw the casualties of the ever-expanding world of power and wealth, its divisive tendence and its potential for corruption and mismanagement. As

Meercraft glibly explains to Fitzdottrell (ever ready, like the foolish bird that Jonson has made him, to swallow anything):

> We see those changes daily; the fair lands
> That were the clients', are the lawyers' now:
> And those rich manors there of goodman Taylor's,
> Had once more wood upon them, than the yard
> By which they were measured out for the last purchase.
> Nature hath these vicissitudes. She makes
> No man a state of perpetuity, sir.
>
> (II.iv.33–9)

By putting these words into the mouth of his chief crook, Jonson attacks the attempts of such projectors to suggest that their proceedings are all entirely inevitable and part of the natural course of things; and by extension the gullibility of those who believed them. He acknowledged that many of Meercraft's projects were feasible, but was not persuaded that these would benefit any other than the projectors themselves. The inevitable revolutionary effect upon society would be felt through its damaging repercussions on individual life; and the projectors' level of care and concern for all this is brilliantly imaged in Meercraft's outline:

> We'll take in citizens, commoners and aldermen
> To bear the charge, and blow them off again
> Like so many dead flies, when 'tis finished.
>
> (II.i.42–5)

In moments like this Jonson reveals the connection between the new and the old style of rogues; despite all his business pretensions, Meercraft betrays himself as a cousin of Face and Subtle under the skin, while his fluency in business jargon confirms the identification. While not against these developments in themselves (Jonson was no atrophied reactionary resisting all change) he reserved the right to assess them critically. And in his considered judgement such practices were found wanting, since Jonson confronted the rise of capitalism and its associated practices with standards and attitudes not formed in the world of mercantile enterprise. Significant economic developments had, for Jonson, to measure up against the known reality of the traditional morality inherited from the Middle Ages, with its stress upon the organic community and the interdependence of one social order upon another within it.

In dramatizing and satirizing the social effects of economic developments, and the inescapable evils and abuses which they had generated, Jonson showed how much his capacity for analysis had changed and matured. In the construction of *Volpone* (1606) he had handled greed, cupidity and acquisitiveness almost wholly in personal and psychological terms. By 1616 he had developed his skills of analysis to the point where he could authoritatively sketch in the wider social implications: that the unequal distribution of wealth robs society, and damages its weaker members.

The Devil is an Ass provided Jonson with his first public platform to attack a specific, topical, up-to-the-minute social abuse, as opposed to the earlier, more generalized techniques. This new focus combined with the treatment of vice and folly through the witchcraft theme to give the play a tremendous satiric bite:

> Sir, money's a whore, a bawd, a drudge,
> Fit to run out on errands; let her go.
> *Via pecunia!* when she's run and gone,
> And fled and dead, then will I fetch her again,
> With *aqua-vitae* out of an old hogshead!
> While there are lees of wine, or dregs of beer,
> I'll never want her! Coin her out of cobwebs,
> Dust, but I'll have her! Raise wool upon eggshells,
> Sir, and make grass grow out of marrowbones
> To make her come.
>
> (II.i.1–10)

In this animated, surrealistic vision of the relation of the moneymaker to his adored and despised creature, money, Jonson transfixed and preserved the type to posterity like a butterfly on a pin. Through an assortment of moments like this, in *The Devil is an Ass* Jonson created a nexus of significant comments on the key developments of what Christopher Hill has named 'the century of revolution'.

And even within the framework of comedy, Jonson made no attempt to evade or to palliate the uncomfortable truths that his analysis threw up. At this late stage of his dramatic career, he was even more implacably opposed than previously to the soothing formulae and comforting conclusions of romantic comedy. His handling of the story of Mistress Fitzdottrell, for instance, is stark and uncompromising; the presentation of a woman married to a coarse and degraded partner anticipates a familiar situation of Restoration comedy of over half a century later, *The Provoked Wife*, for instance. If ever Jonson wrote with his vaunted 'truth to nature', it is here, in the study of a woman who has to live the horror that Grace Wellborn only anticipates, when however wretchedly married, 'they that cannot work their fetters off, *must wear them*' (III.v.286–7).

Jonson's handling of Mistress Fitzdottrell is the more interesting in the context of the Jonson canon at large, since it is the only genuinely compassionate study of a woman that he ever made in drama. This portrait showing her 'the wife / Of so much blasted flesh, as scarce hath soul / Instead of salt, to keep it sweet' (I.vi.88–90) goes on to extend the picture of misery that is the Fitzdottrell marriage; and Jonson gives full weight to the suffering that underlies Mistress Fitzdottrell's 'I must obey' (line 59), in the face of the domination of a despised master.

Even more telling than the action, however, is the image pattern by which Jonson consistently associates this young woman with small, pitiable and helpless creatures. She is introduced to us, in her idiotic husband's condescending term, as 'a niaise', which Jonson himself glosses as 'a young hawk, taken crying out of the nest'. Subsequently this image chain unfolds to present the character as a bird in a cage, in a net, or waiting to be caught. Such is the sympathy that Jonson arouses for Mistress Fitzdottrell that her situation seems initially to be an evocative reworking of the *Volpone* motif when he assures Celia, 'Thou hast, in place of a base husband found / A worthy lover . . .' (III.vii.186–7). But in the astringently unsentimental and satirical perspective of *The Devil is an Ass*, the audience knows very clearly that there can be no escape from this woman's situation.

The handling of Mistress Fitzdottrell in this full way is the more interesting in comparison with the treatment of the play's other female characters. The fashionable harpies Lady Tailbush and Lady Eitherside are lineal descendants of the collegiate ladies of *Epicene*, voluble, self-possessed gorgons, characterized but not personalized, and drawn entirely after the 'humours' manner, rather than in Jonson's subtler and more penetrating style. This is not to say, however, that they sit uneasily with the characterization of Mistress Fitzdottrell; on the contrary, this tender presentation of her plight is entirely consonant with the depiction of her natural predators, made all the more telling since they are of her own sex.

As this suggests, *The Devil is an Ass* is a crowded, subtle and resonant play alive with topical relevance, side by side with questions of eternal human importance. Possibly Jonson, in the maturity of his genius and the fullness of confidence, attempted too much. In contrast with the relative looseness of *Bartholomew Fair*, this piece can seem overplotted, its narrative too dense as the spectator is required to follow its convolutions around the adventures of Pug, the complications of Fitzdottrell's 'get-rich-quick' manoeuvres, and the (eventually abortive) love interest of Mistress Fitzdottrell and her suitor Wittipol. Criticism has also centred on the contemporary nature of the satire, on the grounds that this renders the main action inaccessible to post-seventeenth-century audiences, and on the difficulties that Jonson clearly experienced in rounding off an arguably overfull plot; the explosion of the action appears to take place in the fourth act, when Wittipol makes his declaration to Mistress Fitzdottrell and is discovered by her husband, so that the resolution of all the complications in the fifth act has been found rushed and perfunctory.

Yet these objections are more apparent than real, based upon the experience of reading the play in the study rather than enjoying it in the theatre. *The Devil is an Ass* was rightly rated by Swinburne as one of the author's crowning masterpieces, and complaints against it result from the imaginative failure to place it in its proper home, the world of the stage. In performance, for instance, the play is continuously, inventively funny in a way that the text alone would not suggest, as successful revivals at Edinburgh and Birmingham have shown. It communicates its points forcibly through a humour that ranges from the subtlest irony to the broadest farce. Not only Mistress Fitzdottrell but the grossest of Jonson's villains are handled with the same light touch; Meercraft, for instance, attempting to cut short a rambling tale, elegantly advises, 'Spare your parenthesis.' Within a line, his small stock of patience quite exhausted, he crudely demands, 'Well, and went you to a whore?' (V.i.21–3). In the linguistic descent from the Greek phraseology to the native vulgarity, the character is instantly exposed for our scrutiny. *The Devil is an Ass* abounds richly in exchanges like this, where Jonson's penetration of character and motive is effortlessly matched by his dramatic expertise in developing it.

At the other end of the scale, Jonson's talent for farce is equally given its full rein in this play. His fascination with disguise is evident in all his plays; but this is the first occasion on which he introduces a device deeply embedded in the English performance tradition if nowhere else, the 'drag' routine of a male actor impersonating a female. The situation in this play is the more highly charged as Witttipol in his female disguise both fends off the unwelcome affection of other women and takes the opportunity to court his

205

mistress when her husband has thought her safely disposed among a gaggle of women. Like the sequences in *As You Like It* where Orlando courts a boy playing a girl disguised as a boy pretending to be a girl, the situation is rich in sexual ambiguities that call for the playing of skilled and sophisticated actors to draw them out to the full.

Equally attractive and distinctive is the tone of the play, the result of a unique combination of old style with new subjects. Jonson concentrated his dramatic exposure on a critique of the most up-to-the-minute social abuses of his day, through the medium of some of the oldest characters and situations of English drama. The on-stage appearance of the devil, for instance, enlivens such antique Elizabethan interludes as *The Longer Thou Livest, The More Fool Thou Art* (? 1564) and *Like Will to Like* (1568), for example. Jonson's sources for this play include the old prose history of Friar Rush; Dekker's play *If This be not a Good Play, The Devil is in It*, which itself was founded upon the earlier prose account: the anonymous *Grim the Collier of Croydon* (1600); and *The Merry Devil of Edmonton* (1602), to which he jokingly alludes in the prologue.

Jonson makes this ancient and well-worn material work for him in two ways. On the first level, all the old devil and witchcraft literature is deeply and endearingly rural, which allows Jonson to establish an apposition between urban simplicity and rural cunning. The devil Pug, who ought to be the embodiment of all evil, can think of nothing more frightening as a demonstration of his powers than 'laming a poor cow or two', or 'entering a sow, to make her cast her farrow' (I.i.8—9). Even at the end of the play, after his induction into advanced wickedness on a human level, this remains his frame of reference:

> O call me home again, dear chief, and put me
> To yolking foxes, milking of he-goats,
> Pounding of water in a mortar . . . gathering all
> The leaves are fallen this autumn.
>
> (V.ii.1—5)

Although a devil and an accredited agent of Hell, within the context of the play's action, Pug is handled by Jonson like a country gull; he is cozened of his ring, fooled and beaten, and generally taken advantage of by quicker spirits just like the young shepherd in *The Winter's Tale*.

Pug's country-cousinship is shown in sharper perspective by being placed firmly in a city surrounding; as Jonson observed, 'our scene is

London', and this play loses nothing of Jonson's ability of the mature period to make this location work for him by contributing its colour and values to the world of the drama. Before the clod-hopping Pug has even come to earth, the old devil Iniquity has boasted:

> I will fetch thee a leap
> From the top of Paul's-steeple to the standard in Cheap:
> And lead thee a dance, through the streets without fail.
> We will survey the suburbs, and make forth our sallies,
> Down Petticoat Lane and up the Smock-Allies,
> To Shoreditch, Whitechapel, and so to St Katherine's.
>
> (I.i.55–61)

The use of old traditional material enables Jonson to create the 'village within the city' motif (later so useful to Dickens), and to play off one set of values against the other.

The second function of the introduction of these old themes and frameworks is that it permits Jonson to comment not only upon the characters and ideas in his play, but upon the process of play-making itself. As long ago as 1606 Dekker had written, ' 'Tis out of fashion to bring a devil on the [stage]' (*News from Hell*, p. 27). Yet Dekker himself, within a short time, brought the Devil on stage at the Red Bull in *If This be not a Good Play* (1607). As this suggests, presentation of demons, witches or magic on stage belonged not only to an older tradition, but one which Jonson viewed as shallow, crude and risible. Yet he utilized this simple-minded archaism to embody the main truths of his play.

What Jonson draws on, in short, is the continuity of the medieval and Renaissance traditions of dramatic exposition. The morality technique, for all its limitations, formed the appropriate artistic correlative for the thematic burden that Jonson was trying to discharge; it epitomized the transition between older modes of expression and newer states of consciousness. Jonson was building upon a firm traditional base, summed up by a contemporary commentator, John Gee, as follows:

> It was wont when an interlude was to be acted in a country town, the first question that a hob-nailed spectator made, before he would pay his penny to get in, was, whether there be a Devil and Fool in the play? And if the Fool get upon the Devil's back, and beat him till he roar, with his coxcomb, the play is complete.
>
> (*The Foot out the Snare*, 1624, p. 68)

207

Earlier in his career, Jonson himself had derogated this familar piece of ancient stage business as 'fools and devils as antique relics of barbarism' (dedication to *Volpone*, lines 79–80). His introduction of such character-types in *The Devil is an Ass* is done with the intention of giving a fresh ironic motivation to the whole business. In Jonson's play, the devil carries off no one at the end, but is himself transported back to Hell after being overcome by the superiority of human wickedness to anything that he can devise.

What remained, of course, was the implicit comment upon the inferiority of popular taste at the same time as Jonson was milking these popular conventions for everything they could afford in terms of vigour and impact. But Jonson here was not only making a literary satirical comment. As he used devils to mock the continuance of the general belief in devils, so he used the theme of illusion to key into one of his abiding preoccupations, the relation between the stage illusion and 'reality'. *The Devil is an Ass* is an ingenious and extended joke upon the dichotomy between the two. On the one hand Jonson presents the audience with a fantasy re-creation of Hell, with Lucifer and his devils; on the other, he insists on strict verisimilitude, with constant references to Fizdottrell going to a play 'today at the Blackfriars'. In pursuance of this line, Jonson cannot resist the incorporation of a series of theatrical in-jokes – he makes Meercraft run down the actors while singling out one of the boy players for special praise (II.viii.61–75).

As this implies, *The Devil is an Ass* is rooted in theatre, and must be experienced and assessed in that medium for its true quality to be appreciated. In Jonson's creation of the play, only the theatre can do justice to such moments of stagecraft as the visual impact of Wittipol's wooing Mistress Fitzdottrell out of one window while she listens to him at another. The public stage of Jonson's day may not have been the most appropriate arena for the airing of the social preoccupations that were concerning him at the time; and contemporary evidence indicates that others found his material offensive and inapposite, since the king himself 'desired [Jonson] to conceal it'. A later age, however, cannot but admire the tenacity of Jonson's purpose, and its successful translation into an exciting, funny, and thoroughly stage-worthy comedy.

When Jonson completed *The Devil is an Ass*, twenty years had passed since his first experiments in comical satire, years of steady progress, development and success. With this play, Jonson can be seen to be bringing a major artistic phase of his dramatic career to a close. In wider terms, too, Jonson had completed his main accomplishment – the Folio incarnates his claim to poetic immortality, and through it he made his subsequently irrefutable assertion of the literary status of the drama. With this Jonson drew his art together to a summation of sorts, in a conclusive display of the range of his mastery of form and language. There was to be no further effort for some time; the Laureate had staked his claim to the attention of posterity, and was content to await its judgement.

10

SHOWS! SHOWS! MIGHTY SHOWS!

In the years following the publication of the First Folio, and his rise to the status of *poeta regius*, Jonson conveys the impression of a man resting on his laurels — justifiably enough, considering how hard he had worked to earn them. There was no new artistic initiative from him during this period from 1619 to 1626; nor was there a continuation of all his 'wonted studies'. Most significantly, there were no plays at all; after the writing of *The Devil is an Ass* in 1616, Jonson embarked upon one of his periodical retreats from the world of the public theatre. This was to be the longest absence of his professional career — Jonson wrote nothing for the stage for ten years.

He was not, however, entirely cut off from drama and performance. His masque production continued unabated throughout these years, which saw the emergence of seven new masques. One of these, *The Masque of the Gypsies Metamorphosed*, was in fact put on three times, in three different versions; this did not mean an entire rewriting for Jonson on each occasion, but the changes were substantial, and involved him in a good deal of extra work. In addition to the formal masques, Jonson also wrote two entertainments for royalty and the aristocracy. These nine pieces taken together form the staple of Jonson's writing achievement over the period.

In between the preparation of these demanding public ceremonials, Jonson carried on what he thought of as the work he was born to do, the writing of poetry. The number of poems definitely ascribable to these years is almost twenty, more than three a year on average; but Jonson certainly wrote more than this, despite the time and care he gave to each one. The poems afford a record of his thoughts and activities, his intellectual and personal preoccupations. They also demonstrate the continuing applicability of Jonson's chosen motto, *tanquam explorator*; Jonson uses his poetry to search and to strive, as an instrument of discovery both technical and emotional, and as a vehicle for his hugely appetitive grasp on life. Their freshness, variety and sense of exploration show clearly that Jonson was merely resting his talent at this stage of his career, and was far from played out as might superficially appear.

The masques of these years equally demonstrate Jonson's continuing artistic vitality, differing from one another in length, form and tone. Of the seven, *The Masque of the Gypsies Metamorphosed* is the most unusual, first because it was commissioned for performance neither for the court, nor at the court; and then because it was very much longer than the others. The occasion was not the by now customary Christmas season, but a visit of the king to the house of his new favourite and creature, Buckingham; consequently the moving spirit and chief performer knew that he had to put on more than a few of the 'capers' with which he had rescued *Pleasure Reconciled to Virtue* from failure in 1618, to reward his royal patron for the recent dukedom.[1]

The Jonson masque commissioned by Buckingham formed a considerable evening's entertainment. It went on long into the night, and in its full and eventual form ran to nearly 1,500 lines in length. Although some of these lines were written for the revivals of the original masque and therefore would have replaced not augmented existing lines, *The Masque of the Gypsies Metamorphosed* is three or four times as long as most of Jonson's other masques and entertainments, and as such is less like any of these than a little play in its own right. It has from the first a non-court feel, jocular and familiar; this friendliness means that it never becomes offensive, despite the personal nature of the teasing.

The fullness and verve of this masque is the more surprising since Jonson had produced not the customary one, but three entertainments in the previous year. For the Twelfth Night masque of 1620, Jonson wrote *News from the New World Discovered in the Moon*; in the summer of the same year he created a christening celebration for the end of May, the *Entertainment at Blackfriars*, and also a masque written for King James, *Pan's Anniversary*. After the performance of the *Gypsies Metamorphosed* in 1621, the *Masque of Augurs* and that of *Time Vindicated to Himself and to his Honours* followed in 1622 and 1623 respectively. But 1624 brought a reversal for Jonson, and with it a break in the pattern. The collapse of the projected marriage between Prince Charles and the Infanta of Spain, to which Jonson had responded rather too enthusiastically in the composition of *Neptune's Triumph for the Return of*

Albion, meant that his masque was first put off and then abandoned entirely. There must have been some consolation for 'the King's poet' when he was commissioned to write for Prince Charles the country entertainment that became *The Masque of Owls* in July of 1624. But the production of *The Fortunate Isles and their Union* in January 1625, less than three months before King James died, brought to an end Jonson's career as the royal masque-maker – a career that had lasted for over twenty years.

During this penultimate stage of Jonson's masque-making his inspiration shows little sign of petering out. In each of these pieces Jonson continued to try to exploit and vary the limited resources of a restricted form. He further strove to retain the dramatic elements that he had introduced into the static masque original by injecting some life into the anti-masque or non-traditional masque elements. *News from the New World Discovered in the Moon*, for instance, opens with five characters, all speaking parts, whose choric opening modulates into naturalistic dialogue of great directness and impact:

HERALD 1: News, news, news!

HERALD 2: Bold and brave news!

HERALD 1: New as the night they are born in;

HERALD 2: Or the fantasies that begot them.

HERALD 1: Excellent news!

HERALD 2: Will you hear any news?

PRINTER: Yes, and thank you, too, sir; what's the price of them?

HERALD 1: Price, coxcomb! what price, but the price of your ears? As if any man used to pay for anything here!

(lines 1–11)

This device of low-life characters or simpletons wandering by chance into the high life of court festivities was one of Jonson's most serviceable starting-points for a masque. In *The Masque of Augurs* two years later, Jonson again relied upon these characters to get the show off the ground, characters unsophisticated in courtly ways, but as Londoners street-wise after their own fashion. Here, as Jonson tells the reader in an introductory stage direction, 'the presenters were from St Katherine's', a parish hard by the Tower of London, whose situation on the river and varied trades and activities afforded Jonson the personae of 'Notch, a brewer's clerk', 'Slug, a lighterman', 'Lady Alewife' and her two women, and 'Urson the bear-ward', with his amazing dancing bears. These city characters are made to display the time-honoured dauntlessness of the chirpy Cockney – as one of them observes of the court official, 'I am sure I am a greater man than he out of the court, and I have lost nothing of my size since I came into it' (lines 20–2), following this with a request to deal with someone of 'less authority and more wit'.

This sprightly use of the 'outsider' motif contrasts with the purpose Jonson puts it to in the preceding *Masque of the Gypsies Metamorphosed*; there, the outsiders are country clodhoppers, overflowing with good nature rather than bulging with brains. Later, within the same *Masque of Augurs*, Jonson engineered another contrast and variation on the same theme, when low comedy characters give way to the high figures of allegorical abstraction with which the masque concludes. Jonson's range of technical responses to an old and conventional device is ample illustration of his continued skill and vivacity in creation.

The Masque of Augurs holds considerable formal interest in terms of Jonson's masque-making. As this suggests, Jonson reverted to his earlier style in the contrivance of an elaborately mythological ending. The whole piece is more self-consciously classical than most of Jonson's more recent productions; the central conceit, the divination of the future from the scrutiny and assessment of portents, in particular the behaviour of birds, is borrowed from the Romans. In this, and in the heavy panoply of textual notation with which the masque was equipped for publication, *The Masque of Augurs* strongly resembles *Hymenaei* of 1606, and suggests Jonson harking back to a previous success.

The erudite and conscientious scholar, however, is only one of Jonson's many voices. In his work for the public theatre, for instance, he spoke very differently. In addition, working for the court meant a perennial tension between the dramatic material which Jonson's imagination so readily provided and shaped, and that proper to the masque. In *Time Vindicated to Himself and to his Honours* (1623) Jonson attempted a marriage between the sort of personal satiric attack that had marked a much earlier phase of his career, and the 'high fantastical' conclusion of Saturn, Venus, Cupid, Diana, Hippolytus, 'their Votaries' and a Chorus. There is some discrepancy between Jonson's different materials, which an overall classical gloss cannot dismiss. Jonson seized upon the opportunity of the time to use the anti-masque as a personal attack upon the rival but inferior satirist George Wither, and his castigation was unmerciful: Withèr was a

213

> . . . wretched impostor,
> Creature of glory, mountebank of wit,
> Self-loving braggart . . .
>
> (lines 96–8)

The victim of this attack was finally assured that 'Fame doth sound no trumpet / To such vain, empty fools'. Even the shrouding of Wither's identity under the classical name of 'Chronomastix' ('Whipper of the Time') could not obscure the connection of this type of writing with the 'War of the Theatres', so many years before; nor provide a link with the purely allegorical and mythological figures of the main part of the masque.

The Wither episode, however, although problematical in its own time (contemporary comment recorded that Jonson was 'likely to hear further' from the authorities for daring to introduce the topic) went to indicate Jonson's recurrent difficulty in remaining within the confines of any given form. This natural, temperamental artistic difficulty could only be maximized when the form itself was as rigid and limited as was the masque. All Jonson's masques of this phase show the constant change and experimentalism that proceeded from his dissatisfaction with the masques both as they stood and as he was making them. The ill-fated *Neptune's Triumph for the Return of Albion* (1624), aborted before performed, had essayed a more low-key opening than Jonson commonly employed, a naturalistic duologue in which a poet and a cook discuss the relative merits of their callings as confectioners to royalty and ticklers of sophisticated palates. This simple prologue was repeated in *The Fortunate Isles and their Union* (1625), which incorporated much of the material of its unperformed predecessor, but with a new inflection. Here, the duologue takes place between one mythological and one realistic character, as 'an airy spirit of Jove' engages 'a poor student' in debate. Despite surface dissimilarities, the openings of these two masques are structurally identical as Jonson deploys two voices only, before leading into the fuller and more rounded masque proper.

Jonson's fluctuating sense of the capacity of the masque form is nowhere more evident than in his handling of the anti-masque. The greater stress upon dramatic, and particularly upon comedy intrusions, inevitably strengthened the anti-masque in apposition to the masque proper. Jonson clearly clung on to his original concept of the anti-masque as a strong contrast of the grotesque, the ridiculous even, with the formal ceremonial. *Pan's Anniversary* (1620) offered an anti-masque danced by the 'Boys of Boetia', a region legendary in classical times for stupidity and clumsiness; *The Masque of Augurs* provided two anti-masques, one of bears, and the other 'a perplexed dance of straying and deformed pilgrims, taking several paths, till with the opening of the light above, and breaking forth of Apollo, they were all frighted away' (lines 270–3).

Yet for all his evident fertility in devising strange new anti-masque ideas, Jonson held certain fundamental reservations about this device, reservations that characteristically enough he used the masque form itself to discuss. Jonson's critical view of this glamorous but flimsy form is hinted at, to say the least, in the character of Vangoose, the 'rare artist' and 'projector of masques' who appears in *The Masque of Augurs*. To the reasonable enquiry, 'What has all this to do with our masque?', Vangoose is made to reply:

> O Sir, all the better, for an antimasque; de more absurd it be, and vrom de purpose, it be ever all de better. If it go vrom de nature of de ting, it is de more art.
>
> (lines 265–8)

The multiple levels of irony here, including the implicit self-deprecation, are too subtle to be picked up all at once, especially in the speed of performance. But Jonson reverted to and developed the point in *Neptune's Triumph for the Return of Albion*, in an important exchange between the Poet and the Cook concerning the arts of court concoctions:

> COOK: But where's your antimasque now, all this while?
> I hearken after them.
> POET: Faith, we have none.
> COOK: None?
> POET: None, I assure you, neither do I think them
> A worthy part of presentation,
> Being things so heterogene to all device,
> Mere by-works, and at best outlandish nothings.
>
> (lines 215–20)

The immediate and vehement attack of the Cook on this 'ignorantly simple' declaration of the Poet, with his offer to produce 'a metaphorical dish' of his own out of the kitchen by way of anti-masque as an illustration of 'how a good wit may jump', does nothing to undermine the poet's statement. It is further given authority within the masque by being put into the mouth of 'the Poet'. This

215

character is certainly too complex to be summed up as no more than the mouthpiece of the real 'poet', Jonson himself; but among the objects of Jonson's ironical reflection in this tightly packed little sequence, there is no reason to think that he exempted himself from satiric self-scrutiny. His self-presentation in this masque may seem indeed to be unduly harsh to later audiences unaware of Jonson's artistic situation at the time. In response to a query from the Cook as to where he fits into the King's establishment, Jonson's Poet sardonically categorizes himself as 'the most unprofitable of his servants, I, sir, the Poet. A kind of Christmas engine; one that is used at least once a year for a trifling instrument of wit, or so' (lines 34–6).

Such moments as this, coupled with Jonson's perpetual variation in search of the magic combination of the excitingly new with the comfortingly conventional, hint at a writer not entirely at home with the form he is using. *The Masque of the Gypsies Metamorphosed* is unusual in being an unchallengeable and harmonious success; written in an easy and warm manner for a known group of performers and spectators, it capitalizes upon the 'in-joke' situation to produce a delightful entertainment, not without bite but free of strain. The picture of the newly made Duke of Buckingham and his family (whose comet-like rise and consequent engrossment of rewards and perquisites had caused much comment) as a pack of thieving gypsies, is clearly not without some satiric purchase. But in the context of the performance, where the beloved handsome 'Steeny' himself represents the Captain of the Gypsies in a private show before the doting master from whom he has received these good things, then the aspersion takes on the nature of well-judged teasing on Jonson's part, a piece of cheek amply balanced by the full and extended praise elsewhere in the masque lavished upon King James, his wit and his judgement.

In other masques of the period, however, Jonson can be seen pushing his material in directions it will not so readily take. The conceit of the 'new world discovered in the moon', for instance, of the 1620 masque, could be interpreted in a variety of ways. Where earlier Jonson would have handled this in a straightforward allegorical mode, as he did with the concept of the Niger in the masques *Of Blackness* and *Of Beauty*, for instance, now the fantasy was developed along more discriminating and satirical lines to provide a reflection of life on earth; fantasy became a critical rather than an allegorical instrument. Again, the enchanting world of the timeless pastoral in *Pan's Anniversary* is made to give way to the low comedy contrast of the tooth-drawer, the corn-cutter, the bellows-mender and the tinderbox man, with the incidental satire on 'a subtle shred-bearded sir, that hath been a politician but is now a maker of mouse-traps, a great engineer yet [still]' (lines 127–8). From these realistic and down-to-earth jibes, Jonson did not always achieve an effortless transition to the higher realms of ritualized adoration which remained the prime function of the masque:

CHORUS.

The courtly strife is done, it should appear,
Between the youths and beauties of the year;
We hope that now these lights will know their sphere,
And strive hereafter to shine ever here.
Like brightest planets, still to move
In the eye of Time, and orbs of Love.

(*Time Vindicated to Himself
and to his Honours*, lines 450–5)

Stylistically, too, there is a faint sense of unease in Jonson's masque-writing at this time. On the immediate level it provides a constant parade of Jonson's technical virtuosity, since he never repeats himself once, and in each masque experiments with some new way of opening the masque, of unfolding the conceit with all its appositional strands and finally of uniting and elevating the disparate elements to the requisite climax. *News from the New World Discovered in the Moon* makes its 385-line journey through 300 lines of prose dialogue interspersed only with four short songs. *The Masque of the Gypsies Metamorphosed*, in strong contrast, moves from a verse prologue through low-life prose, song and comic verse to a flowing musical climax. Jonson also allowed himself to indulge his running preoccupation with the abuse of language, as he makes the Gypsy Jackman say:

If here we be a little obscure, it is our pleasure, for rather than we will offer to be our own interpreters, we are resolved not to be understood. Yet if any man doubt of the significancy of the language, we refer him to the third volume of reports set forth by the learned in the laws of canting, and published in the gypsy tongue.

(lines 106–11)

Jonson's skill and command is evidence throughout the texture of these pieces, often in touches which must have been almost too subtle

217

for the spectators to absorb on first hearing. The Curious, for instance, in *Time Vindicated to Himself and to his Honours*, are presented by Jonson as petty, degraded creatures whose nature makes them contemptible:

> The curious are ill-natured, and like flies
> Seek Time's corrupted parts to blow upon.
>
> (lines 266–7)

But Jonson does not merely dictate this characteristic; he demonstrates it through the use of short broken verse lines whose brevity and triviality indicate the essential meanness and limitation of the Curious:

EARS: What? what? Is it worth our ears?
EYES: Or eyes?
NOSE: Or noses?
EYES: For we are curious, Fame; indeed, the Curious.
      We come to spy.
EARS: And hearken.
NOSE: And smell out.

> (lines 6–12)

The masques and entertainments of this period abound in arresting moments like this, where Jonson strove for and attained the appropriate vehicle for his varied effects. Yet there remains a disturbing sense of restlessness in the constant shift between prose, blank verse, heroic couplets, short rhyming verses and song stanzas. The attentive reader is left with the impression that the poet had not ultimately found the linguistic medium to satisfy the artistic demands he was making of it, and of himself. No matter what successes Jonson achieved in naturalistic prose, in heroic abstraction, in varying line lengths or short repetitive comic doggerel, he was certain to try something different in the next masque. Who could fault the lyric sweetness of the opening songs of *Pan's Anniversary*?

NYMPH II.

> Strew, strew the glad and smiling ground
> With every flower, yet not confound
> The primrose drop, the Spring's own spouse,
> Bright day's-eyes, and the lips of cows,
>   The garden-star, the Queen of May,
>   The rose, to crown the holy-day.

NYMPH III.

Drop, drop you violets, change your hues,
Now red, now pale, as lovers use,
And in your death go out as well
As when you lived, unto the smell;
    That from your odour, all may say
    This is the shepherds' holy-day.

Yet despite the Arcadian elegance of this (contrast it with the
comedy of vulgar dispute between the dry- and the wet-nurse in the
Entertainment at Blackfriars (1620), for instance) and Jonson's ability
to range through a variety of tones and moods, when all is said and
done the best of these moments remained always literary in temper.
As such, they were inescapably at the mercy of the other elements in
an essentially non-literary form. Despite the consistent strength and
skill of Jonson's writing, his masque success was rendered uneven
through the simple fact that he was not always able to come up with a
strong visual central concept that was rich in its power of suggestion
and spectacular in effect. *The Masque of the Gypsies Metamorphosed*, for
example, works splendidly in visual terms; the 'tattered nation' of
'tawny faces' afforded an exotic disguise full of raffish glamour for the
silken exquisites of the court to assume; and the gypsies' practices
gave the hint for a strange and startling opening:

Enter
A Gypsy, leading a horse laden with five little children bound in a trace
of scarves upon him. A second, leading another horse laden with stolen
poultry, etc. The first leading gypsy speaks, being the Jackman.

Room for the five Princes of Egypt, mounted all upon one
horse. . . . Gaze upon them as on the offspring of Ptolomy,
begotten upon several Cleopatras in their several countries . . .
                                                    (lines 51–61)

But often Jonson's notions do not translate so well into eye-
catching show. The spectacle of augury, however learnedly argued,
does not supply the feast for the eye that it may for the mind. In other
masques of the period, the vivid and memorable moments are
non-verbal; they were provided by the 'antimasque of tumblers and
jugglers brought in by the Cat and the Fiddle, who make sport with
the Curious and drive them away', in *Time Vindicated to Himself and to
his Honours* (lines 261–3). Jonson was certainly capable of thinking in

visual terms; a relatively late piece, the 1624 *Masque of Owls*, is built around the notion of an eccentric presenter mounted upon a hobby-horse making a series of six owls pop up and display themselves to the spectators. But as with the Printer, the Chronicler and the Factor of *News from the New World Discovered in the Moon*, Jonson's starting-point is all too frequently drawn from the world of the word, rather than that of the image. Consider how literary *The Fortunate Isles* is: not only does the alchemical and supernatural material lean heavily on Jonson's own *The Alchemist* and *The Devil is an Ass*; all the characters in the anti-masque are literary figures like Skelton, and Jonson even writes in imitation of Skelton's verse form.

But the literary, however high its level, does not count for much in terms of masque success. Jonson's masques became less and less the frameworks for the dancing that had stimulated their origin and remained their *raison d'être*; while musically they became very much more elaborate as the musical knowledge of both practitioners and audiences became more sophisticated. *The Masque of Augurs*, despite Jonson's battery of classical learning, depended for its effect at its key moments upon a greatly increased use of music, and in particular the substitution of plain speech for recitative. Jonson generously credited the music-makers for their part, and cannot have been blind to the take-over of the spoken by the sung elements, and in particular the reliance upon music to achieve the required elevation of the ending.

Ultimately, however, the threat to Jonson's position as masque-maker did not come from the musicians, who still required a libretto for their work and could not mount a masque from their music alone. Jonson's contribution was being overshadowed by that of his colleague Inigo Jones, the brilliance of whose 'shows' was beginning to make Jonson's endeavours look pale. In *Time Vindicated to Himself and to his Honours*, for instance, Jonson gave the spectators 'the scene opening', changing, vanishing, becoming a wood, and so on, with apparent ease. This masque also had two elaborate anti-masques; terse stage directions minimize or negate the prime importance of this. Jonson himself indicated the shape of things to come in a defensive, but not ungenerous, comment on one of the copies of *The Masque of Augurs*:

> For the expression of this, I must stand: the invention was divided betwixt Mr Jones and me. The scene, which your eye judges, was wholly his, and worthy his place of the King's

Surveyor and architect, full of noble antiquity and high present-
ment.

(HS VII, 625)

Jonson's own awareness of the need for balance in performance is
shown in his comment through the Herald in *News from the New World
Discovered in the Moon*, that '"Tis time to exercise their eyes, for their
ears begin to be aweary' (lines 291–2). On the other side, Jones's work
was not always so ingenious and elaborate; *Neptune's Triumph* opens
very simply with two pillars framing a tableau. But in the gradual
ascendancy of the spectacular was incorporated the literary decline.
Jonson's efforts both of theory and practice, his attempts to use the
masque form in a Platonic way to make its forms symbolic of a higher
reality, were superseded by the glory of 'shows! shows! mighty
shows!' The soul of the masque, on which Jonson had placed so much
importance, gave way to a stress upon the novelty of the device.

This was, of course, one of the factors which made the masque
increasingly moribund; a play can be seen ten times, with a sense of
discovery on each occasion, but once a moving mountain, floating
island, or opening cloud has been seen, the effect is consumed like
lightning at the moment of impact. This was the source of Jonson's
divergence from Jones; in a dispute that was as much theoretical as
personal, it proceeded from Jonson's fixed concept of the structure of
the masque, and the relation within that structure of the various
parts. To Jonson, it was the poet's invention alone that could provide
the unifying force and spiritual significance, and that alone could save
the masque from becoming a hollow spectacle.

Jones, not accepting this analysis, found pretentious Jonson's
efforts to dignify what to him were 'nothing else but pictures with
light and motion'.[2] Jones's own professional standards were high – his
machines were brilliantly innovative, and he brought a wide assortment of skills and abilities to his side of the task. But he could not see
why masques need be any more than colours, scenes, lights, music
and dancing. Jonson had put up a splendid fight on behalf of his view
of the masque – it is no exaggeration of partisanship to say that all the
great and lasting achievements in the masque were his – but he was
losing now, and fast.

Given the adverse circumstances that for Jonson attended the writing
of plays and masques, it is hardly surprising that he continued to
solace himself with the regular production of his beloved poetry. For

this he had no need to await a commission from a captious and exigent patron, or strive to satisfy the demands of an audience he despised. He was not at the mercy of temporary fashion, nor of the shortcomings of colleagues. He could choose and fashion his material in any way he pleased; for poetry was his created universe, in which he was both god and man.

Yet whatever the breadth of his range, his starting-point was very often himself. Jonson used his poetry as an instrument of self-definition, but without a hint of the self-conscious or pompous. Consider the little poem which Jonson sent back to his Caledonian host, Drummond of Hawthornden, after he returned to England:

'My Picture Left in Scotland'

I now think love is rather deaf than blind,
    For else it could not be
        That she
Whom I adore so much should so slight me,
    And cast my love behind;
I'm sure my language to her was as sweet,
    And every close did meet
In sentence of as subtle feet.
    As hath the youngest he
That sits in shadow of Apollo's tree.

(*Underwood* 9)

This subtle piece, with its multiplicity of interlocking ironies, is the quintessence of Jonson's later poetic mode. Although on one level writing only of his own thoughts and actions, he was in fact using the self as a springboard, from which he moved off to the discussion of other topics; here, youth and age, the nature of love, and the making of poetry.

Jonson was of course following hallowed classical precedents, both in the self-reflexive nature of his verse and the employment of the medium to comment upon other relations, especially social and moral. Both these considerations meet in the relation between poet and patron, which Jonson debates at full in the grave and lengthy 'Epistle to Sir Edward Sackville', *Underwood* 13. The extensive borrowings in this poem from Seneca are not alone responsible for the Senecan morality of the finished result. Jonson's attitude to his patron has nothing of the humble or servile about it; even as he sternly castigates 'proud, hard, or ungrateful men' he conveys his sense of an honourable transaction between the giver and the recipient, where the generosity of the patron is matched by the worth of the poet, in an exchange that demonstrates the magnanimity of both and dignifies their endeavours:

> For benefits are owed with the same mind
> As they are done, and such returns they find . . .
> You cannot doubt but I, who freely know
> This good from you, as freely will it owe.

Such a meeting of true minds, in Jonson's analysis, offers a microcosm of the ideal in society. The true subject of this poem, then, is not merely the 'courtesy' of Sackville, even though this gracious and ancient attribute is understood in its fullest sense. It establishes the standards by which such qualities may find their expression between members of society. As such it is more than a simple epistle; it is a small sermon on the 'skill / Or science of discerning good and ill', and on the art of living by the light of this discovery.

Jonson's poem to Sackville is in the nature of a quiet duologue; the poet outlines his ideas and reflections, and creates the presence of the benefactor within the poem by means of his favourite technique of direct address: 'If, Sackville . . .', 'you cannot doubt . . .', 'No!', 'you, sir, know it well. . . .' Elsewhere, however, Jonson's verse strongly indicates its kinship with his plays, as he fills it with striking *dramatis personae*. Poetry thus becomes for Jonson a theatre of the imagination where he can stage his figures without interference or restraint. Here he marshals a Morality pageant of the craven and contemptible who are so 'bogged in vices' that all hope of honour passes them by:

> Look on the ambitious man, and see him nurse
> His unjust hopes with praises begged, or (worse)
> Bought flatteries, the issue of his purse,
> Till he become both their and his own curse!
> Look on the false and cunning man, that loves
> No person, nor is loved . . .
> See the grave, sour and supercilious sir –
> In outward face, but, inward, light as fur
> Or feathers – lay his fortune out to show,
> Till envy wound or maim it at a blow!
> (*Underwood* 15, lines 11–22)

In the bold line-drawing of the character sketches, in the imagery of fur and feathers even, this recalls Jonson's writing in the vein of comical satire; the tone rather darker than before, and not so shrill, but displaying its descent in both matter and manner.

Yet it would be inaccurate to imply that satire was a mode Jonson had left behind. Two of these pieces are expressly designated as 'A Satirical Shrub' in the 'underwood' of Jonson's verses, and 'A Little Shrub Growing By'. The second of the two sounds off in Jonson's most harsh and Martial tones, mingling moral reproof with physical disgust in a way that anticipates Pope's technique of a century later:

> Ask not to know this man. If fame should speak
> His name in any metal, it would break.
> Two letters were enough the plague to tear
> Out of his grave, and poison every ear.
> A parcel of court-dirt, a heap and mass
> Of all vice hurled together; there he was
> Proud, false, and treacherous, vindictive, all
> That thought can add; unthankful, the lay-stall
> Of putrid flesh alive; of blood the sink;
> And so I leave to stir him, lest he stink.
>
> *(Underwood* 21)

Of the other objects of Jonson's satirical scourge, chief among them were women; and the scornful *Underwood* 20, the 'satirical shrub' on 'a woman's friendship', rapidly moves on from the unlikelihood of this possibility to a general arraignment of the sex on the grounds that 'their whole life was wickedness, though weaved / of many colours' (lines 10–11). The poem builds up to a climax of rabid anti-feminism which makes an amusing comment by contrast with the rueful adoration expressed in 'My Picture Left in Scotland':

> I could forgive her being proud, a whore,
> Perjured and painted, if she were no more:
> But she is such as she might yet forestall
> The devil, and be the damning of us all.
>
> (lines 21–4)

Both here and elsewhere there is a remarkable continuity both of attitude and expression in the sexual themes first dealt with in the *Epigrams* – demurely and disingenuously described by Jonson as 'my chaste book'. The same preoccupation with the loose morals of the fashionable world boils up in Jonson's stigmatizing of the 'court-filly' who thinks it smart to prostitute herself to the 'lace and starch' of 'Stallion'; the close-textured jumbling of Jonson's favourite clothes metaphors with those drawn from the animal world of uncontrolled sexual service, demonstrates his rumbling indignation. Later in the same poem (*Underwood* 15) Jonson took up some hints from Juvenal to push his farmyard vision of womankind to almost absurd lengths; his treacherous whores 'firk, and jerk', as if 'a breeze were gotten in their tail':

> And laugh, and measure thighs, then squeak, spring, itch,
> Do all the tricks of a salt lady bitch.

> (lines 75–6)

These coarse and vulgar lines do not, however, undermine the self-portrait of Jonson as a lover that so touchingly peeps forth in the *Underwood* (not only 9, but also 40, 41, 42), and also in the ungathered verse that can definitely be related to this period. They are simply further demonstration, if any were needed, of Jonson's enormous range of poetic personae. Contrast the strength and assurance of this satire, with the almost tentative poetic stance expressed in the 'Epitaph on Master Philip Gray': 'If such men as he could die / What surety of life have thou and I?' Elsewhere in this collection we see Jonson as 'the king's poet' paying his dues to royalty (*Underwood* 48) and turning off an equally complimentary but quite different ceremonial greeting to Lord Bacon (*Underwood* 51); these courtly gestures are balanced by two tributes of friendship as Jonson used his verses to give those of others a literary send-off (*Ungathered Verse* 24 and 25). As with the *Epigrams* Jonson comes before the reader as one equally at home in high or low life, as friend or enemy, as lover or as hater of humanity; as, in short, 'the poet'.

Yet by the time of this later collection of poems, undated save for their posthumous publication in the two-volume Second Folio of 1640–1, 'the poet' has both shifted and deepened his centre of poetic interest. The exploration in this later phase is rather of the worlds of thought and work, than of the busy social milieu of the earlier days. The crowded canvas of the *Epigrams*, with characters freely and swiftly drawn, has given way to longer, and more reflective pieces, like the epistles and elegies. Jonson's technique now is to give the reader the familiar scene, but to set himself apart within it. *Underwood* 42, 'An Elegy', for example, takes the familiar starting-point of the poet's sensibility, here expressed as a defiant assertion of the individual and unique in a happy combination of personal and classical streams of thought:

> Let me be what I am: as Virgil cold,
> As Horace fat, or as Anacreon old.
>
> (lines 1–2)

Yet this individualism was located within a comparative framework whose points of reference are all great poets of the classical era. Similarly in social matters, in a tone of voice curiously evocative of *Epicene*) Jonson was concerned to display the paradox that he is at once familiarly involved in court and city, yet at the same time critically detached from them:

> It is a rhyming age, and verses swarm
> At every stall; the city cap's a charm.
> But I who live, and have lived, twenty year
> Where I may handle silk as free and near
> As any mercer, or the whale-bone man
> That quilts those bodies I have leave to span;
> Have eaten with the Beauties and the wits
> And braveries of court, and felt their fits
> Of love and hate, and came so nigh to know
> Whether their faces were their own, or no
> It is not likely I should now look down
> Upon a velvet petticoat, or gown.
>
> (lines 27–38)

In these lines Jonson's description of the making of fine clothes and the painting of faces alerts the reader to consider the whole question of art and artifice; this ties in with the main theme of the poem, that of the poet as maker, and his relation to his outside world. Jonson's treatment here fuses present and past, as he picks out the details of the fashionable scene, yet places his participation in it in the past.

This impression of Jonson's heightened awareness of, and willed separation from, the busy throng of his previous characters, both real and fictional, is reinforced by a reading of what is undoubtedly the most considerable piece of these years, 'The Execration upon Vulcan' (*Underwood* 43). The nominal occasion for this poem was the destruction by fire of Jonson's study, and all that it contained, in November 1623. This blow, however, provided the impetus for a thorough review of all his works, past and present. These productions of one who, as a poet, is dedicated to 'making', are ironically contrasted with

226

the 'works' of the god of destruction; certain famous fires are brought forward as Vulcan's *chefs d'oeuvre*. This notion of interpreting a random disaster as the conscious handiwork of Vulcan enables Jonson to interlock a series of comments upon ruin and decay, with a summary of the powerlessness of humankind to avert or resist them.

Yet underlying the accounts of the fall of 'the Globe, the glory of the Bank', underlying also the relation of all of Jonson's that perished in his fire –

> I dare not say 'a body', but some parts
> There were, of search and mastery in the arts

– lies the proud claim that the work of the poet will outlast time and all temporal vicissitudes. This emerges through the humorous personalization of the fire as a deliberate visitation by Vulcan on Jonson: 'And why to me this, thou lame lord of fire?' The poet wryly acknowledges Vulcan's superiority in brute force, 'thus to devour / So many my years' labours, in an hour'. But where the poet has his muse, and is beloved of Apollo, Vulcan remains a crude joke and butt of the divinities:

> Thou woo Minerva! Or to wit aspire!
> 'Cause thou canst halt, with us, in arts and fire!
>   (lines 109–10)

This strong central conceit, of a tussle between the poet and the god, is worked out right through the poem until the last defiant insult – 'Thy wife's pox on thee, and Bess Broughton's, too!' As in the best moments of Jonson's drama, his bedrock of classical knowledge combines with and enriches a reference of more recent growth to the advantage of each. The satirical casting of the goddess of love as a rotten whore equivalent to a well-known contemporary of Jonson's gives the poem a powerful and explosive climax whose reverberations linger in the mind. This wonderful poem has proved too long, at 216 lines, to be readily anthologized. It is also tightly argued and densely packed with a multitude of allusions, personal, literary, classical and modern, and both these factors have inhibited its wider knowledge and appreciation. But the confident fusing of the high and low, the mundane and divine, the coarse and the elevated, the personal and the general, is not excelled anywhere in Jonson's poetry.

The conversion of what was in life a great loss, into a poetic victory, fully exemplifies Jonson's profound and cherished views of the role of poetry and the obligations of the poet. These themes are rehearsed once more, but in a different tone, in the 'Epistle Answering to One that Asked to be Sealed of the Tribe of Ben' (*Underwood* 47). This compelling piece knots up Jonson's personal, social, literary and poetical preoccupations into one minor masterpiece of brooding commentary upon himself, his position, and his relation to others, written under the smart of rejection as masque-maker for a great royal celebration. The poem moves through various stages of argument in which Jonson reviews his position. His reflections upon being passed over, early in 1624, for the ceremonial reception then under way for Prince Charles's proposed bride the Spanish Infanta, supply a valuable counterweight to the public eulogy of the court and court proceedings which Jonson more generally felt called upon to offer:

> . . . that's a blow by which in time I may
>   Lose all my credit with my Christmas clay
> And animated porcelain of the court;
>   Aye, and for this neglect, the coarser sort
> Of earthen jars may there molest me too.
>
> (lines 51–5)

The metaphors of fragility, brittleness and artifice which Jonson uses, in designating his court patrons and followers as 'animated porcelain', indicate his judgement of their intrinsic worthlessness. Pursuing the image of vessels of a finer or baser material, Jonson comments with a fine delusive self-irony in the first line:

> Well, with mine own frail pitcher, what to do
>   I have decreed; keep it from waves and press,
> Lest it be jostled, cracked, made nought, or less;
>   Live to that point I will, for which I'm man,
> And dwell as in my centre as I can,
>   Still looking to, and ever loving Heaven;
> With reverence using all the gifts thence given.
>
> (lines 56–62)

As always, Jonson's declaration of personal integrity settles upon 'that one talent, which 'tis death to hide', as Milton was to put it in the next generation, the gift of poetry.

One conclusion is inescapable, that the hidden imperative in all the poems of Jonson, was to comment upon the making of poems. From the delicate punning of *Underwood* 9, 'My Picture Left in Scotland', on 'the subtle feet' of poetry, and the 'sweet' language of his verse, we sense 'the poet' standing behind, and at a distance from, the lover. In many similar touches in this collection we are reminded of the poet's conscious attempt to engage our awareness of the mechanism of a poet:

> Reader, stay;
> And if I had no more to say
> But 'Here doth lie, till the last day,
> All that is left of Philip Gray',
> It might your patience richly pay . . .
>
> *(Underwood* 16)

From the bold, broken-line opening, with the challenge that it issues to the reader, we are drawn into Jonson's conception of every poem (even one as short as this) as a mutually active transaction between its maker and its fortunate recipient.

Jonson's deep consciousness that every poem is as much about the writing of it as it is about the nominal subject, is one of the factors that lend even his so-called 'occasional pieces' an enduring weight and significance. It is also a measure of the importance that Jonson attached to poetic style. The majority of these pieces take the form of the rolling pairs of noble couplets that Jonson in this era made his own, and which, he told Drummond, he valued above any other verse form. But this is not to say that he dismissed other verse forms as beyond his ability or notice. A frequent resort in his masque-writing was the rhyming quadrameter, the rhythm traditionally associated with sub- or superhuman creatures, and hence invariably pressed into service for the delineation of witches, fairies, or the like. But Jonson never elsewhere used it to such purpose as in the 'Epitaph on Master Vincent Corbett', where the simple trotting beat of the verse line aptly catches up the unaffected simplicity of the subject of the poem:

> Dear Vincent Corbett, who so long
> Had wrestled with diseases strong,
> That though they did possess each limb,
> Yet he broke them, ere they could him,
> With the just canon of his life;
> A life that knew nor noise, nor strife . . .
> His mind as pure and neatly kept
> As were his nurseries . . .
>
> (lines 7–16)

Inevitably not all Jonson's verse is as smooth and successful as this. The simple artlessness of this mode is a rare one for Jonson; generally

229

he prefers the art that displays art, even at the cost of appearing strained and effortful. He courts disaster when he turns his Latin tropes straight into English, a medium that will not readily accommodate its habitual contractions and elisions. At such moments Jonson produces a stiff hybrid and compacted diction, clotted with undigested Latinisms, which bears little resemblance to the natural shape and movement of the parent language:

> Or if he did it not to succour me
> But by mere chance, for interest, or to free
> Himself of farther trouble, or the weight
> Of pressure, like one taken in a strait?
> All this corrupts the thanks; less hath he won
> That puts it in his debt book ere it be done . . .
> *(Underwood* 13, lines 29–34)

Such episodes, however, are rare. While Jonson's verse is never limpid in its clarity – he always retains the requirement that the reader come at least half way to meet him by making some effort – nevertheless the characteristic style of the later period is one of great directness. Jonson does not cease to employ his poetry as the true arena for the airing of his concerns, of all kinds. He does, however, search for, experiment with, and discover, increasingly effective ways of communicating them.

For Jonson the years from 1619 to 1625 were relatively free from the pressures to produce in artistic fields that he did not freely choose; and his continuance of his poetry demonstrates his desire to proceed with the production of what he could enjoy and value, rather than what he had to do. This almost fallow time, however, was not to last; a combination of constraints were coming into play to disturb Jonson's peace and his self-chosen role of 'poet' above all.

HE PRAYS YOU'LL NOT PREJUDGE
HIS PLAY FOR ILL

The closing years of Jonson's life saw a crucial change in his professional pattern. As King James's poet laureate he had been able to take life in a leisurely way, producing at last only the sort of work he deemed compatible with his position and status. With the accession of Charles I in 1625 the old poet had to begin again under a new master, with new customs and fashions at court. A growing insecurity, together with a steadily deteriorating financial situation, drove Jonson to resume working in what should have been his retirement. In the eight years following 1626 he wrote four full-length plays, *The Staple of News*, *The New Inn*, *The Magnetic Lady* and *A Tale of a Tub*. Although these were the years of Jonson's final defeat as court masque-maker by Inigo Jones, he nevertheless also received commissions for four masques in this time. Even under such pressure, Jonson did not stop writing his occasional verse – now more than ever he needed to make his poems his friends, as Horace said – and he was, additionally, engaged in various prose ventures. After the disastrous fire of 1623 Jonson was provoked to try to re-create for posterity his lost work on English grammar while he also continued to use the commonplace book method of collecting and refining those insights and pronouncements that became his critical handbook, *Timber, or Discoveries*.

Yet despite their variety and commitment, Jonson's late-flowering endeavours traditionally failed to please. The four plays in particular suffered irreparably from Dryden's branding them as Jonson's 'dotages', although they nowhere display the ineffable feebleness that this verdict implies. On the contrary, Jonson's writing at the end of his career does not soften into slackness, but becomes more strenuous and taut. The control becomes more rigid and mechanical, but it results too in unexpected flickers of nervous brilliance. Until very recently, modern theatrical revivals of Elizabethan and Jacobean plays have tended to avoid Jonson's later and lesser drama; without any life in the theatre they are therefore condemned to be experienced only in the study, where they are at their greatest disadvantage.

Yet no real grasp on Jonson is possible without an understanding of this phase of his creative career. These four plays demonstrate above all how much Jonson had been and remained a craftsman of great singleness of purpose. His methods and standards varied little with the variations of form that he employed. For the basis of all his concepts and practices was essentially intellectual, a faith in the rational and controlling powers that experience had done nothing to shake. His dramatic pattern, never remarkably flexible, had begun to harden as he clung ever more fiercely to the structuring and schematizing of characters and dramatic action in an over-cerebral and mechanistic way. Nowhere else in Jonson's drama is his audience so aware of the dramatist's criteria, his presence, and his intentions.

This declension into the didactic expressed itself dramatically in a move towards allegory. Where previously Jonson had felt able to represent the greed and cupidity of the characters in *Volpone* or *The Devil is an Ass*, then leave the spectators to draw their own conclusions about the evils of money as a motivating force, now in *The Staple of News* he had to bring on 'Lady Pecunia' courted by many suitors to demonstrate the corruption of men's attempts to attract and obtain 'Lady Money'. The symbolism is baldly stated and obtrusively paraded within the play; Jonson is to be seen reverting to his old mode of the comical satires by making his moral too painfully clear. Here the avaricious Pennyboy Senior dilates to Lady Pecunia upon her power and importance:

> . . . your services, my princely lady,
> Cannot with too much zeal of rights be done,
> They are so sacred . . .
> Yourself scarce understands your proper powers.
> They are almighty, and that we, your servants,
> That have the honour there to stand so near you,
> Know; and can use too. All this nether world
> Is yours. You command it and do sway it,
> The honour of it and the honesty,
> The reputation, ay, and the religion . . .

Is Queen Pecunia's. For that style is yours,
If mortals knew your grace, or their own good.

(II.i.26–44)

Earlier in his dramatic career Jonson had been content simply to bring the world of money-worshippers into existence, demonstrate their antics, and leave the moral implications for the audience to draw unaided by any promptings of this nature. In *The Staple of News* the bones of the schema are to be seen and felt poking out through the body of the play. To create these abstractions, Jonson draws on the native tradition in English drama and particularly its Morality elements, a drift adumbrated in *The Devil is an Ass*, but not there realized with such prominence. Critics have pointed to the use of the Prodigal Son motif in the handling of Pennyboy Junior, who has to undergo the ritual reduction to rags before he can be reconciled to his father, the father who in disguise has attended him all along, awaiting his reformation and return to the fold of family love. Pennyboy Canter is also to be seen as an example of the type of the 'beggar-fool', familiar from and popular in numerous plays of the period, like Chapman's *An Humorous Day's Mirth*, for instance. This romantic-mythic story of loss, suffering and redemption is of the same order as *Pericles*, earlier dismissed by Jonson as 'a mouldy tale'. Additionally the motif of the disguised father waiting upon his ungrateful son had been used twenty years earlier by Marston in *The Fawn* (1606), and by John Day in *Law-Tricks* (1608). Old or not, this material was now what Jonson felt he needed to use.

There are other ways too in *The Staple of News* in which Jonson seems to side-step or neglect the advances won in his maturest drama in favour of earlier techniques. In the figure of Pennyboy Canter, the wronged father and the play's central virtuous character, Jonson reverted to the figure of the choric pointer and dramatic regulator within the action for the first time since Horace in *Poetaster* (1601). He also felt compelled to get the play off with a stern instructional prologue, informing the audience that the poet would

. . . have you wise
Much rather by your ears than by your eyes,
And prays you'll not prejudge his play for ill
Because you mark it not, and sit not still.

(lines 5–8)

From this insulting estimation of his spectators' limitations, stressing their fatuous desire for show over substance and their

233

inability even to sit still long enough to listen, Jonson moved the prologue on to a glorification of the poet as one of 'those few [who] can think / Conceive, express, and steer the souls of men'. Claiming kinship with this exalted fellowship, Jonson then dared the audience not to admire this poet's play:

> Mark but his ways.
> What flight he makes, how new. And then he says,
> If that not like you that he sends tonight,
> 'Tis you have left to judge, not he to write.
>
> (lines 27–30)

The most striking example, however, of Jonson's nervous over-controlling of the audience lies in his revival of the Induction, a device he first employed in *Every Man out of his Humour* in 1599. Jonson's introduction of the four playgoing women, the Gossips Mirth, Tattle, Expectation and Censure, has an overtly didactic function – as they crowd chattering on to the stage at the start of the play, demanding seats, news of the play, and 'delights', the actor playing the prologue is made to instruct them firmly to 'expect no more than [they] understand' (lines 30–1) – an expressive resurgence of the perennial Jonsonian compulsion 'to make the spectators understanders'. In addition to open directives of this sort, Jonson further attempted to control the audience's response by anticipating, satirizing, and hence deflecting popular response, taking pains to reintroduce his four ignorant, garrulous commentators as an 'intermean' at the end of each act where their comments are clearly intended to spike the guns of any disapprovers in the audience:

CENSURE: Why, this is duller and duller, intolerable, scurvy! Neither devil nor fool in this play! . . .
MIRTH: How like you the Vice i'the play?
EXPECTATION: Which is he?
MIRTH: Three or four: Old Covetousness, the sordid Pennyboy, the moneybawd who is flesh-bawd too, they say.
TATTLE: But here is never a fiend to carry him away! Besides, he has never a wooden dagger.

> (Second Intermean, lines 1–11)

Jonson's mockery of unsophisticated expectations of fiendish carryings-on was not only handled much more subtly in *The Devil is an Ass*; in that play, ten years earlier, Jonson had succeeded in incorporating this material into the action in a thoroughly dramatic manner, rather than in this externalized and detached way.

All this exemplifies Jonson's by now almost total lack of faith in his audience's powers of understanding. As Jonson moved towards 'the close or shutting up of his circle', his play world had grown dangerously self-contained. Now he became primarily involved in creating his own reality, as he grew more and more out of the habit of a real audience and into the fictionalizing of the ideal reader, spectator and 'understander'. He was engaged, in effect, as he had been at times before, in the business of making the dramatic into the essentially non-dramatic, to devise ways of addressing, moulding, even fantasizing the 'understander' who would replace the idle auditor of his experience.

For *The Staple of News* this meant an undue weight of extra-formal material, and a heavy reliance upon devices like prologue, induction and the direct introduction of authorial commentary. The poet indeed makes his monitory appearance in person in the Induction, where Jonson endearingly introduces his professional *alter ego* as 'within . . . in the tiring house . . . rolling himself up and down like a tun [barrel] in the midst of [the actors]', frothing and sweating (lines 58–60). Throughout the play the poet labours non-stop to insinuate his own presence, to internalize his own values, to direct the attention of the audience, and to underscore his own aims.

Jonson's mistrust of his audience is the more interesting since the themes with which he concerned himself in this play were of serious concern to every member of the Jacobean commonwealth. The 'staple' of his title is both the physical centre and symbol of the fast-growing news industry. Jonson had noticed this as a feature of contemporary life deserving of attention as long age as 1620, when he made the Factor, in *News from the New World Discovered in the Moon*, declare:

> And I have hope to erect a staple for news ere long, whither all shall be brought and thence again vented under the name of Staple news.
>
> (lines 45–7)

To Jonson the idea of a news office, where information was brought in, processed and then 'vented' upon the public for money, had an irresistible whiff of quackery about it. He viewed it in the same light as the machinations of Face and Subtle, seeing these pioneer news-hounds as no more than con-men – one of them, Fitton, is even equipped with a name whose dialect meaning is 'a lie'. He it is who boasts of the quality of the Staple's news and reports: 'All are alike true and certain.' When asked 'Is't true?', he replies in a brilliant equivocation with the perfect truth, '*As true as the rest.*'

The News Office afforded Jonson a richly rewarding subject for his satire, since both the crooks who produced the news and the fools who credulously consumed it were ripe for exposure and derision. More generally, these early practices of newsmongering highlighted what to Jonson was another social vice, the pursuit of novelty and the relish of idle gossip. The foolish gossips of the Induction, commenting upon the Staple in the Third Intermean, find the news there 'monstrous, scurvy and stale'; Tattle boasts, 'I have had better news from the bakehouse, by ten thousand parts, in a morning' (lines 14, 19–20). Jonson's declared method of exposing the news business lay 'in raising this ridiculous office of the Staple, wherein the age may see her own folly or hunger and thirst after published pamphlets of news, set out every Saturday, but made all at home, and no syllable of truth in them, than which there cannot be a greater disease in nature, or a fouler scorn put upon the times' ('to the Readers' between Acts II and III).

The development of the news industry, with the related treatment of news as a commodity to be bought and sold, also linked in Jonson's mind with other contemporary economic abuses. For the idea of the Staple of News was that it should be set up as a monopoly:

> Where all the news of all sorts shall be brought,
> And there be examined, and then registered,
> And so be issued under the seal of the Office
> As Staple News, no other news be current.
>
> (I.ii.33–6)

In this play Jonson took up, after a ten-year gap, the preoccupations expressed in *The Devil is an Ass* with money and its misuse. Like the projectors of the earlier play and in the same imagery Fitton is castigated as 'a moth, a rascal, a court rat / That gnaws the common-wealth with broking suits' (IV.iv.142–4). Once again Jonson demonstrated his awareness of interlocking political, economic and social issues. He returned to the attack on monopolies, which not even his loyalty to King James had earlier prevented him from pursuing, with an analysis that spelt out the social and economic damage they caused, yet which laid the responsibility firmly at the individual projector's door.

For Jonson was unique among dramatists of the time in his ability to grasp the importance of money and the role of the individual financier. Others continued to thunder in the medieval style against the religion of Lady Meed and the sin of making money a god. But only Jonson, as seventeenth-century England moved from an agrarian subsistence economy to a capitalist economy of plenty and conspicuous consumption, diagnosed the way in which 'Lady Pecunia' was becoming 'the Venus of the time and state'.

These were the elements that Jonson sought to combine in his new play; the Prodigal Son tale of Pennyboy Junior and his father, the worship of Lady Pecunia, and the satiric attack on the novel social phenomenon of the news office. Jonson's solution to the technical problems so presented was twofold; he handled the characters in the method he had perfected for his 'humours' study, and he plotted the action rigidly in precise conformity to the academic principles of the five-act structure. Pennyboy Senior, for instance, the rich uncle, guardian and servant of Lady Pecunia, is satirically linked with the Vice of the old morality play. But he is in fact a pure 'humour' of Avarice, and in his self-denying, life-denying habits, – he prides himself on keeping alive 'like an old hoary rat, with mouldy pie-crust' (II.i.18) – a cousin-german to Morose in *Epicene*. The courtiers, men-about-town and 'jeerers' who feed and frequent the Staple are also drawn after the 'humours' method, while Pecunia, labouring under the twin disadvantages of Jonson's perennial difficulty with female characters and the pre-designation of her role as symbolic, has no chance of attaining even this limited vitality. The same is true of her waiting-women Mortgage, Statute, Band and Wax; while the women of the Induction, gossips delimited by their names of Tattle, Censure and so on, share this one-dimensional creation.

If the personae are therefore not achieved as characters, there is a similar rigidity and contrivance about the dramatic action. To link his plot elements Jonson has to bring together Pennyboy Junior and Lady Pecunia, and he arranges this transaction at the Staple itself; both come to view the news office and to experience one of the novelties of the town. But the characters are rather manoeuvred alongside one another than successfully interlocked; there is no meaningful exchange or interaction between them. As Pennyboy brings his 'princess' Pecunia to the Staple and she passes among the officers of the new industry favouring one or other with a kiss, the force of the symbolism effectively precludes other considerations.

Despite the tightness of Jonson's plotting, however, and the attention given to the consistent through-working of theme and action, the play lacks unity. In part this occurs because the three plot elements remain disparate, and are never raised to that level at which an emotional, philosophical, or artistic synthesis is achieved. Additionally, Jonson's use of the 'magnetic field' device is less assured in *The Staple of News* than it is elsewhere. He had in the past found serviceable the idea of something – a court, a fair, even an ordinary house if Face and Subtle were running it – that irresistibly attracts the characters of the play world and brings their interests together. Here, the Staple serves that function, but the conceit is not followed through. Jonson builds strongly throughout Acts I and II to the climactic scene in the pivotal third act when Pecunia and Pennyboy at last visit the news office together. This episode of strong, sinewy satire is one of the most successful in the play. But when it is over, the Staple is abruptly dropped. For reasons not clear within the terms of the play, but with an effect that is noticed most disapprovingly by the gossips, the Staple is 'let fall most abruptly' and no more is seen of it.

Structural uncertainties such as this have been attributed to Jonson's flagging grasp in the last plays, with his use of native dramatic material as a regression from his previously achieved modes. It is perhaps more helpful to think of Jonson's continuing conviction that what determined the success of any play was the dramatist's power of assimilation and transmutation of his materials. Never in his working career had he gone for the safety of a single-action plot, preferring always to create in large and challenging patterns whose unity resided in the force of the ideas behind them.

This unity *The Staple of News* ultimately fails to achieve. It has moments of great brilliance in the satirizing of the news staple as 'a weekly cheat to draw money', and in the savage caricatures of such corrupted members of society as Pennyboy Senior the rich usurer and the cheating lawyer Picklock. The writing often rises to the achieved level of Jonson's most blistering satire, as in the wronged father's sardonic praise of his son's worthless activities:

> Sir, I say this is
> A very wholesome exercise, and comely,
> Like lepers showing one another their scabs,
> Or flies feeding on ulcers.
>
> (IV.i.33–6)

These images of disease and parasitism are part of a wider image pattern that combines with the themes to give *The Staple of News* a considerable sub-structural unity. And as this suggests, the play is thoroughly Jonsonian throughout, and manifestly of a piece with itself and with Jonson's earlier work. Ultimately, only the experience of the play in the theatre could accurately pinpoint the true source and nature of its weaknesses and strengths.

The central issue of *The Staple of News* concerns its degree of success within its chosen mode. *The New Inn* has posed a problem for critics of an entirely different order.[1] After a working lifetime devoted to the creation of satire in various forms – central satirical elements are to be found not only in Jonson's comedies and verses but in his two Roman tragedies – Jonson confounded the taste he had himself created, by producing in this last phase an unabashed and old-fashioned romance. To the Inn of the Light Heart that gives the play its name comes the Lady Frampul, attended by her waiting-woman and courtier admirers, to establish for a day of sport a little Court of Love. Fortuitously in residence is Lovel, who, as his name implies, is nursing a true but hopeless love for the lady. She is an orphan, having lost mother, father and sister many years before. At the climax of the action Lovel wins Lady Frampul, when it is suddenly revealed that all the other members of her family are living unknown to one another under the same roof; her father as 'mine host' of the inn, her mother deeply disguised as a one-eyed drunken Irish gypsy woman, and her sister who has been passed off as a boy all her life.

Any summary of the play tends to highlight its eccentric features, but the central difficulty of accounting convincingly for its composition remains. Its central theme is love, in its courtly and platonic mode; Lovel not only cherishes such a feeling, which he expresses through his behaviour, but at the Court of Love, in the pivotal third act, is made to act as mouthpiece for a defence of this view:

> For what else
> Is Love, but the most noble, pure affection
> Of what is truly beautiful and fair?
> Desire of union with the thing beloved?
> (III.ii.72–5)

Warming to his theme, in a peroration of over one hundred lines, Lovel soars into hyperbole:

> Love is a spiritual coupling of two souls,
> So much more excellent as it least relates
> Unto the body; circular, eternal;

Not feigned or made, but born; and then so precious,
As nought can value it, but itself. So free,
As nothing can command it, but itself.
And in itself so round and liberal
As where it favours, it bestows itself.

(III.ii.105–12)

Jonson's previous programme of poetic study had given precious little attention to the love that 'least relates / Unto the body'; his chosen field was always rather 'the fury of men's gullets, and their groins' (*The Staple of News*, III.iv.4). Yet throughout his work there runs a lyrical, idealizing strain from which *The New Inn* must trace its descent if it is to establish any link at all with the productions of Jonson's earlier career. And in making this study of love in its most elevated guise – indeed, in making any extended study of love at all – was Jonson seeking to repair a gap in his poetic repertoire that he had elsewhere shown himself to be aware of? *The Forest* had opened with Jonson's account of 'Why I write not of love', and both there and in the *Underwood* Jonson had examined both love itself, and the idea of himself as a lover. The masques too had centrally depended upon the theme of love, handled in the very form and phraseology that Lovel employs. Only in the major arena of the theatre had Jonson never significantly drawn on this primary aspect of human experience.

The difficulty lies in reconciling this explanation with the fact of Jonson's lifelong opposition to romance. To construe *The New Inn* as a romantic comedy means accepting that Jonson had significantly shifted a stance that he had held passionately for many years. For Jonson resorts here quite unblushingly to the pure romance theme of mistaken identity. Of the four members of the Frampul family only one, Lady Frampul, enjoys her rightful name and status. Her father is sheltering under a false beard, her mother under an eye-patch and a whisky bottle, and the sister has taken refuge in the opposite gender. This final character of Laetitia, a girl disguised as a boy pretending to be a girl who is in reality a boy actor, employs the Ganymede motif from *As You Like It* that Jonson had already deployed, to striking satiric effect, in *Epicene*. The telling difference between Shakespeare's method and Jonson's, however, lies in the dramatist's attitude to the device. Where Shakespeare wants the audience to share in and relish the complexity of the situation, Jonson chooses to keep the spectators in the dark as to 'Frank's' true identity until the final denouement. By so doing he denies himself any possibility of exploiting the multiple levels of awareness of the situation, and maximizes the danger of a charge of implausibility, something never levelled against Shakespeare's Rosalind, for instance.

Equally incongruous with Jonson's previous methodology is the final offering of love as the ultimate harmonizing, reconciling force. The love both symbolized and incarnated by Lovel is the major statement of a variety of handlings of this theme in the play. Love is sought, attempted, held up to the process of trial, and at last achieved; *The New Inn* terminates with a welter of unions and reunions to ensure that every Jack has his Jill. Yet undeniably Jonson achieves something akin to a Shakespearean consummation in the warm words of the Host to his new son-in-law:

> LOVEL: Is this a dream now, after my first sleep?
> Or are these fantasies made in the Light Heart
> And sold in the New Inn?
> HOST: Best go to bed
> And dream it over all. Let's all go sleep
> Each with his turtle.
>
>   (V.v.120–4)

Yet even at a moment such as this Jonson's characteristic sense of humour cannot be long suppressed. Within a dozen lines or so, the Host is unromantically categorizing love and marriage in the old proverbial vulgarism as no more than 'four bare legs in a bed'. Within the romance framework, vestigial traces of Jonson's customary mode of comedy-writing constantly break through the blandness of the surface. The characterization retains elements of his 'humours' technique – Lord Frampul, for instance, has demonstrated his madcap humour to follow the gypsies and leave his wife and family, and within the play itself, as 'mine host' of the Light Heart Inn, he is nothing but a walking humour of joviality and goodwill, self-situated where he may most feed his humour of enjoying other men's humours. He is made from the outset to summarize his aim 'in keeping this Light Heart':

> Where, I imagine, all the world's a play . . .
>   and if I have got
> A seat, to sit at ease here i' mine Inn
> To see the comedy; and laugh and chuck
> At the variety and throng of humours
> And dispositions, that come jostling in

BEN JONSON

And out still, as the one drove hence another:
Why, will you envy me my happiness?
(I.iii.128–37)

The jolly inn-keeper is handled within a framework which includes
other lingering suggestions of Jonson's former 'humours' typology.
His daughter, Lady Frampul, is 'as cock-brained as ere the father was',
'of so bent a fantasy / As she thinks nought of happiness but to have / A
multitude of servants' – it is her humour to be so 'frampul', or
self-willed.

At times in *The New Inn* Jonson's habitual satiric slant both
determines the material incorporated and colours the presentation.
One such episode, harshly out of keeping with the love business, and
evocative of the cruellest of Jonson's corrective satires, is that of Stuff
and his wife Pinnacia. The treatment of this couple catches up several
perennial Jonsonian preoccupations. The idea of the tailor whose
sexual obsession necessitates copulating with his wife in the fine
clothes that he has made for his customers harks back to *Underwood*
42, where the mention of 'a velvet petticoat or gown' caused Jonson to
reflect:

> Whose like I have known the tailor's wife put on
> To do her husband's rites in, ere 'twere gone
> Home to the customer; his lechery
> Being, the best clothes still to preoccupy.
> (lines 39–42)

Further variations on the theme of women being forced to serve men's
sexual perversions were also considered by Jonson in *Epigrams* 25 and
78.

In *The New Inn* this perverted and underhand dealing is linked with
another form of deception, that of the 'fine lady would-be'. Dressed in
the clothes intended for Lady Frampul, Pinnacia Stuff passes herself
off as a countess. When the truth comes to light she is 'dis-ladied' and
'dis-countessed' in a motif reminiscent of the uncasing of Sir Pol in
Volpone. Despite the fact that she has been acting under her husband's
compulsion, the woman is then savagely punished with all the
penalties and humiliations inflicted upon a convicted whore, in a
disturbing upsurge of Jonson's anti-feminism:

HOST: Pillage the Pinnace.
LADY: Let his wife be stripped.
BEAUMONT: Blow off her upper deck.

242

LATIMER: Tear all her tackle.
LADY: Pluck the polluted robes over her ears . . .
HOST: And send her home
   Divested to her flannel, in a cart.
LATIMER: And let her footman beat the basin afore her.

(IV.iii.90–9)

Other characters of the play are also handled on this satiric-realistic level, although not so fiercely, and are likewise outside the world of courtly love to which the principals belong. These are the low-life, below-stairs dwellers, who potentially at least are of the calibre to hold their own with Jonson's other dramatic creations in this vein. Fletcher thought well enough of the horse gossip between the stable companions Pierce, Tipto, Ferret and Trundle to borrow some of it for his own play *Love's Pilgrimage* (see HS II, 198–200, for a full comparison and analysis); and in the unusual character of Fly, major-domo and 'parasite of the Inn', 'one that had been a strolling gypsy, but now is reclaimed, to be an inflamer of the reckonings' (HS VI, 403), Jonson had the makings of a latter-day Mosca, crossed with Face. The problem with these characters stems from a lack of verve and commitment on Jonson's part; they are not drawn with sufficient vividness, they fail to become integrated with the main action of the play but sit uneasily on its perimeter, and they are firmly dropped by Jonson as the play nears its conclusion, having no place in the Court of Love, or in the multiple unmaskings and reconciliations which form the real business of the resolution.

As this suggests, Jonson's development of *The New Inn* is not haphazard; the drama is spared the loose rambling sprawl that afflicts much romantic comedy. The poet clung to the five-act structure as academically prescribed; he employed his favourite double-action structure, in which the low characters enact a parody of the higher action above-stairs; and he created the action to conform to the classical unities with the same location employed throughout, and stage time mimicking real time within the compass of a single day. The same intensity of purpose denotes the characterization of the main parts; Lovel is conceived in Jonson's own words as 'a complete gentleman, a soldier and a scholar' (HS VI, 402); so he is drawn, and so remains. Equally the Host, Lady Frampul, and Prue her maid, all exemplify throughout what they are to begin with and as such consistently reinforce the message of the play.

Is that message then satirical or romantic? It is, certainly, hard to account for Jonson's late resort to a fanciful Arcadian mode with multiple disguise and crossed love of the sort that he had so copiously despised. It is, too, a radical change for Jonson to make this type of appeal to an audience, aiming for the tolerant, the consensual, and comforting response, rather than seeking to puncture the spectators' complacency in order to send them away aroused and disturbed. It is, however, harder still to account for the play as a satire either upon the conventions of romantic comedy, or, more remotely, upon the 'cult of courtly love' playfully revived at the court of Charles I's queen, Henrietta Maria. Satire is not a hesitant or delicate instrument, whose objects have to be teased out by analysis. In other Jonson plays there is no difficulty in detecting where the satiric attack is directed. Had Jonson wished to satirize these subjects, his readers and spectators would have been aware of it. In all his productions of the previous thirty years, Jonson never left any doubt as to what had provoked his scorn and displeasure, or had been the occasion for the composition.

Another pointer to Jonson's intention is to be found in the Epilogue to *The New Inn*. Its tone is far humbler than is customary with Jonson, and he shares with the audience some hints of his hopes for the play, and the artistic decision by which he tried to ensure its success:

> Plays in themselves have neither hopes nor fears,
> Their fate is only in their hearers' ears.
> If you expect more than you had tonight
> The maker's sick, and sad. But do him right,
> He meant to please you; for he sent things fit
> In all the numbers both of sense and wit,
> If they have not miscarried! . . .
>   He could have haled in
> The drunkards, and the noises of the inn
> In his last act; if he had thought it fit
> To vent you vapours, in the place of wit.
> But better 'twas that they should sleep or spew
> Than in the scene t'offend or him, or you.
>   (HS VI, 490)

The unfamiliar desire to please, the uncertainty of the play's reception, both point to an attempt on Jonson's part to introduce something new to the spectators. Finally, the decision to suppress the low-life satirical-realistic characters before the resolutions of the last act conclusively suggests that the play is not to be read as a satire.

Whatever the focus of the drama, Jonson did not succeed in clarifying it sufficiently to let the audience into the secret. Yet there are many good things in this play to which critical comment is only recently beginning to do full justice.[2] When Jonson treads familiar ground as in his handling of the theme of the dichotomy between appearance and reality, the ideal and the actual, he shows himself still capable of powerful effects. In *The New Inn*, the discussion of love in these terms is subtly linked with that of dress and behaviour, with the implicit question of the authenticity of experience underlying both. Lovel's defence of true valour is one of many moments in the play when these issues are considered in a recognizable Jonsonian tone and phraseology:

> It is . . .
> A certain mean twixt fear and confidence;
> No inconsiderate rashness, or vain appetite
> Of false encountering formidable things;
> But a true science of distinguishing
> What's good or evil. It springs out of reason
> And tends to perfect honesty.
>
> (IV.iv.38–45)

Like most of what Lovel says, this speech has a heroic dignity. But it highlights one final difficulty of the play. The tendency to create long oracular pronouncements for his characters was a weakness of Jonson's dramaturgy from his earliest days. In the middle phase he resolved this difficulty with the use of more action in his plots, and with the discovery of how to express dramatic developments through action as well as speech. In *The New Inn*, partly at least through the initial choice of the 'Court of Love' debate formula, Jonson reverted to the creation of a much higher proportion of speech over action.[3] The price of this is paid in the static, undramatic nature of much of the play. Lovel's speeches, and Lady Frampul's responses, are fine, grave and eloquent pieces of writing. But they are not inherently theatrical, and it is hard to imagine how in production they could be made so.

In the event, they were not. The original production was hooted from the stage. Jonson was baffled and enraged by its failure. Apart from the hostile activities of his enemies, the play faltered through the audience's uncertainty about what kind of dramatic experience they were undergoing. In his later 'Dedication to the Reader' Jonson attacked those spectators who by their behaviour offered proof positive 'of their not understanding one scene' (HS VI, 397). It is an interesting reflection that subsequent readers, despite the heavy battery of notes, explanations and other non-dramatic material later added by Jonson, are still in much the same position in regard to this fascinating play.

A gap of three years had separated *The New Inn* from its predecessor, *The Staple of News*. Another three years brought forth another new play from Jonson, and a new dramatic impetus and change of direction. *The Magnetic Lady*, produced in Jonson's declining years of age and sickness, had little of the palsy about it, but was a vigorous attempt on an unusual tale. The 'Magnetic Lady' of the title is seeking to marry off her niece, and the plot concerns the efforts of assorted suitors, of varying degrees of desirability, to secure the prize.

As the title suggests, the most immediate feature of the play is its overtly allegorical framework. The magnetic centrepiece is Lady Loadstone, whose capacity it is to draw 'gentlewomen, male guests / Of several humours, carriage, constitution / Profession, too' (I.i.5–7). As she is the centre, the twin pillars of the drama are provided by two young heroes, the friends Compass and Ironside, who embody true values and act throughout on the side of right. The two heroines both symbolize what men desire in a young bride; their interchangeability is attested by the fact that Jonson gives them both the same name, one in English and one in Latin. These female leads, Placentia and Pleasance, suffer the same fate as Pecunia in *The Staple of News* – their characters remain abstractions and never spring to dramatic life. The 'magnetic centre' device, one of Jonson's tried favourites, has now assumed the visible centre of the play, instead of serving as a main underpinning as before; the foundations of the dramatic construction are now plainly in view on the surface.

This framework of masque-like formalism is carried through into the structural movement of the play. As in *The Staple of News*, where Pecunia is brought on, beset, and finally triumphs (echoing the format of the 'Triumph' type of masque), so here Compass circumscribes and controls all the action, regulating it and keeping it within bounds. In lesser developments of the plot, the Placentia/Pleasance duo are also tried and proved, to establish which is the false and which the true heroine; while Ironside is drawn to the love and service of his 'magnetic mistress' Lady Loadstone in a movement that has been solidly set up from the start. As the local prelate is made to observe,

More work then for the parson; I shall cap
The Loadstone with an Ironside, I see.

(V.x.154–5)

The very naming of these characters leads the audience to expect that the magnet will attract the iron before the play is out.

But *The Magnetic Lady* is a far livelier production than this might imply. Jonson returns here to the source and centre of his strength, the satire of contemporary types and modes. In the thirty years that had passed since the creation of *Poetaster* and despite the stir he had caused then, Jonson had not ceased to find lawyers both humorous and suspect. His lawyer Practice in *The Magnetic Lady* is not the sharpest villain ever to go in a black coat and wig – his own Picklock from *The Staple of News* is a more sinister creation – but Jonson obtains some innocent fun by the reverse process of showing one described as 'the only famous counsel in the kingdom . . . sharp Practice' (IV.ii.42 and 45), being outwitted in a piece of legal dealing by a simple device of Compass's.

Parallel with the satire upon lawyers is that of another fashionable and problematical social group in Jonson's day, the courtiers. In an interesting cluster of motifs running back to Jonson's earliest comment upon this theme, Sir Diaphanous Silkworm is made to embody Jonson's profound reservations about those whose exquisite exterior masks an inner void, who are thus shallow, soulless, non-human:

All men are worms: but this no man. In silk
   'Twas brought to court first wrapped, and white as milk;
   Where afterwards it grew a butterfly,
   Which was a caterpillar. So 'twill die.

(Epigram 15)

The vain Silkworm in *The Magnetic Lady* is not handled in such a darkly sardonic mode as this. But his essential hollowness and obsessional concern with his clothes and appearance are fully brought out. At the point in the action when Silkworm has suffered an assault from the down-to-earth, right-thinking Ironside, and the lawyer Practice is urging him to go to law, with the enthusiastic offer, 'Let me pack your jury!', Silkworm voices his main injury:

SILKWORM: There's nothing vexes me, but that he has stained
   My new white satin doublet, and bespattered
   My spick and span silk stockings, on the day
   They were drawn on. And here's a spot in my hose, too.

247

COMPASS: Shrewd maims! your clothes are wounded
  desperately,
And that, I think, troubles a courtier more
An exact courtier, than a gash in his flesh.

(III.iv.6–12)

Lawyers and courtiers are the principal objects of Jonson's satire in the main plot of *The Magnetic Lady*. It is, however, a remarkable tribute to the old playwright's continuing fertility of stagecraft that this play contains the most representative social group of any he had so far assembled in one drama, when its full range from highest to lowest is taken into account; the characters include a scholar, soldier, parson, doctor, midwife, doctor's boy, nurse, and steward, as well as a financier and a statesman.

All these are deeply involved in the false religion of the world, worshipping money, power, food, clothes and success, or, more rarely, standing outside it as its critics. To handle these types and themes, Jonson deliberately reverted to his 'humours' method of so many years ago. *The Magnetic Lady* is subtitled 'Humours reconciled', a phrase Jonson thought it worthwhile to spend some time explaining to his audience:

> The author, beginning his studies of this kind, with *Every Man in his Humour*, and after, *Every Man out of his Humour*, and since, continuing in all his plays, especially those of the comic thread, whereof *The New Inn* was the last, some recent humours still, or manners of men, that went along with the times, finding himself now near the close, or shutting up of his circle, hath fancied to himself in Idea this magnetic mistress. . . . he makes that his centre attractive, to draw thither a diversity of guests, all persons of different humours to make up his perimeter. And this he hath called 'Humours Reconciled'.
>
> (Induction, lines 99–111)

The tone of this is more temperate than much of Jonson's earlier humours work. Within the play too, the portrayals of Practice and Silkworm are essentially benign, their humours interpreted in the undeveloped sense of 'affectation' rather than as a gross deformity in nature. But in the character of Sir Moth Interest, the third of the unholy trio of these 'caterpillars of the commonwealth', Jonson is working within his true 'humours' style to created a telling indictment of a very different kind of man. Interest, the 'usurer and money-bawd', is asked for his reaction to public disapproval of his practices. His reply betrays his kinship with the prince of Jonson's money-magnificos, Volpone:

> Let 'em exclaim and envy; what care I?
> Their murmurs raise no blisters in my flesh.
> My monies are my blood, my parents, kindred:
> And he that loves not those, he is unnatural.
> I am persuaded that the love of money
> Is not a virtue only in a subject
> But might befit a prince.
>
> (II.vi.37–43)

In the wretched narrowness of his compulsion, Interest descends directly from the desperate, avaricious Sordido of *Every Man out of his Humour* (himself an offspring of the frantic miser Jaques in Jonson's first extant play *The Case Is Altered*), with elements of Morose from *Epicene* thrown in; and he meets a fate symbolically tailored to his humour when in the pursuit of his ruling passion he falls down a well.

The Magnetic Lady is also vitalized by another development in Jonson's running battle with the audience. Even so near to 'the close, or shutting up of his circle', Jonson did not give up his attempts to school the spectators in the correct response as the play went along. His method here was to introduce, as an Induction to the drama, two gentlemen playgoers who come along to the theatre as to a 'poetic shop', to try the latest fashions in 'fine fancies, figures, humours, characters, ideas, definitions of lords and ladies, waiting-women, parasites, knights, captains, courtiers, lawyers' (lines 2–4). Jonson repeats here not only the induction device first developed in *Every Man out of his Humour*, but also the notion of having the cavillers and complainers against his play up on the stage, to anticipate and disarm adverse criticism – this had been used with the gossips of the Intermean throughout *The Staple of News*.

Here, however, Jonson devised a modification that significantly improved this piece of business. He staffed his 'poetic shop' with a bright little salesboy, who proves more than a match for the grumbling gentlemen Probee and Damplay. In the character of the witty boy, who responds to the patronizing Damplay's fragment of Latin by completing his quotation and correctly attributing the authorship – 'I understand that, Sir, since I learned Terence in the third form at Westminster; go on, Sir' (Induction, lines 46–7), the old poet paradoxically discovered his most successful mouthpiece; for any precocious youngster can dispense instruction and pour scorn with much more charm and humour than an irascible adult. Equally, it is a much more effective method of disposing of the objectors, to stage them with the answer to their quibbles right at hand.

The Induction and choruses of *The Magnetic Lady* therefore constitute a series of lively dramatic entertainments in their own right as the 'poet's boy', with some assistance from Probee, takes it upon himself to teach the ill-informed Damplay the intricacies of dramatic structure with such lordly demands as, 'Now, gentlemen, what censure you of our *protasis*, or first act?' (Chorus 2, line 1). The discussion of the action led by the boy further ensures that these choruses are fully integrated into the play experience – they act as a series of playlets within the play, in a framing and distancing manner, constantly placing the action for the audience, though not too insistently.

Another valuable function of the Induction and choruses lies in providing a further arena for Jonson's satire. The 'shop' framework reflects Jonson's contempt for commercialism, and for the consumerist pursuit of whatever is newly 'in'. When these values of the world of trade are applied to the 'sacred poesy' and the drama, then Jonson is scathing in his attack upon the shallow desire to take up the fashionable 'poet of the day'. Nor is the stage itself exempt from Jonson's scorn; he seizes the opportunity to make the boy outline the correct theory of dramatic construction, sarcastically dismissing the stage techniques of old-fashioned romance narrative as he does so:

> So, if a child could be born in a play, and grow up to a man in the first scene, before he went off the stage; and then after to come forth a squire, and be made a knight; and that knight to travel between the acts, and do wonders in the holy land, or elsewhere; kill paynims [pagans], wild boars, dun cows, and other monsters; beget him a reputation, and marry an Emperor's daughter for his mistress; convert her father's country; and at last come home lame, and all to be laden with miracles.
>
> (Chorus 2, lines 16–24)

None of these features, incidentally, is ever employed by Jonson, even in *The New Inn*. The fiction that drama could cover any time or space never failed to enrage the poet reared on the classical unities.

But Jonson is not simply riding all his old hobby-horses in *The Magnetic Lady*. There are some interesting new elements in its construction suggesting that Jonson's imagination was running strongly and was far from played out. Jonson here makes his first sustained satirical attempt upon a rich topic hitherto neglected by him, the process of courtship and marriage. As the suitors gather around the rich Placentia about to be given in marriage by her aunt, for the sole purpose of prising her portion out of her wicked uncle Interest, Jonson exposes not only the pretensions of the aspirants, but the corruption of those who feed upon the process like the go-between Parson and the waiting-women who have to be bribed for their goodwill. The pursuit of the bride is sardonically exposed for the sordid transaction it is, when the news breaks that she is 'brought to bed of a bouncing boy' even as the negotiations are being clinched. In a commodity market, the all-desired property is now shop-soiled, 'cracked in the ring', and valueless. Her demotion is completed with the revelation that Placentia is not, in any case, the real heiress but a substitute. Pleasance is then promoted to her true eminence, and quickly snapped up by the well-placed Compass.

Like all Jonson's heroines, these two girls are colourless characters acted upon by others, to whom they can only palely react. Their portrayal, however, is complemented by the studies of the low-life females who serve as a counter-weight to the 'ladies'. *The Magnetic Lady* is of interest not only in having a larger number of female characters than is usual with Jonson; but also in having two drawn with a vigour and verve unequalled by Jonson since he pilloried the collegiate women in *Epicene*. The confidante and parasite Polish and the nurse Keep are splendid satiric portraits, refreshingly reminiscent of Ursula in *Bartholomew Fair*, and bringing the same powerful gust of the real world with them whenever they enter. As Jonson creates the quarrel that ensues after the discovery that Placentia, their charge and Polish's concealed daughter, is pregnant, the pair recall Face and Subtle at the start of *The Alchemist*:

> POLISH: Out, thou caitiff witch!
>   Bawd, beggar, gypsy! anything indeed
>   But honest woman!
> KEEP: What you please, Dame Polish,
>   My lady's stroker. . . .
> POLISH: Thou art a traitor to me,
>   An Eve, an apple, and the serpent too,
>   A viper, that hast eat a passage through me,
>   Through mine own bowels by thy recklessness. . . .
>   Sleepy unlucky hag! Thou bird of night,
>   And all mischance to me.

KEEP: Good Lady Empress!
Had I the keeping of thy daughter's clicket
In charge? Was that committed to my trust?
POLISH: Soft, devil, not so loud.
KEEP: You'ld have the house hear and be witness, would you?
Let all the world be witness. Afore I'll
Endure the tyranny of such a tongue –
And such a pride –
POLISH: What will you do?
KEEP: Tell truth, and shame the she-man-devil in puffed
sleeves.
POLISH: Not so high! . . . And must you be so loud?
KEEP: I will be louder.

(IV.iv.1–32)

Jonson's interest in women's secrets had earlier flashed out only intermittently, as in the dialogue between the wet- and dry-nurses in the *Entertainment at Blackfriars* twelve years before. In *The Magnetic Lady*, for the first time, he made space to develop this theme at leisure.

The interest of *The Magnetic Lady* has never been fully realized. Sabotaged at its first performance by Inigo Jones and his hostile claque in the light of which Jonson's prior creation of Damplay ('Damnplay') takes on a prophetic significance, it has never in the intervening years been reclaimed or rediscovered for the stage. Inevitably it is not on the level of Jonson's greatest works; by his own highest standards, the plotting is somewhat slack, as Compass has things far too much his own way, some of the characters are under-realized, and the construction is too often achieved in long speeches and indigestible chunks of verse used in effect as building blocks. As with *The Devil is an Ass*, Jonson does not quite pull off his favourite technique of the fourth-act plot explosion, with another set of pyrotechnics at the climax. Once the revelation has been made that the two girls were exchanged at birth, nothing quite lives up to this as a plot surprise. But *The Magnetic Lady* retains powers of attraction for which it has not received credit. It is a sprightly, comical piece fully deserving of that life in the theatre that from its birth it was refused.

Sadly, the same cannot be said of Jonson's final production, the curious *A Tale of a Tub*. This was the last play of Jonson's ever to be staged, in 1633, but the speed with which it appeared at the beginning of the year, only a matter of months after *The Magnetic Lady*, would in itself indicate that it was not newly written. The play in fact was an ill-advised revival of one of Jonson's earliest comedies, those he had told Drummond were not in print, and which he had not considered worthy of inclusion in the 1616 Folio. Now, smarting under the deliberate wrecking of *The Magnetic Lady* by Inigo Jones, Jonson cast about for a vessel of his wrath to be directed against his enemy. But when, laced with satirical shafts against Jones the play came before the Master of the Revels, it was refused a licence. Further rewriting was demanded before permission for performance was granted.

The text that was eventually printed in Jonson's second Folio of 1640 incorporates, then, all three strata of its evolution.[4] At the base level lies the original play, clearly a very early example of Jonson's comedy-writing. Overlaid on this, as the entry in the Revels book relates, was a personal satire on Jones under the name of 'Vitruvius Hoop', with a foolish piece of stage business designed to make the Surveyor look ridiculous, described by Herbert, Master of the Revels, as 'the motion of the tub' (HS III, 3). That this satire had some bite and venom is evident from Jones's taking 'exceptions' to it 'as a personal injury unto him'. The inclusion of the 'motion' also demonstrates that Jonson attacked Jones both personally and professionally – although employed as the Surveyor of the King's Works for his skill in architecture and design, Jones's reputation rested substantially upon the moving machines, stage effects, lights and shadow-plays which he devised for masques and court performances.

Some traces of this caricature remain, to indicate how Jonson handled the man whom he had previously condemned to Prince Charles as '*the greatest villain in the world*' (HS I, 145). Not surprisingly, Jonson twitted his opponent with the desire to lord it unchallenged in the world of masque-making that had precipitated the final rift between them:

> He'll do it alone, sir, he will join with no man,
> Though he be a joiner; in design he calls it
> He must be sole inventor.

> (V.ii.35–7)

From the scornful designation of Jones as a 'joiner' emerges Jonson's view of him as nothing but a glorified carpenter; but one with pretensions, claiming his work to be the art of 'design'. Jonson further incorporated into the portrait certain of Jones's verbal affectations, and gave him an overweening confidence in his professional ability to make a 'motion' out of the most unpromising subject matter: 'I can express a wash-house (if need be) / With a whole pedigree of tubs' (V.ii.47–8).

As satire this version of Jones is very small beer, since Jonson had been compelled to delete whatever had the power to injure his adversary. These deletions, and the substitution of Vitruvius Hoop by In-and-In Medlay (so called for the craft of his godfather the weaver, and for his own joinery, both of which required the operatives to lay their work 'in, and in') both weaken and confuse the scenes in which he appears. He is not well sorted with his fellow rustics and yet is denied the special skills which the prototype character must have had to set him apart from them. There is an uneasy matching of the original satire with the enforced changes, and the joinery of Jonson himself is all too visible.

The strain existing between these elements, however, is small in comparison with the incongruity between the new satirical inserts and the old original material of the play itself. For A Tale of a Tub in manner and form pre-dates Jonson's 'humours' work and satirical comedy. It is a comedy of intrigue whose closest relation in the Jonson oeuvre is the similarly unsophisticated The Case Is Altered. The attempts of Toby Turf the village constable to get his daughter Audrey married in the teeth of interference from a disappointed suitor, his disgruntled mother, an amorous magistrate and a mischievous parson, are handled in Jonson's earliest style. The humour obtained at the expense of the blundering officer and the local peasantry is of the warmest, almost Shakespearean tone; none of the opportunities provided by the plot for keen mockery or sharp scorn is taken up.

For this is a world of almost prelapsarian innocence, one of well-intentioned simpletons whose worst offence is no more than dullness and muddle. A somewhat ambivalent prologue asserts the values of the piece:

> No state affairs, nor any politic club
>   Pretend we, in our tale here of a tub.
> But acts of clowns and constables today
>   Stuff out the scenes of our ridiculous play.
> A Cooper's wit, or some such busy spark
>   Illumining the high constable, and his clerk
> And all the neighbourhood, from old records,
>   Of antique proverbs, drawn from Whitsun Lords,
>   And their authorities, at wakes and ales,

> With country precedents and old wives' tales;
> We bring you now, to show what different things
> The cotes of clowns are, from the courts of kings.

Shakespeare continued to keep alive in his work the countryside of his early imagination, but this was a world where Jonson had always been frankly out of place.

The difficulty, in the existing state of the text, is to divine Jonson's artistic intentions. The play is noteworthy in its presentation of this small group of villagers, with a lady of the manor and a parson, but with no person of greater worldliness to set them off. Even amid a group of clowns, the heroine, Audrey, is a girl of such remarkable dullness that even the most besotted of her wooers is forced to comment on the fact, while to an audience she appears to be virtually mentally defective. Here Jonson presents her sublimely disconnected response to a proposal of marriage:

> POL-MARTIN: Are you disposed to marry?
> AUDREY: You are disposed to ask.
> POL-MARTIN: Are you to grant?
> AUDREY: Nay, now I see you are disposed indeed.
> POL-MARTIN: (I see the wench wants but a little wit
>   And that defect her wealth may well supply.)
>   In plain terms, will you have me, Audrey?
> AUDREY: In plain terms, I tell you who would have me . . .
>
>   (IV.v.79–85)

Remarkable, too, is Jonson's setting of the play in England, with numerous references to Kentish Town, Islington, Kilburn and Hampstead. The use of a native rather than an Italian or classical location is more readily associated with the later phase of Jonson's career, and as part of his rewriting it is likely that he 'Englished' *A Tale of a Tub*, as he had done *Every Man in his Humour* for the 1616 Folio.

What, however, seems more remarkable still is the fact that Jonson revived the play at all. It is in almost every regard so weak and flat that only rage and desperation can account for Jonson's decision to exhume it from the merited obscurity to which he had previously consigned it by his decision to exclude it from his First Folio. It fails on the simplest level as a comedy of intrigue and disguise, since the elements borrowed from Roman comedy cannot combine to provide it with a plot. All it can offer is the central situation of the girl who wants to be married never minding who is to be the groom, and the father who has determined on the match but cannot bring it about. The play unfolds by simply repeating the thwarting of the father, and resolves itself in a trice when an unlikely outsider pops in to snatch the dim-witted bride from under the nose of prior claimants. The tricky vicar, Canon Hugh, who helps to make the mischief of the play, is given an alias of Captain Thumbs, and is brought on at one point disguised as a soldier, in a clear anticipation of Brainworm and even Face. But lacking a structural base either in the parent Plautine comedy, or in a well-knit dramatic situation, Sir Hugh floats free in a limbo of mirthless implausibility.

Not only the overall construction of the plot, but the minor details similarly appear beyond Jonson's range. The opening scenes progress by means of that heart-sinking exposition in which characters are brought on to inform one another of facts that they both already know: 'Tub, I should call him too, / Sir Peter was his father . . . who left his mother' (I.i.12–14). And so on. Stranger still from the author of what Coleridge considered to be one of the most perfect comedies in English is the poor quality of the humour contrived here. This is posited almost entirely on the assumption that to equip a character with a ridiculous name and a regional dialect will automatically raise a laugh. Here, for instance, is 'Ball Puppy' in full flight:

> Vaith, vor mine own part,
> I have zupped up so much broth, as would have covered
> A leg of beef o'er head and ears in the porridge pot,
> And yet I cannot sussifie wild nature.
>
> (III.viii.35–8)

From the poet of *The Alchemist* and *Bartholomew Fair*, even *The Devil is an Ass*, this lamentable groping after comic effect constitutes a descent almost too painful to contemplate.

A Tale of a Tub represents a complex of so many textual problems that Jonson's artistic or dramatic intentions cannot now be recovered with any clarity. What cannot be in any doubt, however, is the total failure of the piece on every level. Posterity has tacitly dismissed *A Tale of a Tub* from Jonson's *oeuvre* and it is virtually unknown. It constituted in its time a violent declension even from Jonson's later standard and the most poignant termination to a dramatic career full of glories. The very title, with its proverbial self-deprecation, is an indication of the slightness of the work in Jonson's estimation. He made *A Tale of A Tub* his swan-song, and thereafter wrote no more for the public stage.

12

NEAR THE CLOSE OR SHUTTING UP OF HIS CIRCLE

With *A Tale of a Tub* Jonson made his farewell to the stage. The form with which he had first made his way into public notice was the first he was forced to lay aside under the pressure of failing faculties and changing times, when the dramatic craftsmanship he had struggled so hard to master was no longer serviceable to him and to his ideas. His masque-making lasted longer, as a few commissions continued to come in. Yet as the last plays had displayed a marked stiffening of their allegorical sinews, becoming more and more like masques, so his masques too were hardening into ever more rigid and rarefied forms. And as his play-writing fell off, so too as a masque-maker Jonson was drawing 'near the close, or shutting up of his circle' – during these years he wrote only two masques for the court, and two country entertainments.

These final masques were effectively a pair, since the king first offered *Love's Triumph through Callipolis* to the queen as his Twelfth Night tribute, and the queen then responded with *Chloridia* to repay and return the compliment. Both *Love's Triumph* and *Chloridia* by their very nature and from their inception strengthened the tendency of the Caroline masque to turn in upon itself, becoming increasingly self-reflexive and self-congratulatory. As such it departed irrevocably from the mode Jonson had made his own, that of the offering of the court to the king, and of the king to his devoted people.

Love's Triumph through Callipolis was a most important commission for Jonson, since he had not written a court masque for the last six years. But when the chance came, it was not to be his alone. Jonson now had to share the role of 'inventor' with Inigo Jones, and from his own account of the 'debate of cogitation' between them (HS VII, 736) it is clear that the device was a joint production. The effect of this was to increase the primacy of the visual element as Jones worked in those

257

themes and characters most conformable to his particular skills. The anti-masque, where Jonson had previously developed some of his wittiest and most innovative flights of fancy, was now reduced to a list of characters:

> A glorious, boasting lover
> A whining, ballading lover
> An adventurous Romance lover
>
> A fantastick umbrageous lover
> A bribing, corrupt lover
> A forward, jealous lover . . .

Twelve of these 'depraved lovers' were introduced, to dance 'a distracted comedy of love . . . in the scenical persons and habits of the four prime European nations' (HS VII, 736). They have no dialogue, and evidently provided far more scope for Jones than for Jonson. Vestiges of Jonson's 'humours' theory linger on in the presentation of the characters; in their exaggerated, one-dimensional behaviour, for instance, and in the movement of the masque to purge the masque world by driving 'such monsters from the labyrinth of love' (line 378). But the main interest of the 'depraved lovers' lay in the designs that Jones created for them; drawn from the *commedia dell' arte* and enriched with themes from France, Italy, Spain and Holland, these were elaborately worked out and stunning in effect (see HS X, 677–9, for a description of the designs in full).

After the anti-masque, the main theme of the evening's entertainment, the visit of Love to Callipolis, the city of Beauty or Goodness, was introduced in a song. Jonson's verses for this are never less than dignified and powerful:

> Joy, joy to mortals, the rejoicing fires
>   Of gladness, smile in your dilated hearts!
> Whilst Love presents a world of chaste desires
>   Which may produce a harmony of parts!
>
> Love is the right affection of the mind,
>   The noble appetite of what is best
> Desire of union with the thing designed,
>   But in fruition of it cannot rest.
>
> (lines 50–7)

But again, given the importance of the music and singing, as well as the visual effect of this character Euphemus descending and taking the stage, Jonson's contribution, the verbal, is automatically thrust into second place.

Visually, the masque was both sumptuous and full of surprises. After the songs, as Jonson's description tells us:

> The Triumph [a moving machine] is first seen afar off, and led in by Amphitrite, the wife of Oceanus, with four Sea-Gods attending her . . . it consisteth of fifteen lovers, and as many Cupids, who rank themselves seven and seven a side, with each a Cupid before him, with a lighted torch, and the middle person, which is his Majesty, placed in the centre.

The presentation of the triumph, with the true lovers and King Charles, was succeeded by the surprise appearance of 'Euclia, or fair glory' up above the action in 'the heavens'. After the revels the scene changed to a garden, the heavens opened, and four new characters appeared, the divinities Jupiter, Juno, Genius and Hymen, 'in form of a constellation'. Subsequently Venus appeared in a cloud and descended to the earth, 'when presently the cloud vanisheth, and she is seen sitting in a throne'. After her song the throne disappeared, and Jones produced his masterpiece: 'there shooteth up a palm tree with an imperial crown on the top, from the root whereof lilies and roses, twining together and embracing the stem, flourish through the crown' (lines 205–8). Jones's ability to conjure up such spectacular displays, which were far in advance of anything that the theatre could contrive, was a source of never-ending delight to his contemporaries.

But however visually impressive, the masque was textually thin. The verbal element was decisively submerged in the struggle with the other masque elements of spectacle, song and dance. The concern with love links *Love's Triumph through Callipolis* thematically with *The New Inn* of two years before and several of Lovel's speeches would not be out of place in the choric sections of the masque. But Jones's intervention denied Jonson the autonomy by which he could work through one central unifying concept. The necessity to bring in ill-assorted personages purely for their spectacular effect resulted in such anomalies as the appearance of various sea-gods who have no relevance whatsoever to the theme. The masque becomes in the final analysis a hodge-podge of ideas and motifs, without the integrity of construction through which Jonson had formerly raised it to the level of whatever significance it could attain.

Such verse as Jonson did contribute to *Love's Triumph through*

Callipolis shows that he was still capable of creating at a higher standard than he was allowed to achieve. The lines are both smooth and taut, the rhythms varied and unexpected, the rhymes true and crisp:

> So love, emergent out of Chaos, brought
> The world to light!
> And gently moving on the waters, wrought
> All form to sight!
>
> Love's appetite
> Did beauty first excite
> And left imprinted on the air
> Those signatures of good and fair
> Which since have flowed, flowed forth, upon the sense,
> To wonder first, and then to excellence,
> By virtue of divine intelligence!
>
> (lines 155–65)

But whatever its virtues, this pellucid and unostentatious verse could not compete with floating sea-gods and sprouting palm trees. The emblematic climax of lilies and roses flourishing through the crown imperial was purely visual, a special effect rather than a thematic resolution.

The production of *Chloridia* within a few weeks of *Love's Triumph through Callipolis* involved a reproduction of the same set of problems. For this piece, the queen's return of love and duty to the king her husband, the 'inventors' had decided upon the form of the pastoral. Henrietta Maria was cast as Chloris, the goddess of the flowers, while the framework of the masque was to be a service of worship of her beauty and goodness. For Jonson, the brief was to create a fantasy on the theme of spring, with soft breezes, showers, and fresh growth abounding. The lyrical idealizing strain of Jonson's imagination was well suited to this subject, while there was ample precedent in both ancient and contemporary literature for the treatment of the theme.

The subject was, however, equally congenial to Jones, who lost no opportunity for elaboration and embellishment. Despite the extreme strain of relations between Jones and himself, which were shortly to erupt in the final explosion of bad feeling, Jonson was ready to pay tribute to Jones's work:

> The curtain being drawn up, the scene is discovered, consisting
> of pleasant hills, planted with young trees, and all the lower

banks adorned with flowers. And from some hollow parts of those hills, fountains come gliding down, which, in the far-off landscape, seemed to all to be converted to a river.

Over all, a serene sky, with transparent clouds, giving great lustre to the whole work, which did imitate a pleasant spring.

(lines 19–27)

And as in *Love's Triumph through Callipolis*, once again the masque began with music. The whole of the introductory section was sung, making the masque more akin to the world of opera than that of the drama where, in spite of all, Jonson still had his artistic home.

With the anti-masque comes the first section in which Jonson was able to work relatively untrammelled by the need to provide for Jones's 'shows'. It was performed by 'a dwarf-post from hell' who burst in as the rude intruder of masque formula to disturb the harmony of the revels, and to threaten the supremacy of the central character. The part was played by Queen Henrietta's dwarf, who made his entrance riding upon a docked pony,[1] after which Jonson launched him into a racy prose monologue. This chirpy little 'postilion of hell' is cast in the form of a cockney gossip, armed with all the latest news of the inhabitants. This anti-masque perfectly fulfils the Jacobean requirement of its function, that it should provide a total contrast to the masque proper.

But simple contrast is not enough. Theoretically, the anti-masque should be both in balance with and apposition to the main theme. The mounted dwarf's entry cannot but be a *coup de théâtre* – it is faintly reminiscent of the Gypsy Jackman with his mounted horse in *The Masque of the Gypsies Metamorphosed* from twelve years before – but its relevance to the spring theme, or to the framework of the rites of the goddess, is quite obscure, indeed non-existent. Then again, Jonson had indulged himself, in writing the dwarf's speech, with various indecencies of the grosser sort that King James had relished but which the fastidious King Charles most certainly did not. Describing his entry into the court, the 'dwarf-post' is made to declare that he was only allowed in 'by the favour of one of the guard who was a woman's taylor, and held ope the passage' (lines 155–6). The king was not amused.

The dwarf's main function is to introduce the persons of the anti-masque, to open in effect the Pandora's box of evils that will disturb the harmony of the proceedings. These are, however, as in

Love's Triumph through Callipolis, wordless characters who dance and exit, with the climax of the anti-masque being not a verbal response but one of Jones's ingenious scene changes. For the rest of the masque, all Jonson's words are sung, while further scenic marvels feed the eyes of the spectators. At the close of the action, such unity as the piece has possessed as a pastoral is shattered by the sudden appearance of four allegorical figures of Poetry, History, Architecture and Sculpture, attended by Fame, who are all brought on to praise Chloris and to dignify her rites. These personages, seated on a hill that Jones contrived to raise from the earth, provided him with a splendid series of design opportunities. For Jonson they simply posed the problem of their convincing integration into the world of flowers. And as with the companion piece to this masque, the final moment and climax of the piece was visual, as these allegorical figures made their appearance, declared their nature, and then sank away again when their hill disappeared.

Such was the ending of Jonson's career as the court masque-maker – one not unworthy of his long service, but far removed from his own criteria of what the masque should be. With his last two productions in this genre Jonson was on happier ground; away from the court and commissioned to create the kind of country welcome with which he had first come to the attention of the royal family at the start of James's reign in 1603. The two entertainments with which Jonson concluded both this type of production and his public writing career as a whole, are again a linked pair like the masques; the second was devised as a sequel and response to the success of the first. And like the masques again, they are quite dissimilar to one another, and in no aspect a repetition of what has gone before.

The King's Entertainment at Welbeck in Nottinghamshire, to give it its full formal title, is much longer, and more masque-like, than its successor, *Love's Welcome, the King and Queen's Entertainment at Bolsover*. Opening with a sung dialogue between the passions of Doubt and Love, it follows the debate formula so familiar to the masque structure. Working with his usual care 'to make all fitting', Jonson introduces a reference of geographical aptness to 'old Sherwood' and the area in which the masque was taking place. Following the formal welcome came a kind of anti-masque; as the king was about to mount his horse, two curious characters were 'discovered' in the crowd.

These two, Accidence and Fitzale, are the local teacher and antiquary respectively, and in their combination of affected learning with simple ignorance, recall Shakespeare's Holofernes and Sir Nathaniel from *Love's Labour's Lost*. In a variety of verse forms, and with a good deal of gentle humour, the pair introduce rustic games and combat for an impending country bridal. The similarity of the theme to that of *A Tale of a Tub* clouds rather than clarifies the attribution of that play to any particular phase of Jonson's creative career. What seems clear, though, is that Jonson drew on the raw material of the drama to body out his entertainment. The country sections have a sweetness and lack of sophistication not normally used by Jonson in his work for the court:

> Six hoods they are, and of the blood,
> They tell, of ancient Robin Hood.

Here the six hoods presented themselves severally, in their livery hoods [i.e., men wearing different coloured hoods] . . .

> Red-hood, the first that doth appear,
> In stamel [a coarse woollen cloth]; scarlet is too dear.
> Then green-hood. He's in Kendal green
> As in the forest colour seen.
> Next blue-hood is, and in that hue
> Doth vaunt a heart as pure and true
> As is the sky (give him his due)
> Of old England the yeoman blue . . .

(lines 171–81)

Jonson clearly knew better than to tread upon the king's limited Stuart interest in the doings of his poorer subjects – he caused the rustic revels to be swiftly broken up by 'a Gentleman' who enters with the rebuke 'Give end unto your rudeness.' This modulates easily into a discussion of the king and finally into a praise and blessing to confirm the 'welcome, welcome, welcome' of the opening strains.

Jonson here calculated with all his old accuracy of judgement. King Charles liked the *Entertainment*, and Jonson was once more called upon to create a welcoming show when the royal visit was repeated in the next year, 1634. But *Love's Welcome, the King and Queen's Entertainment at Bolsover*, was another new departure for Jonson. The entertainment opened in the manner of the later masques, with a song in three parts, to deliver the introduction and make the initial welcome:

COMPLIMENT.

Could we put on all the beauty of all creatures,
Sing in the air, and notes of nightingales,
Exhale the sweets of Earth, and all her features,
And tell you, softer than in silk, these tales,
Welcome should season all for taste.
                                        And hence
At every real banquet to the sense,
Welcome, true welcome, fill the compliments.

                                    (lines 26–32)

But Jonson daringly followed this stately formality with another part of the show in which, by way of anti-masque, he introduced a satiric portrait of Inigo Jones, under the names of 'Coronell Vitruvius' and 'Iniquo'. The proximity of this masque to the *Tale of a Tub* indicates that in fact the king and queen were treated to the caricature of Jones that the enraged designer had had suppressed in that play. In this instance, Jonson had the last word. He seems not to have incorporated the full satiric study in all its fierceness – this 'Vitruvius' is neither a very long nor a harsh study – but he did not hold back from showing the king his Surveyor as a foolish fuss-pot always trying to look busier than he was. The clumsy, garrulous showman with his rattling prose patter is succeeded by a verse dialogue between Eros and Anteros, a motif borrowed from Jonson's own *A Challenge at Tilt* of so many years before, and the entertainment concluded with a speech reconciling these disputants and exalting the royal spectators who by their presence had converted the place to a 'school of love'. As Jonson's letters to his patron the Earl of Newcastle indicate, he had taken anxious pains over these pieces and his care was not defeated.

Of all Jonson's productions in these final years, the least problematic for him were his poems. In the theatre of his verse he could construct the ideal audience, one that would not abuse his work by destroying it through malice or misunderstanding. He could, too, rely upon the actors in his poetic theatre not to mangle or misperform their parts, since they were entirely at his command. The volume of poetry he wrote testifies to the importance it played in his life; the *Underwood*[2] contains ninety pieces of varying length, and Jonson was also regularly contributing commendatory verses to the work of others, in addition to other occasional pieces now brought together as his *Ungathered Verse* in modern editions.

Unfortunately the *Underwood* has not çome down to us in the finished shape perfected by the poet, as the *Epigrams* and *Forest* have done. Jonson had begun to put the collection together, as a prefatory note to the reader explaining the title shows:

> With the same leave [that] the ancients called that kind of body *sylva* or ῞γλη, in which there were works of diverse nature and matter congested, as the multitude call timber trees, promiscuously growing, a wood or forest; so I am bold to entitle these lesser poems of later growth by this of *Underwood*, out of the analogy they hold to *the Forest* in my former book, and no other.
>
> Ben Jonson.

The sequence as it was eventually printed displays some signs of order. It opens with three religious poems, followed by 'a celebration of Charis in ten lyric pieces', the songs of sacred love off-setting the secular in a thoroughly Jonsonian arrangement. Nine lyrics of love and womankind, all short and light, are succeeded by four grave and lengthy poems addressed to men close to Jonson and dealing with the theme of friendship; again, the classical apposition of women's love with the weightier and more valuable relationships with men is clearly traceable not only to the substance of Jonson's reading, but to the practices of his life. Thereafter the poems have no discernible pattern, and jumble together a variety of pieces of differing lengths and contrasted poetic modes. Lyric, elegy, ode and epigram are all represented, some, interestingly, from much earlier in Jonson's writing career, like *Underwood* 25, 'An Ode to James, Earl of Desmond, Writ in Queen Elizabeth's Time, Since Lost, and Recovered'.

As this suggests, the *Underwood* is an unusual collection and despite Jonson's somewhat tentative description of its contents as 'lesser poems of later growth', one of great power. Although the level of the writing is uneven, individual poems or groups of poems rank with the most accomplished and moving of all Jonson's work. Jonson here extends his range considerably, pushing forward into areas of thought and experience which he has previously explored little, if at all. First of these, to give them the primacy they hold in the collection itself, are the three poems of devotion: one addressed to the Holy Trinity, one a 'Hymn to God the Father', and one 'A Hymn on the Nativity of my Saviour'. These three pieces, none of which is longer than forty-eight lines, are almost the only witness to the religious basis of

Jonson's thought, an element of profound significance although so little visible.

For the only connection that they make with any of Jonson's previous verse is with the climactic poem of *The Forest*, 'To Heaven'. Jonson's explicitly religious poems are to be distinguished from those on moral themes like epigrams 34, 'On Death', and 80, 'Of Life and Death', or his many epitaphs, all of which contain a reflective or philosophical element. In making the selection and arrangement of the opening poems of *Underwood*, Jonson picked up the theme with which he had closed the earlier collection, of 'great and good God'. *Forest* 15, 'To Heaven', however, is rather a poem about the difficulty of making the correct religious response, than an examination of a spiritual state like the three poems in *Underwood*. Its exasperated opening

> Great and good God, can I not think of thee
> But it must straight my melancholy be?

demonstrates Jonson's concern not to be misunderstood in his religious observations, when his impulses of piety are interpreted as signs of 'disease', a depressive malady. His sense of frustration acts as a stumbling-block to the expression of his feelings:

> Yet dare I not complain, or wish for death
> With holy Paul, lest it be thought the breath
> Of discontent; or that these prayers be
> For weariness of life, not love of thee.
>
> (Forest 15)

In the poems of the *Underwood*, this resentful awareness of the unsympathetic outsider is entirely absent, and the poet takes the reader directly to the experience of a limed soul struggling to reach its maker:

> O holy, blessed, glorious Trinity
> Of persons, still one God in unity,
> The faithful man's believed mystery,
>   Help, help to lift
>
> Myself up to Thee, harrowed, torn and bruised
> By sin and Satan; and my flesh misused,
> As my heart lies in pieces, all confused,
>   Oh, take my gift.
>
> ('Poems of Devotion', I.i, lines 1–8)

266

Moments like this remind us, however faintly, of Jonson's long association with that other mighty spiritual wrestler, John Donne. There are echoes, too, of Herbert, whose first collection, *The Temple*, was published in 1633, in the final piece of this trio of devotional poems, the 'Hymn to God the Father':

> Hear me, O God!
> A broken heart
> Is my best part;
> Use still thy rod,
> That I may prove
> Therein thy love . . .
> ('Poems of Devotion',
> I.ii, lines 1–6)

The short verse line and the varied stanzaic patterns in themselves indicate Jonson's departure from his normal poetic mode; and in these unaffected poems of deep emotion there is a welcome freedom from Jonson's tendency towards strenuous poeticization. There is no sense of the poet's performance of his role and feelings which mars some of the other poems, but rather a realization of some fine and subtle impulses of great simplicity.

Jonson's sacred verses, although few in number, go some way to repairing a gap in his poetic repertoire. During this period of his creative life Jonson also chose to pay his dues to another neglected deity, the god of love. *Underwood* 2, the 'Celebration of Charis', is an elaborate poem of ten linked pieces, on 'His Excuse for Loving', 'How He Saw Her', 'What He Suffered', and so on. In the search for any illumination or amplification of the desert area of Jonson's love relationships, biographers have seized upon some of the twenty-seven love poems in the *Underwood* for a personal interpretation. This is not borne out by external evidence; apart from the difficulty of finding the lady and identifying the object of Jonson's autumnal passion, it is hardly conceivable that a man as gossiped about as Jonson was could have pursued a love affair of any significance without anyone in the small world of London society observing and recording the fact.

But clearly the Jonson of this phase recognized love and courtship as a poetic field that he had so far left untilled. More significantly, he had reached the stage at which Horace, his guide and standard, had made poetic material out of the inappropriateness of love, begging Venus not to renew her torments of a man who had safely attained his old age (*Odes* IV, I, 'To Venus'). Jonson's combination of classical and conventional motifs with material that yet is still evidently drawn from direct personal experience makes for a constantly shifting perspective and tone in these love pieces. The echo of Horace is heard in the opening invocation to Charis:

> Let it not your wonder move,
> Less your laughter, that I love;
> Though I now write fifty years,
> I have had, and have my peers . . .
> (*Underwood* 2, i, lines 1–4)

Other pieces in this 'celebration' are purely conventional, and as such indeterminately applicable; two of the three stanzas in the fourth poem of the sequence consist of the song with which Wittipol courts Mistress Fitzdottrell in *The Devil is an Ass* of 1616. Others again are so purely impersonal that they have the appearance, although not the feel, of a poetic exercise, like *Underwood* 36, 'A Song':

> *Lover*
> Come, let us here enjoy the shade,
> For love in shadow is best made.
> Though envy oft his shadow be,
> None brooks the sunlight worse than he.
>
> *Mistress*
> Where love doth shine, there needs no sun,
> All lights into his one doth run;
> Without which all the world were dark,
> Yet he himself is but a spark.
>
> *Arbiter*
> A spark to set whole worlds afire,
> Who more they burn, they more desire,
> And have their being their waste to see,
> And waste still, that they still might be.
>
> *Chorus*
> Such are his powers, whom time hath styled
> Now swift, now slow, now tame, now wild;
> Now hot, now cold, now fierce, now mild;
> The eldest god, yet still a child.

Strongly contrasted with such pieces are the poems in which Jonson draws overtly upon his own self for poetic material, and in particular upon his own body, the source of so much matter on themes other than love. Jonson's age, his twenty-stone weight, his massive belly and blasted visage are employed as foils to the traditional expectation of youth and beauty in a lover, to draw out, through Jonson's pervasive irony, the complexities of this emotion. Occasionally, however, the poet takes the reader below the glittering ironic surface to share the pain and anxiety that attend the experience of age and love:

> Oh, but my conscious fears,
>   That fly my thoughts between
>   Tell me that she hath seen
>   My hundred of grey hairs,
>   Told seven and forty years,
> Read so much waste, as she cannot embrace
> My mountain belly, and my rocky face;
> And all these through her eyes have stopped her ears.
>   (*Underwood* 9, lines 11–18)

Throughout the poems that went to make up the *Underwood*, Jonson displays a far greater readiness to employ this sort of material than he had done earlier. Now, all his life experience became grist to the mill, as opposed to the carefully selected elements deployed by Jonson 'The Epigrammatist' in his first collection of poetic pieces. There the persona of the moral arbiter and scourge of the times had boxed the poet into a constant display of his own self-control and superiority to others. Freed of that constraint Jonson could colloquially confess ' 'Tis true, I'm broke', or share with a friend his sense of grievance at being rejected for the state preparations for Prince Charles's Spanish bride (*Underwood* 38 and 47). This greatly extended the range of his possible subjects and stances, with a corresponding deepening of the emotional impact of the poems.

Yet the abandoning of the persona of the snarling satirist did not mean that Jonson denied himself any expression of his satirical genius. Two linked pieces in the *Underwood*, 20 and 21, are devoted to a savage fling at the expense of their unnamed victims. In the first, ironically entitled by Jonson 'A Satirical Shrub', the poet paraded his lifelong and now hardened anti-feminism, waxing sarcastic about the possibility of the existence of such a thing as 'a woman's friendship', and going on to attack the sex in general: 'their whole life' is 'wickedness', 'their whole inside full of ends and knots'. This woman is only typical of her sex:

> Do not you ask to know her; she is worse
> Than all the ingredients made into one curse,
> And that poured out upon mankind, can be!
> Think but the sin of all her sex, 'tis she!
> I could forgive her being proud, a whore,
> Perjured and painted, if she were no more:
> But she is such as she might yet forestall
> The devil, and be the damning of us all.
>
> (lines 17–24)

The parallel attack upon the male is not couched in these generalized terms. But it is composed in Jonson's most brutal satiric manner, with the subject of this 'Little Shrub Growing By' vilified as a 'plague', a 'poison', 'a parcel of court-dirt, a heap and mass / Of all vice hurled together'. The 'dirt' metaphor is pursued to its conclusion when the man is finally designated as a 'lay-stall' (dung-heap).

These extracts can hardly do justice to the range and variety of the subjects through which Jonson moves in the *Underwood*. Noble epistles, epigrams, warm epistles to friends, courtly salutations to his patrons and everyday exchanges with ordinary people make this theatre of Jonson's poetry thoroughly representational of his intellectual and personal preoccupations. Particularly poignant are those poems from Jonson's closing years, when the old poet had to master a form he had never before had to attempt, the 'Epistle Mendicant' (*Underwood* 71). Meanwhile the roll-call of epitaphs and exequies testifies to the series of deaths Jonson was called upon to notice in the midst of his own difficulties. Clearly the ability to have emotional resort to his poetry maintained its importance in Jonson's life, if anything increasing as the years went by.

Jonson's own sense of the value of his poetry is evidenced from the unsparing pains he took over each piece. Inevitably some betray the characteristic Jonsonian fault of seeming to be only versifications of the occasion that provoked them. But none is less than deliberately and finely wrought, manifesting Jonson's by now enormous technical competence, his versification so smooth and persuasive as to appear effortless. For 'the poet' persevered still with his 'wonted studies', and the *Underwood* consistently reveals Jonson's classical scholarship not only in its ease and range of classical allusion and reference, but also in the pieces of translation from Petronius, Martial and others, with which the collection ends.

A translation from the Latin was Jonson's other main poetic task in his last years, and one of at least equal importance in his eyes. His version of Horace's *Art of Poetry*, turned into an English that would both describe and exemplify the desired qualities, had been on the stocks since Jonson was writing *Sejanus* in 1603. The fire of twenty years later had destroyed the version that Jonson had by then written, and later again he undertook the labour of recalling or reconstructing this piece – these actions amply suggestive of the primary place that he accorded it among his poetic productions.

The result is a lengthy act of piety to the old Roman master of Jonson's professed art, which won some admiration in his own time but has had scant attention since. The reason for this may be deduced from the poem's opening lines:

> If to a woman's head a painter would
> Set a horse-neck, and divers feathers fold
> On every limb, taken from a several creature,
> Presenting upward a fair female feature
> Which in some swarthy fish uncomely ends . . .

Jonson's translation is so knotty, so literal and so compacted, that the reader can hardly understand it without benefit of the original Latin to throw some light on the meaning. Jonson encounters throughout the problem of trying to turn a language of tremendous resonance and compression into one which does not have the same powers of suggestion. In the interests of faithful translation, he resisted the natural solution of expanding the Latin, and constricted himself too by his choice of his preferred form, the tight couplet, as the medium. The result is a stiff, clotted piece of some 680 lines in a rigid, unnatural English bristling with quite unnaturalized versions of Latin construction and syntax, like 'the very root of writing well and spring / Is to be wise' (lines 440–1). Here Jonson's attempt to reproduce the Latin word-order of Horace ('*Scribendi recte, sapere, est et principium et fons*') produces a sentence in which 'spring' becomes detached from 'root' which it should accompany, and seems, confusingly, to be linked with 'well', thus rendering the meaning hopelessly obscure. It is a saddening reflection that the hours of painful labour which must have gone into the poem 'Horace, of the Art of Poetry' were so misplaced; and that the piece so laboriously produced has given no

271

subsequent reader the pleasure Jonson both took in and expected of it
– see HS VIII, 303–55 for the parallel texts in English and Latin.

Jonson's ungathered verse is of interest rather as cataloguing the
names and numbers of his friends, since the majority of it consists of
poems which Jonson contributed by way of commendation to the
poems or works of other writers, than as poetry in its own right. This
group contains, however, Jonson's justly celebrated lines on
Shakespeare (*Ungathered Verse* 26), some of which have passed into a
proverbial immortality: 'He was not of an age, but for all time!' (line
43). There are, too, pieces of hate as well as of love, like the
'Expostulation' with 'Tire-man, Mountebank, and Justice Jones'
(*Ungathered Verse* 35), in which Jonson not only vented his spleen at
Jones's arrogance, imperfect Latin and social climbing, but also
developed some of his views on the nature of the visual element in
court entertainment:

> O shows! shows! Mighty shows!
> The eloquence of masques! What need of prose
> Or verse, or sense, to express immortal you?
> (*Ungathered Verse* 34, lines 39–41)

But Jonson's concerns were not exclusively with his personal relations. Two distinguished epitaphs, 28 and 31 in this collection,
written on the aunt and the mother of Jonson's patron, the Earl (later
Duke) of Newcastle, indicate some of the other strands in Jonson's
professional life.

These occasional and incidental pieces, found among Jonson's
papers after his death, or garnered from the pages of the often obscure
and undistinguished books they were written to grace, do not all
proceed from the last few years of Jonson's life – the earliest,
Ungathered Verse 1, comes from 1598. But those examples from the
final phase bring to an impressive total the poems which Jonson
composed at a time when his resources were never more strained. That
he could continue to create poems with so little evidence of strain, and
with no sustained diminution of his standard and ability, witnesses to
his true attainment of his chosen role of 'the poet'.

As a poet, Jonson's chief preoccupation was always with language,
and with his enormous intellectual tenacity and thoroughness he
made the time during his crowded working life to acquaint himself
thoroughly with the tools of his trade. The result of Jonson's studies of
language and syntax came together as his *English Grammar*. Like the

translation of Horace, this was another attempt on a subject whose original version had perished in the study fire of 1623; in the 'Execration upon Vulcan', *Underwood* 43, Jonson lamented the loss of 'a grammar', whose purpose was 'to teach some what their nurses could not do, / The purity of language' (lines 91–2). Jonson valued the *Grammar* sufficiently highly to undertake the labour of rewriting it; and a substantial work, in two books of thirty-one chapters all told, had been written, although not completed, by the time of Jonson's death.

In the revision Jonson's fuller intentions were made clear. The work was designed to be an aid both to foreigners seeking to master English and to native speakers desirous of understanding or improving their grasp of the language. As Jonson explained in his brief preface:

> The profit of Grammar is great to strangers, who are to live in communion and commerce with us; and it is honourable to ourselves. For by it we communicate all our labours, studies, profits, without an interpreter.
>
> We free our language from the opinion of rudeness, and barbarism, wherewith it is mistaken to be diseased; we show the copy of it, and matchableness with other tongues; we ripen the wits of our own children and youth sooner by it, and advance their knowledge.
>
> (HS VII, 465)

To Jonson, grammar as the foundation of language was a matter of supreme importance, for in one of his jottings he had noted: 'Language most shows a man! speak, that I may see thee' (HS VIII, 625). Again, in one of the Latin tags that Jonson had laboured to collect he had stated his belief that 'a delight' in words is the beginning of eloquence' (HS VIII, 621). In the furtherance of his crucial task, then, Jonson employed both his resources of scholarship, a questing, independent mind and a deep search of all available materials and accounts. Other teachers, grammarians and writers had made attempts on the Herculean task of unravelling the tangles of English etymology, spelling, pronunciation, and syntax. Jonson faithfully consulted whatever authorities he could discover, not limiting himself to those who had addressed themselves to English – James Howell had procured for him the Welsh grammar of Dr Davis, and one of the writers whose work Jonson leaned on most heavily was the Parisian grammarian and Latinist Pierre de la Ramée.[3]

The result is an engaging production, highly idiosyncratic and often mistaken, but an undoubted achievement in an age that had no facility for the comparative or scientific study of language. Jonson's perennial bent towards Latin was responsible for a consistent degree of misinterpretation; he was possessed of the conviction that the principles of English usage must not only be illustrated with Latin examples, but must be based upon Latin, and this misled him. But he was the first English scholar to try to work through a consistent system of phonetics as applied to English speech, and to tackle the problem of the classification of English verbs. Further, in an age which saw a good deal of false etymology through a pedantic desire to dignify native words with inauthentic Latin or Greek roots Jonson urged the return to essential simplicities, and placed as the value above all others in speech and writing the cultivation of what was sound, natural and unaffected.

Jonson was also touchingly conscious of the possible shortcomings of his study. Of one topic he remarks in passing,

This would ask a larger time and field, than is here given for that examination: but since I am assigned to this province, that it is the lot of my age, after thirty years' conversation with men, to be *elementarius senex* [an old man struggling with first principles] . . . to the end [that] our tongue may be made equal to those of the renowned countries, Italy and Greece . . . and as for the difficulty, that shall never withdraw, or put me off from the attempt. For neither is any excellent thing done with ease, nor the compassing of this any whit to be despaired.

(HS VIII, 501)

With the increase of knowledge, linguistic studies have progressed beyond Jonson's possible area of competence, and his *English Grammar* has not stood the test of time either as technical treatise, or as a piece of prose to be read for its own sake. But it demands to be thought of as a work that absorbed an enormous amount of Jonson's time and energy in proportion to the achieved result, and one on which Jonson's claim to be a serious scholar, rather than a comedy playwright with intellectual pretensions, must be based.

Jonson's other work of scholarship, albeit of a more random and informal nature than the *English Grammar*, also dates substantially from the last period of his working career after the 1623 fire. Unlike the *Grammar*, the 'Explorata, or Discoveries', entitled 'Timber' in the

274

1640 Folio, has had a considerable and respectful readership in the modern period, despite its irregular, indeed unclassifiable format. What it consists of is a series of notes, jottings and short essays on moral, political and literary themes, supported with many Latin quotations, and classical or modern examples of what is under consideration. Early critical approaches to the 'Discoveries' made much of Jonson's originality and power of thought – subsequent investigation revealed that almost half of Jonson's critical remarks on poetry, for instance, were translations or paraphrases of another critic's work, the *De Tragoediae Constitutione De Satyra* of the European scholar Heinsius.[4] The work in fact incorporates extracts culled from a wide range of classical and Renaissance authors and critics – Seneca, Plutarch, Buchler, Vives, Lipsius, Scaliger and Hoskyns.

In effect, the *Discoveries* represents a commonplace book of Jonson's reading and study – and by no means his only or even principal work in this mode, since he stoically recorded in the 'Execration upon Vulcan' (*Underwood* 43) the loss of his records of his 'search and mastery in the arts', especially some 'twice twelve years' stored-up humanity', the gleanings of his lifetime's reading in innumerable works of poetry, drama, languages, the law, and all the numerous interests to which Jonson's known library of books bears witness. It is impossible to know whether or not Jonson ever intended the *Discoveries* for publication. This seems unlikely, since the purpose of a commonplace book was quite other than this, and most of the material is of the sort which Jonson clearly had in mind to use for something else; as a suggestion for an epigram, for instance, or an incident that could be bodied out for a scene in a comedy, while others seem to have an educative purpose, if only that of the daily practice of self-improvement which Jonson had been trained to at Westminster.

Certainly the *Discoveries* can never have been meant for publication in its extant form. Jonson's papers were evidently thrown together for the press to accompany the 1640 Folio and are scrappily edited throughout, with no attempt to maximize the links that already exist quite fortuitously between some areas of the writings. Many of the short sententious passages on moral or ethical themes, for instance, could have been grouped together with advantage, but have been printed apparently in the order in which they were discovered. Later critics have both censured the arrangement as it stands, and attempted the task of rearranging the extracts in a more coherent form.

But even as it stands, *Discoveries* is a work of deep interest and delight. These pieces, of varying lengths, all share one key unifying factor – they all were selected for their meaning and power of suggestion to Jonson. His habits of mind were ingrained and consistent; his borrowings were made in accordance with his living and working principles of forty-odd years of study and thought. This it is that lends these comments and notes their sombre authority, their resonance, strength and sinew. They were gathered to feed one of the hungriest and most powerful minds of the age; and cannot therefore but have an underlying consistency, and a corresponding capacity to nourish the thought and feeling of others:

> I know of no disease of the soul, but ignorance; not of the arts and science, but of itself. Yet relating to those, it is a pernicious evil; the darkener of man's life, the disturber of his reason, and common confounder of truth; with which a man goes groping in the dark no otherwise than if he were blind. Great understandings are most wracked and troubled with it; nay, they sometimes will choose to die, than not to know the things they study for. Think then what an evil it is; and what good the contrary.
>
> (HS VIII, 588)

For as this shows, none of Jonson's extracts is simply lifted bodily from its original context and dropped down in Jonson's pages; it passes first through the filter of Jonson's subtle and sensitive thought process, taking on the peculiarly Jonsonian colour on the way. In addition, Jonson draws freely upon his own experience to exemplify the truths he garners, and this is one of the principal elements giving the book its charm and fascination. In a discussion of writing for the stage, Jonson will casually remark, 'I remember the players have often mentioned it as an honour to Shakespeare, that in his writing, whatsoever he penned, he never blotted a line '(HS VIII, 583). Such off-hand insights permeate the *Discoveries* like a multitude of unexpected good things.

But however informal, Jonson's effects were not achieved unawares. The collection functions throughout as the working tool of a writer of conscious art, striving endlessly to refine the moral basis of his thought, his ethical capacity, his critical theory and his experience of life. The commentary shows the constant evidence of the play of Jonson's mind on every issue no matter how significant or how trivial. Jonson made no attempt to synthesize his heterogeneous material, whose value to him lay in its very diversity and range. His confidence here gave him the ability to cut through a good deal of extraneous matter on a given issue, and to penetrate directly to the essentials, never letting pedantry or obscurity hinder his grasp, as in these observations on style:

> Custom is the most certain mistress of language, as the public stamp makes the current money. But we must not be too frequent with the mint, every day coining. Nor fetch words from the utmost ages, since the chief virtue of a style is perspicuity, and nothing so vicious in it as to need an interpreter. Words borrowed of antiquity do lend a kind of majesty to style, and are not without their delight sometimes. For they have the authority of years, and out of their intermission do win to themselves a kind of grace like newness. But the eldest of the present, and the newness of the past language, is the best.
>
> (HS VIII, 622)

As a record of Jonson's thought the *Discoveries* holds a unique place in the Jonson canon. It serves too, as an indication, however skeletal, of Jonson's body of teaching, largely lost to posterity in the absence of a Boswell who could have shared and preserved encounters with the numerous individuals and groups who came to learn from him. Principally, however, the *Discoveries* embodies and preserves Jonson's unwearying compulsion not only to express his critical ideas, but to reincarnate the underlying classical conceptions of truth and beauty of which his critical theories and moral beliefs alike were the product. All these come together in gentle pedagogic moments such as this: 'A poem, as I have told you, is the work of the poet, the end and fruit of his labour and study. Poesy is his skill, or craft of making' (HS VIII, 636) – here are the authentic accents of 'Father Ben'.

With the *Discoveries* Jonson came to the close of his circle. Even when he could no longer undertake the labour of shaping up a play for the stage, and found that his muse of poetry only peeped out once in a hundred days as he reported in *Underwood* 71, he nevertheless kept on with the consolation of his reading and study. This collection of accumulated wisdom is an appropriate final monument for one who above all fought against that 'disease of the soul [called] ignorance': Jonson never ceased to seek the profit of the mind even as his bodily frame decayed.

And at the end, as the *Discoveries* shows, Jonson reverted ever more strongly to his intellectual origins, the creative wellspring of his poetry-making, his 'wonted studies', the classics. To the last 'the ancients' provided the main grist to his literary mill, and the principal yardstick by which his productions were to be judged. Yet he was never, as generations of critics and cavillers have had it, a 'mere translator' or 'plagiary'. Certainly Jonson could and did take a Greek or Latin original and turn it into English with an almost ferocious fidelity, so that the native sinews are stretched to cracking-point in his determination to accommodate the heavy and unwieldy foreign phrases. But in general his method was that of the 'mere empiric', his motive to develop and demonstrate his craft in emulation of the greatest 'makers' of the past.

What this meant in practice was very far removed from any mere translation. Jonson's starting-point was to take an idea, an image, or even a phrase, and build from there, gathering materials as he needed but letting his own muse shape and determine the end product. One of his most famous and beloved lyrics, for example, is rather dismissively stigmatized by Herford and Simpson as 'a cento adroitly pieced together from the *Epistles* of Philostratus' (HS XI, 39). Subsequent research, however, has demonstrated that Jonson knew the piece both in the original Greek and in a later Latin version, and worked carefully from both in order to polish up his own version. So successful is the poetic method, so seamless the patchwork, that who can detect the ancient skeleton beneath the newly fleshed form?

> Drink to me only with thine eyes,
>   And I will pledge with mine;
> Or leave a kiss within the cup,
>   And I'll not look for wine.
> The thirst that from the soul doth rise
>   Doth ask a drink divine;
> But might I of Jove's nectar sup,
>   I would not change for thine.
>
> I sent thee late a rosy wreath
>   Not so much honouring thee
> As giving it a hope that there,
>   It could not withered be.
> But thou thereon didst only breathe,
>   And sentst it back to me;
> Since when it grows and breathes, I swear,
>   Not of itself, but thee.
>
> (*Forest* 9)

Only in the creation of such pieces was Jonson able to engage most closely and directly with the classical heritage that gave him what he needed in the way of form, subject-matter and an absolute standard. But his classicism was never mere pedantry; it was an impulse too broad and profound to expend itself in technical exercises. He strove always for the timeless classical virtues of unity, symmetry, clarity and proportion. His poetry demonstrates his continued confidence in the stability of these values, both as moral and technical attributes. It was this confidence, unshaken through a lifetime of professional vicissitude, rather than any shortage of poetic inspiration, that caused Jonson to return so frequently to the writers of ancient Greece and Rome. He lived not merely his intellectual life, but his whole existence in and through the ancient great; everywhere he found their comments and discoveries validated by his own. For him the worlds of classical literature and personal experience were one, the past continually illuminating the present that as continually echoed it. This meant that Jonson's classicism was never dry or academic but remained fresh, newly vitalized by his everyday living; the past linked with the present, and the chain of human experience passed on to the future generations. It was one of Jonson's proudest hopes, to be a simple link in this chain. And if the ear of the trained classicist hears in Jonson's verse the tread of Martial, Horace, Seneca and a host of others, then the poet would only have retorted with impatience that he would have expected no less.

Jonson's classicism began as a reference back to a source of undisputed authority, whose worth was proved by its endurance through the ages down to the present day of Jonson's lifetime. His use of the classics became more eclectic as his craftsmanship developed, as he increasingly mined the ancient writers for materials and forms which would support and develop his own views. The danger of Jonson's classicism to his evolution as an artist came when his use of this reference point hardened into a blind faith in the authority of the classical precedent; when his adoption of classical modes became rigid and ungiving. It led him to deny the importance of the romantic and the sensuous, and made him eventually implacably hostile to appeals other than to the power of the mind. It brought an unamiable pedantry, too – Jonson always tried to classicize the spelling of Greek and Latin derivatives in English, which led to such monstrosities as 'tragœdie', 'æmulation', and 'prætext'. Classicism thus became a matter of linguistic dogma which he adopted with a campaigning zeal. The result of all this was a threatening stiffness, a stifling of the vitality that Jonson by nature possessed in abundance, and which alone could lift his work to the highest standards of excellence that he craved.

This was the constant tension that Jonson spent his life's work in the attempt to negotiate, between the native springs of his vitality and the frameworks and forms he found necessary to control it. The classical framework supplied the discipline; but sometimes at the expense of the free-flowing movement, the dynamic of the individual idea. In life, too, there was an opposition between his classical ideals of moderation and decorum, his contemporary conditioning and nurture, and his fervent nature and animal high spirits. Thus the didacticism of much Latin literature takes a distinctively Christian and Renaissance turn in Jonson's hands, while the punitive and hostile attitudes of the medieval theorists animate his satirical thinking.

In the work of Jonson and in that of his contemporaries, the sustained intensity and acerbity of the satiric literature of the sixteenth century surpasses even that of the bitterest of the classical satirists. Jonson's work contains much classical learning, but a strongly modified classical technique. Generations have thought of Jonson as an intellectual, but many of his plays and poems contain a physical, even gross element; the purge and vomit sequence in *Poetaster*, for example. Jonson also had a decided taste for the indecent and the obscene, indeed the frankly filthy, which is likewise masked by his pose as the venerable classical scholar, and his repeated claims never to have been foul. He usually kept his vulgarities in character and context. But he obviously relished a spice of the salacious, even though he could also attack audiences who 'swallow up the garbage of the time' in preferring bawdy and old jests to solid matter.

From this conflict proceeded Jonson's irritability of disposition, and the paradox of his behaviour. He *was* the grave and reverend classical poet. He was also the boastful boozer and ungoverned layabout. The lapses from the classical standard, the *via media*, all too frequently expressed themselves in a lack of emotional distance, a failure of detachment, which brought shameful consequences in their wake. But whenever Jonson fell below his own ideals, it was by the standards of the classical world that he judged his failure; and in the language and phraseology of the classical writers that he castigated his own imperfections along with those of the rest of erring humanity.

The mature Jonson, at the height of his powers, unquestionably gave life to everything he touched. As a writer, he may not have been gifted with what Sidney in *Astrophil and Stella* called 'thoughts of gold', inspirations so pure and perfect that they simply needed casting into words to prove poetic coin. For Jonson, the labour was integral to the transmutation, and a great effort, with a certain amount of luck, went into making the finished result genuine tender. In later life Jonson's powers of synthesizing began to fail him, and his chosen subjects, recalcitrant to the tried and tested Jonsonian method, by and large declined to be brought to full creative life. This, however, is no indictment of the method, of Jonson's dedicated, polished craftsmanship; nor yet of the art which at its highest it achieved.

And at the last, Jonson himself knew that like his 'beloved' Shakespeare, 'he was not of an age, but for all time'. He could, at 'the close, or shutting up of his circle', look back on a working lifetime of continuous commitment to the highest goals, and to an achievement over a range of subject areas unequalled by any writer of his age, or indeed of any other. The enduring philosophy of the *Discoveries* offers a final apt comment on the often startling vicissitudes of this life:[5]

> Ill fortune never crushed that man whom good fortune deceived not. I therefore have counselled my friends, never to trust to her fairer side, though she seemed to make peace with them; but to place all things she gave them so as she might ask them again without their trouble; she might take them from them and not pull them, to keep always a distance between her and themselves. He knows not his own strength, that has not met adversity. Heaven prepares good men with crosses; but no ill can happen to a good man.
>
> (HS VIII, 563)

Discoveries also affords a glimpse of Jonson's last mellow musings on his life's most precious endeavour, 'the craft of making':

> These three voices differ, the *Poem*, the *Poesy* and the *Poet*. Now the *Poesy* is the Art, nay rather the Queen of Arts . . . but before we make court to the Art itself as a Mistress, I would lead you to the knowledge of our Poet. . . . For to Nature, Exercise, Imitation and Studie, *Art* must be added, to make all these perfect. And though these challenge to themselves much in the making of our Maker, it is Art only can lead him to perfection and leave him there in possession, as planted by her hand.
>
> (HS VIII, 636 and 639)

Art and craft, craft and art – in this perennially fruitful and self-reflexive circle Ben Jonson mastered both 'the Poem' and 'the Poesy' to become that highest thing of all: *the Poet*.

EPILOGUE

Even after his death, Jonson's creative career could not be neatly wrapped up. *The Sad Shepherd* and *Mortimer His Fall*, two fragments discovered among his papers, have continued to puzzle literary critics. Of the two, *The Sad Shepherd* is the more considerable, since its two and a half acts constitute half of a complete full-length play. The accompanying list of characters, description of the scene, and prose 'argument', give further indications of how the play was intended to turn out; although in its imperfect state the exact conclusion which Jonson proposed for it remains in doubt.

Doubtful too is what stage the manuscript of Jonson represented. Was this a finished composition, of which the latter half had gone astray? Jonson did lose his work occasionally; in the ten-part elegy on the death of Lady Digby (*Underwood* 84), the printer had to inform the reader that 'a whole quaternion [quire of four sheets folded in two] in the midst of this poem is lost', as was the tenth poem, 'her inscription and crown'. Similarly the 'Ode to James, Earl of Desmond' (*Underwood* 25) was lost and subsequently recovered. But Cary's comment in his epitaph on Jonson (HS XI, 436) indicates that Jonson was at work on a pastoral when he died. Cary's slight description of the piece, with the reference in the prologue to *The Sad Shepherd* describing the poet as 'one that hath feasted you these forty years', combine to suggest strongly that this was the last play of Jonson's penultimate working years, and that disease and death had prevented its completion.[1]

Even completion, desirable though that consummation would be, could hardly resolve the riddles posed by this extraordinary production. *The Sad Shepherd* offers a new Jonson from that with which 'the poet' had familiarized his public over so many decades. The greatest English dramatizer of the purely urban turned at last to the strange world of the pastoral, with nymphs and shepherd swains displacing sharks and gulls from his centre of attention. The plot concerns a bereaved lover Aeglamour searching for his lost love Earine; his story is set against the rustic background of a band of Sherwood Foresters, with Robin Hood and Maid Marion, while the evil plots of Maudlin, the wicked witch of Papplewick, are brought in to ensure that the course of true love will not run smooth.

Reduced to its essentials like this, the outline of *The Sad Shepherd* sounds as if Jonson must have undergone softening of the brain in his latter days. But the play fragment in itself is not only a charming and persuasive piece of writing; it is far more consonant with Jonson's known habits and ideals of composition than could appear on the surface. In taking a form which is in its origins classical, and reworking the material 'of Sicily, or Greece' into a thoroughly English scene of Sherwood Forest, Jonson is following a method which he devised in his first play extant, *The Case Is Altered*. This technique of reinterpreting classical myths and motifs in a native and contemporary form Jonson also applied to his non-dramatic poetry, throughout the epigrams, for instance. The allegorical suggestion in the naming of the characters as 'The Kind', 'The Courteous', 'The Proud', and so on, links both with Jonson's masque work and with his later employment of morality devices in plays like *The Devil is an Ass* and *The Magnetic Lady*. Finally, it was not beyond Jonson, who in his time had made theatrical fashion, to decide now to follow it; from observations scattered throughout his work it is clear that Jonson knew well the Jacobean form of tragicomedy, and had admired Fletcher's version of it, *The Faithful Shepherdess*.

In turning to the enchanted groves for his subject, Jonson nevertheless imposed his own style on the proceedings. He ruthlessly threw out the conventional Arcadian affectation, and makes his characters speak and act in a normal and easy manner. Even the traditional figure of the melancholy lover is handled without the usual repetitive claptrap, and Jonson achieves with Aeglamour some moments of unexpected tenderness in the expression of his sense of loss:

> Did not the whole earth sicken when she died?
> As if there since did fall one drop of dew
> But what was wept for her!
>
> (I.v.37–9)

And in the development of the theme of love Jonson is continuing his dramatic exploration of the later years, here, perhaps, more successfully than anywhere else. For only in *The Sad Shepherd* does Jonson attempt to represent a mature, happy sexual relationship between two equal partners in love; see the stage directions to the first scene between Robin Hood and Maid Marion (I.vi) with their endearing and unJonsonian insistence, 'He kisses her'; 'he kisses her again'; 'he kisses her again'. This passion is not merely physical, but metaphysical even after the manner of the early Donne:

> MAID MARION: You are a wanton.
>
> ROBIN HOOD: One I do confess
> I wanted till you came, but now I have you,
> I'll grow to your embraces, till two souls
> Distilled into kisses, through our lips
> Do make one spirit of love.
>
> MAID MARION: O Robin! Robin!
>
> (I.vi.9–13)

Although not all the writing in *The Sad Shepherd* is of this type or level, the piece is such as to make it a matter for considerable regret that Jonson's ending for it does not exist.

The second of the Folio's surprise pieces, *Mortimer His Fall*, will bear no comparison with *The Sad Shepherd*. As only two scenes have survived, it is impossible to deduce much from this fragment, which, from its bombastic, ranting style, feels like a product of a phase earlier than any of Jonson's work which we possess. Two points of interest lie in the use of English history as matter for a tragedy, when in Jonson's mature career nothing would serve but 'the matter of Rome'; and the projected use in the play of three choruses. This constructional eccentricity is outlined in the 'Argument' which prefixes the action, and from Jonson's description of the activities of his choruses of 'Ladies', 'Courtiers' and 'Country Justices and their wives', it is clear that their function was purely static and descriptive, failing to advance the action in any particular. This fragment could with difficulty be made into a play as it stands; but it must have had some significance for Jonson for him to have kept it by him for so many years. The likelihood is that he retained enough faith in the power of the subject-matter to feel that it would, one day, be worthy of his maturer attention.

With these contrasted pieces, one from the beginnings and one from the conclusion of Jonson's writing career, the Second Folio gathers up and concludes what was left of Jonson's work.

Appendix

JONSON'S CLASSICAL STUDIES AT WESTMINSTER SCHOOL

The Westminster curriculum at the time that Jonson followed it was constructed in such a way as to suggest that Jonson certainly proceeded beyond the fourth form (see the companion volume to this study, *Ben Jonson: His Life and Work*, p. 18, for discussion of how long Jonson remained at Westminster, and when he left). Apart from his knowledge of Greek, Jonson's interest in the theory of versification is another pointer to a longer stay; at Westminster the lower forms were confined to prose, and the study of verse was not introduced until the upper school. The full curriculum was as follows:

1st form   *Disticha* – Dionysus Cato
            Exercitatae Linguae Latinae – Vives
            Dialogues and *Confabulationes*
            Pueriles – Corderius

2nd form   Terence
            Aesop's Fables in Latin
            Dialogi Sacri
            Colloquies – Erasmus

3rd form   Terence
            Sallust
            Selections from Cicero's letters – Sturmius
            Aesop in Latin

4th form   *Tristia* – Ovid
            De Officiis – Cicero
            Epigrams – Martial
            Catullus
            Terence
            Sallust

Greek: Grammar
        Dialogues – Lucian

5th form Justin
          De Amicitia – Cicero
          Metamorphoses – Ovid
          Horace
          Greek: Isocrates
                 Plutarch

6th ⎫
7th ⎭ form Caesar
          Livy
          Virgil
          Greek: Demosthenes
                 Homer
          Hebrew

The distinction between the two upper forms was purely nominal since they were taught as one. For further information, see John Sargeaunt, *Annals of Westminster School* (1898).

NOTES

1 A MERE EMPIRIC

1 All these extravagant eulogies are to be found in *Jonsonus Virbius* (1638), the collection of verse tributes to Jonson collected and published after his death – see HS XI.

2 The praise is Thomas Carew's, in a verse epistle to Jonson 'upon occasion of his Ode of Defiance annexed to his play of the New Inn' – see J. F. Bradley and J. Q. Adams, *The Jonson Allusion Book* [JAB], 147–8.

3 See appendix for outline and discussion of the Westminster classical syllabus, and the duration of Jonson's experience of it.

4 See Kathryn A. McEuen, 'Jonson and Juvenal', *RES* 21 (1945), 92–104.

5 J. Marshall (introd.), *The Complete Works of Horace* (1911), vii. Wesley Trimpi in *Ben Jonson's Poems: A Study of the Plain Style* (Stanford, Calif., 1962), shows how Jonson developed in detail a rhetorical position that corresponded to the classical 'plain style', and also wrote the largest portion of his works in the genres of comedy, satire, epistle and epigram that correspond to that style.

6 See David McPherson, 'Some Renaissance sources for Jonson's early comic theory,' *Modern Language Notes* 8 (1971), 180–2.

7 *The Works of Thomas Nashe*, ed. R. B. McKerrow (5 vols, 1968), I, 163.

2 BEGINNING HIS STUDIES IN THIS KIND

1 See J. M. Nosworthy, '*The Case Is Altered*', *JEGP* 51 (1952), 61–70, for the suggestion that this play is in fact to be identified with the lost *Hot Anger Soon Cold*, and that Jonson wrote it with Porter; also J. M. Enck, '*The Case Is Altered*: initial comedy of humours', *Studies in Philology* 50 (1953), 195–214, for a discussion of the play as Jonson's.

2 See Frank L. Huntley, 'Ben Jonson and Anthony Munday, or *The Case Is Altered* altered again', *Philological Quarterly* 41 (1962), 205–14, for the opposing suggestion that Munday was implicated in the original version of the play.

3 TO SPEAK THE VICE

1 Professor Alexander Leggatt writes: '"the special intent of the author": I wonder how far Jonson intended the irony implicit in this? Mitis raises only such objections as the author is prepared to rebut; what looks like free criticism is carefully rigged' (private communication).

2 *Cynthia's Revels* is distinguished from Jonson's other plays in that the 1601 quarto is much shorter than the version which appeared in the 1616 Folio. Are the Folio extra passages Jonson's later additions, or is the quarto text a cut one, possibly an acting version? A. C. Judson argues that the additions represent later revisions of the author's original quarto text (*Cynthia's Revels*, *Yale Studies in English* XLV (1912), xxix–xxxii). Herford and Simpson (IV, 17–22) take the opposite view: that the Folio represents the original text, the quarto the version presented at court on 6 January 1601. The excisions thus represent the curb that Jonson found it wise to put upon his satiric spirit for a court audience.

3 W. David Kay, in 'The shaping of Ben Jonson's career: a re-examination of facts and problems', *Modern Philology* 67 (1970), 224–37, dates *Cynthia's Revels* in 'the autumn of 1601'. Herford and Simpson (I, 26) state that the performance was 'most probably in January 1601', but later amend this to December 1600. Ian Donaldson, in *Ben Jonson: Poems* (Oxford, 1975, 44), takes the view that it was written for the Twelfth Night festivities in 1601. See too E. K. Chambers, *The Elizabethan Stage* (1923), III, 364.

4 *Friar Hubbard's Tales* in *The Works of Thomas Middleton*, ed. A. H. Bullen (1885–6), VII, 77.

5 See *Philological Quarterly* 22 (1943), Talbert (193–210) and Gilbert (211–30), for Jonson's moralizing his use of classical allegory.

4 SUNG HIGH AND ALOOF

1 For a full and detailed clarification of all that is known of this curious episode in English theatrical history, see the companion volume by Rosalind Miles, *Ben Jonson: His Life and Work* (1986), Chapter 4, 49–68.

2 For a fuller consideration of Jonson's debt to his many classical sources see the edition of the play by W. D. Briggs (Boston, Mass., 1911), and the Herford and Simpson introduction to *Sejanus*, Volume II.

3 J. A. Bryant discusses the wider implications of Jonson's use of the classics in 'The significance of Ben Jonson's first requirement for tragedy, "truth of argument"', *Studies in Philology* XLIX (1952), 195–213.

4 See D. C. Boughner, *The Devil's Disciple: Ben Jonson's Debt to Machiavelli* (New York, 1969).

5 ROYAL AND MAGNIFICENT ENTERTAINMENT

1 See HS II, 37–46 for a discussion of the relative contributions of the three different writers to *Eastward Ho!*

6 QUICK COMEDY REFINED

1 See Douglas Duncan, *Ben Jonson and the Lucianic Tradition* (Cambridge, 1979).

2 See also Harriett Hawkins, 'Folly, incurable disease and *Volpone*', *Studies in English Literature* 8 (1968), 335–48, in which Jonson's debt to Erasmus' *In Praise of Folly* is considered. The parallels between Jonson and Erasmus were first noted by J. D. Rea, in his Yale edition of *Volpone* (1919).

3 Alvin Kernan analyses this movement at length in *The Cankered Muse: Satire of the English Renaissance* (New Haven, Conn., 1959), 191–2.

4 *Hymenaei* (1606), line 111, footnote; see HS VII, 213.

5 O. J. Campbell, 'The relation of *Epicoene* to Aretino's *Il Marescalco*', *PMLA* XLVI (1931), 752–62.

6 Christopher Hill, *The Century of Revolution 1603–1714* (1961), 74.

7 Jonson's study of alchemy and its literature is outlined in HS X, 46–7, and in Herford and Simpson's commentary upon the play.

7 TO COME FORTH WORTH THE IVY, OR THE BAYS

1 Jonson's debt to his sources for *Catiline* is outlined in HS X, 117–19 and in the commentary on the play. For other and later studies of the source material, see the 1972 edition of W. F. Bolton and Jane Gardner in the Regents Renaissance Drama Series, 176–88.

2 For a full exposition of Jonson's highly wrought symbolism, see D. J. Gordon, '*Hymenaei*: Ben Jonson's masque of union', *Journal of the Warburg and Courtauld Institute* VII (1945), 107–45.

8 THE POET

1 Jonson styled himself *poeta regius*, 'the royal poet', in his letter of 1 January 1620 to the Dutch scholar Morsius (HS VIII, 664).

2 See HS I, Appendix 5; also prefaces to *Every Man in his Humour* edited by Percy Simpson (Oxford, 1919); by G. B. Jackson (the Yale Ben Jonson, London and New Haven, Conn., 1969); and by J. W. Lever (Regents Renaissance Drama Series, 1972). The Lever edition is particularly helpful as it prints the original and the revised text in parallel, so that the reader can identify and appraise all Jonson's changes.

3 See Edward Partridge, 'Jonson's *Epigrammes*: the named and the nameless', *Studies in the Literary Imagination* VI (1973), 153–98.

4 For a detailed account of all these episodes, see the companion volume by Rosalind Miles to this study, *Ben Jonson: His Life and Work* (1986).

9 ALL THY FIGURES ARE ALLOWED

1 See Jonas Barish, 'Bartholomew Fair and its puppets', *Modern Language Quarterly* 20 (1959), 3–17.

2   The details of this imposture are to be found in G. L. Kittredge, 'King
    James and *The Devil is an Ass'*, *Modern Philology* IX (1911), 195–209.
3   See W. S. Johnson's edition of the play in *Yale Studies in English* (New
    York, 1905), lx ff.

10   SHOWS! SHOWS! MIGHTY SHOWS!

1   George Villiers, later Marquis of Buckingham, was the son of an
    insignificant Leicestershire squire, who had found favour with the ageing
    James I through his good looks and graceful dancing. At the Twelfth
    Night performance of *Pleasure Reconciled to Virtue* the king, angered by
    the show, shouted out, 'Why don't they dance? Devil take you all,
    dance!' In the words of the Venetian ambassador, 'Upon this the Marquis
    of Buckingham immediately sprang forward, cutting a score of lofty and
    very minute capers, with so much grace and agility that he not only
    appeased the ire of his angry lord, but rendered himself the admiration
    and delight of everybody.'
2   *Aurelian Townshend's Poems and Masques*, ed. E. K. Chambers (Oxford,
    1912), 83.

11   HE PRAYS YOU'LL NOT PREJUDGE HIS PLAY FOR ILL

1   The consideration of whether *The New Inn* is to be seen as an old-
    fashioned romantic comedy, or as a satire upon it, has occupied a good
    deal of critical attention. To Herford and Simpson, 'No reader can
    mistake the resolute attempt to plot romantically which has determined
    the main lines of the present play' (II, 194). Jonas Barish refers to 'the
    unabashed romance plots of *The New Inn* and *The Magnetic Lady*', in *Ben
    Jonson and the Language of Prose Comedy* (Cambridge, Mass., 1960), 241.
    On the other hand Larry Champion argues that *The New Inn* is nothing if
    not irony, since it contains a flagrant exaggeration of the devices sacred to
    the writers of romantic comedy, which Jonson had always considered a
    degradation of the dramatic art (*Ben Jonson's 'Dotages'*, Lexington, Mass.,
    1967).
2   See, for instance, Harriett Hawkins, 'The idea of a theater in Jonson's *The
    New Inn*', *Renaissance Drama* 9 (1966), 205–26. More recently Anne
    Barton's *Ben Jonson, Dramatist* (Cambridge, 1984) and the 1987 produc-
    tion of the play at the Swan Theatre, Stratford-upon-Avon, have done
    much to rehabilitate this neglected piece.
3   The ratio of talk to action is roughly four to one; see G. B. Tennant's
    edition of the play (*Yale Studies in English*, New York, 1908) xxxii–
    xxxxi, for a schematic breakdown of this.
4   There has been much critical debate as to whether *A Tale of a Tub* is an
    old play revamped, or a new piece in the mixed manner of the last plays.
    See HS IX, 268–75. Muriel Bradbrook, in *The Living Monument:
    Shakespeare and the Drama of his Time* (Cambridge, 1972), argues that it is

not a revision but a new play in the old style. She finds it genuinely festive, and considers that in performance it would succeed as a farce.

12 NEAR THE CLOSE OR SHUTTING UP OF HIS CIRCLE

1 In Jonson's word, a 'curtall'. These horses are no longer seen in England, since the cruel practice of 'docking' (removal of the tail, including the bony section at the end of the spine) was discontinued – for horses, if not for the still-persecuted corgi.

2 Modern scholars suggest that the form 'Underwoods', which appears in the 1640 Folio and in some later editions, is a misprint. There is some confusion in Herford and Simpson, where 'Underwoods' is the form used in the introduction to the poems (II, 337–431), while 'Underwood' is the final form chosen for the edition (Vol. VIII) and the commentary (Vol. XI). See B. H. Newdigate, *Times Literary Supplement*, 7 February 1935, p. 76, and W. W. Greg, *RES* xviii (1942), 159–60, and n., for the case for 'Underwood'.

3 See HS II, 418–19, for a survey of the other authorities that Jonson used in the composition of *The English Grammar*.

4 Paul R. Sellin, in *Daniel Heinsius and Stuart England* (1968), demonstrates that from Jonson's use of Heinsius large portions of the *Discoveries* date from the closing days of Jonson's career, from the period after 1629 (pp. 147–62).

5 For a full discussion of Jonson's fascinating life, including many little-known episodes such as his involvement in the Gunpowder Plot, see the companion volume to this study, *Ben Jonson: His Life and Work* (1986) by Rosalind Miles.

EPILOGUE

1 One date of relevance is 1614, when Daniel had produced *Hymen's Triumph*, to which Jonson makes slighting reference in the prologue to *The Sad Shepherd*. See Joan Rees, *Samuel Daniel: A Critical and Biographical Study* (Liverpool, 1964), and HS X, 365, n. 54.

SELECT BIBLIOGRAPHY

Books are published in London unless otherwise stated.

JONSON'S WORKS

The major edition of Jonson's works is the eleven-volume *Ben Jonson*, edited by C. H. Herford and Percy and Evelyn Simpson (Oxford, 1925–52); for a clear modern edition, see the modernized version of Herford and Simpson, published as *The Complete Plays of Ben Jonson*, ed. G. A. Wilkes (4 vols, Oxford, 1981–3) or the Yale Ben Jonson, published in New Haven by the Yale University Press. For individual plays the modern editions in the New Mermaids Series, published by Ernest Benn Ltd, the Revels plays, published by Methuen, and the Regents Renaissance Drama Series, published by Edward Arnold, are clear and helpful modern-spelling texts. All references to Jonson's poems in this study are taken from *Ben Jonson: Poems*, edited by Ian Donaldson (Oxford, 1975).

COMPANION WORKS

Brock, D. Heyward, *A Ben Jonson Companion* (Indiana and Sussex, 1983).
Brock, D. Heyward and Welsh, James M., *Ben Jonson: a Quadricentennial Bibliography 1947–72* (Metuchen, NJ, 1974).

BIOGRAPHY

Miles, Rosalind, *Ben Jonson: His Life and Work* (1986).
Riggs, David, *Ben Jonson: A Life* (Cambridge, Mass., 1989).

CRITICAL TEXTS: BOOKS

Bamborough, J. B., *Ben Jonson* (1970).
Barish, Jonas, *Ben Jonson and the Language of Prose Comedy* (Cambridge, Mass., 1960).

Barton, Anne, *Ben Jonson, Dramatist* (Cambridge, 1984).

Bentley, G. E., *Shakespeare and Jonson, Their Reputations in the Seventeenth Century Compared* (2 vols, Chicago, 1945).

Boughner, Daniel C., *The Devil's Disciple: Ben Jonson's Debt to Machiavelli* (New York, 1968).

Bradbrook, Muriel, *The Living Monument: Shakespeare and the Drama of his Time* (Cambridge, 1972).

Bradley, J. F. and Adams, J. Q., *The Jonson Allusion Book: A Collection of Allusions to Ben Jonson from 1597–1700* (New Haven, Conn., Oxford and London, 1922).

Chambers, E. K., *Aurelian Townshend's Poems and Masques* (Oxford, 1912).

Chambers, E. K., *The Elizabethan Stage* (4 vols, Oxford, 1923).

Champion, Larry, *Ben Jonson's 'Dotages'* (Lexington, Mass., 1967).

De Luna, B. N., *Jonson's Romish Plot: A Study of 'Catiline' and its Historical Context* (Oxford, 1967).

Donaldson, Ian (ed.), *Ben Jonson: Poems*, see above, under Jonson's Works.

Donaldson, Ian (ed.), *Jonson and Shakespeare* (Atlantic Highlands, NJ, 1983).

Duncan, Douglas, *Ben Jonson and the Lucianic Tradition* (Cambridge, 1979).

Dutton, Richard, *Ben Jonson: To the First Folio* (Cambridge, 1983).

Enck, John Jacob, *Jonson and the Comic Truth* (Madison, Wisc., 1957).

Hill, Christopher, *The Century of Revolution 1603–1714* (1961).

Hudson, H. H., *The Epigram in the English Renaissance* (Princeton, NJ, 1947).

Jonson, W. S. (ed.) *The Devil is an Ass*, Yale Studies in English (New York, 1905).

Johnston, G. B., *Ben Jonson, Poet* (New York, 1945).

Judson, A. C. *Cynthia's Revels*, Yale Studies in English (New Haven, Conn., 1912).

Kernan, Alvin B., *The Cankered Muse: Satire of the English Renaissance* (New Haven, Conn., 1959).

Leggatt, Alexander, *Ben Jonson, his Vision and his Art* (London and New York, 1981).

McKerrow, R. B. (ed.), *Works of Thomas Nashe* (5 vols, 1968).

Marshall, J. (introd.), *The Complete Works of Horace* (1911).

Maus, Katharine Eisaman, *Ben Jonson and the Roman Frame of Mind* (Princeton, NJ, 1984).

Parfitt, George, *Ben Jonson, Public Poet and Private Man* (1976).

Partridge, Edward, *The Broken Compass: A Study of the Major Comedies of Ben Jonson* (1958).

Rees, Joan, *Samuel Daniel: A Critical and Biographical Study* (Liverpool, 1964).

Sweeney, John Gordon, *Jonson and the Psychology of the Public Theatre* (Princeton, NJ, 1985).

Swinburne, A. C., *A Study of Ben Jonson* (1889).

Trimpi, Wesley, *Ben Jonson's Poems: A Study of the Plain Style* (Stanford, Calif., 1962).

Watson, Robert N., *Ben Jonson's Parodic Strategy: Literary Imperialism in the Comedies* (Cambridge, Mass., 1987).

Womack, Peter, *Ben Jonson* (Oxford, 1986).

CRITICAL TEXTS: ARTICLES

Barish, Jonas, 'Ovid, Juvenal and *The Silent Woman*', *PMLA* 71 (1956), 213–34.

Barish, Jonas, 'Bartholomew Fair and its puppets', *Modern Language Quarterly* 20 (1959), 3–17.

Barnes, Peter, 'Staging Jonson', in *Jonson and Shakespeare*, ed. Ian Donaldson (Atlantic Highlands, NJ, 1983), 156–62.

Beaurline, L. A., 'The selective principle in Jonson's shorter poems', *Criticism* viii (1966), 64–74.

Beaurline, L. A., 'Ben Jonson and the illusion of completeness', *PMLA* 84 (1969), 51–9.

Bergeron, David M., 'Harrison, Jonson and Dekker, the Magnificent Entertainment for King James (1604)', *Journal of the Warburg and Courtauld Institute* 31 (1968), 445–6.

Boughner, Daniel C., 'Rhodig and *Sejanus*', *Notes and Queries* NS 5 (1958), 287–9.

Boughner, Daniel C., 'Juvenal, Horace and *Sejanus*', *MLN* 75 (1960), 545–50.

Bredvold, Louis I., 'The rise of English classicism: a study in methodology', *Comparative Literature* 3 (1950), 253–68.

Briggs, W. D., 'Source material for Jonson's *Epigrams* and *Forest*', *Classical Philology* xi (1916), 169–90.

Briggs, W. D., 'Source material for Jonson's *Underwoods* and miscellaneous poems', *Modern Philology* xv (1917), 277–312.

Brown, A. D. Fitton, 'Drink to me, Celia', *Modern Language Review* 54 (1959), 554–7.

Bryant, Joseph A., Jr, 'The nature of the conflict in Jonson's *Sejanus*', *Vanderbilt Studies in the Humanities* I (1951), 197–219.

Bryant, Joseph A., Jr, 'The significance of Ben Jonson's first requirement for tragedy: "truth of argument"', *Studies in Philology* 49 (1952), 195–213.

Bryant, Joseph A., Jr, '*Catiline* and the nature of Jonson's tragic fable', *PMLA* 69 (1954), 265–77.

Burt, Richard A., 'Licensed by authority: Ben Jonson and the politics of early Stuart theatre', *ELH, A Journal of English History* 54:3 (1987), 529–60.

Burton, K. M., 'The political tragedies of Chapman and Ben Jonson', *Essays in Criticism* 2 (October 1952), 397–412.

Campbell, O. J., 'The relation of *Epicoene* to Aretino's *Il Marescalco*', *PMLA* XLVI (1931), 752–62.

Donaldson, Ian, 'Jonson and anger', *The Yearbook of English Studies* 14 (1984), 56–71.

Dorenkampf, Angela G., 'Jonson's *Catiline*: history as the trying faculty', *Studies in Philology* 67 (1970), 220.

Duffy, Ellen M. T., 'Ben Jonson's debt to Renaissance scholarship in *Sejanus* and *Catiline*', *Modern Language Review* 42 (1947), 24–30.

Duncan, Douglas, 'Ben Jonson's Lucianic irony', *Ariel: A Review of International English Literature* 1:2 (1970), 42–53.

Duncan, Douglas, 'A guide to *The New Inn*', *Essays in Criticism* 20 (1970), 311–26.

Enck, John Jacob, '*The Case Is Altered*: initial comedy of humours', *Studies in Philology* 50 (1953), 195–214.

Evans, K. W. '*Sejanus* and the ideal prince tradition', *Studies in English Literature* 11 (1971), 249–64.

Ferns, John, 'Ovid, Juvenal and *The Silent Woman*: a reconsideration', *Modern Language Review* 65 (1970), 248–53.

Furniss, W. Todd, 'Jonson's antimasques', *Renaissance News* 7 (1954), 21–2.

Furniss, W. Todd, 'Ben Jonson's masques', in *Three Studies in the Renaissance: Sidney, Jonson, Milton*, ed. B. C. Nangle (New Haven, Conn., 1958).

Gordon, D. J., '*Hymenaei*: Ben Jonson's masque of union', *Journal of the Warburg and Courtauld Institute* VII (1945), 107–45.

Gordon, D. J., 'Ben Jonson's *Haddington Masque*: the story and the fable', *Modern Language Review* XL11 (1947), 180–7.

Gossett, Suzanne, 'Man–maid, begone!: women in masques', *ELR* 18:1 (Winter 1988), 96–113.

Hawkins, Harriett, 'Folly, incurable disease and *Volpone*', *Studies in English Literature* 8 (1968), 335–48.

Hawkins, Harriett, 'The idea of a theater in Jonson's *The New Inn*', *Renaissance Drama* 9 (1966), 205–26.

Huntley, Frank L., 'Ben Jonson and Anthony Munday, or *The Case Is Altered* altered again', *Philological Quarterly* 41 (1962), 205–14.

Kay, W. David, 'The shaping of Ben Jonson's career', *Modern Philology* 67 (1970), 224–37.

Kirschbaum, Leo, 'Jonson, Seneca and *Mortimer*', in *Studies in Honour of John Wilcox*, ed. A. Dayle (Detroit, Mich., 1958).

Kittredge, G. L., 'King James and *The Devil Is An Ass*', *Modern Philology* IX (1911), 195–209.

Levin, Richard, '*The Staple of News*, the society of jeerers, and Canters' College', *Philological Quarterly* 44 (1965), 445–53.

Levin, Richard, 'The structure of *Bartholomew Fair*', *PMLA* 80 (1965), 172–9.

Levin, Richard, '*The New Inn* and the proliferation of good bad drama', *Essays in Criticism* 22 (January 1972), 41–7.

Loewenstein, Joseph, 'The Jonsonian corpulence; or, the poet as mouthpiece', *ELH, A Journal of English Literary History* 53:3 (1986), 491–512.

McEuen, K. A., 'Jonson, and Juvenal', *Review of English Studies* 21 (1945), 92–104.

McMillin, Scott, 'Jonson's early entertainments: new information from Hatfield House', *Renaissance Drama* NS 1 (1968), 153–66.

McPherson, David, 'Some Renaissance sources for Jonson's early comic theory', *English Language Notes* 8 (1971), 180–2.

Marotti, A. F., 'All about Jonson's poetry', *ELH, A Journal of English Literary History* 39 (1972), 208–37.

Nosworthy, J. M. '*The Case Is Altered*', *Journal of English and Germanic Philology* 51 (1952), 61–70.

Partridge, Edward, 'Jonson's *Epigrammes*: the named and the nameless', *Studies in the Literary Imagination* VI (1973), 153–98.

Redwine, James D., Jr, 'Beyond psychology: the moral basis of Jonson's theory of humour characterisation', *ELH, A Journal of English Literary History* 28 (1961), 316–34.

Ricks, Christopher, 'Sejanus and dismemberment', *Modern Language Notes* 76 (1961), 301–8.

Spanos, W. V., 'The real toad in the Jonsonian garden', *Journal of English and Germanic Philology* LXVIII (1969), 1–23.

Wykes, David, 'Ben Jonson's "Chaste booke" – the *Epigrammes*', *Renaissance and Modern Studies* XIII (1969), 76–87.

INDEX

INDEX